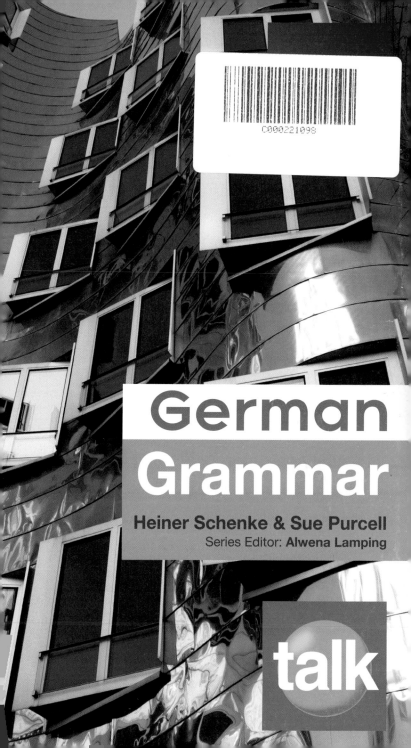

German
Grammar

Heiner Schenke & Sue Purcell

Series Editor: **Alwena Lamping**

talk

Published by BBC Active, an imprint of Educational Publishers LLP, part of the
Pearson Education Group, Edinburgh Gate, Harlow, Essex CM20 2JE, England.

© Educational Publishers LLP 2012

First published 2012.

ISBN 978-1-4066-6975-6

Cover design: Johanna Gale
Cover photograph: © Iain Masterton/Alamy
Insides design: BBC Active design team
Layout: Pantek Media Ltd. www.pantekmedia.co.uk
Illustrations: © Mark Duffin
Publisher: Debbie Marshall
Development editor: Paul Coggle
Project editor: Emma Brown
Marketing: Paul East
Senior production controller: Franco Forgione

Printed and bound in the UK by Ashford Colour Press Ltd.

The Publisher's policy is to use paper manufactured from sustainable forests.

Contents

introduction

Talk German Grammar is the essential handbook for anyone setting out to learn German, at home or in a class. With its straightforward approach and clear layout, it promotes a real understanding of how German works and how it relates to English.

It's much more than an ordinary grammar book. Using the tried-and-tested principles of the bestselling **Talk German** and **Talk German 2**, it demystifies grammar and guides you through the key structures of German in a way that's really easy to follow, even if you have no experience at all of grammar and its terminology.

Its parallel focus is on building a large vocabulary – fast – for you to combine with an understanding of grammar to say whatever you want in German, without having to rely on phrasebooks.

Among its special features you'll find:

- systematic references to **the most significant differences** in the way German and English work;
- clear **jargon-free explanations** of German grammar, set out in units and illustrated by hundreds of **practical examples**;
- **Word power** pages, tailored to individual units. Some of these focus on the similarities between English and German and will help you to recognise German words. **False friends** are highlighted too: words which look as though they might mean one thing but in fact don't;
- great **learning tips and strategies**, positioned just where you need them;
- **dictionary guidance**, with abbreviations and sample entries;
- regular **Checkpoints** with practice activities to reinforce the language patterns and help you remember them. These are also useful as revision or to jog your memory;
- **verb tables**: full tables of commonly-used regular and irregular verbs;
- a **glossary of grammar terms** with examples in English to make them crystal clear;
- a **comprehensive easy-to-use index**.

Talk German Grammar can be used successfully alongside any learning materials, and is the perfect companion for both levels of **Talk German**. The first level has online activities at www.bbc.co.uk/languages/german, where you can also try out the **German Steps** course, which includes some grammar notes.

How to use Talk German Grammar

This book works on several levels – make it work for you!

New to language learning or forgotten everything you've learnt? Or perhaps you already know some German words but have no structure to use them in?
Go to **Getting started** on page 8, which gives you an overview of what grammar is about, introduces you to the keystones of grammar and offers a few short activities to help you recognise and remember them.

New to German but understand the meaning of basic terms such as noun, adjective, verb?
Go to page 10 which prepares you for learning German by highlighting the principal differences between German and English.

Learning German on your own or in a class and need extra support?
Choose the unit you want, work through it then complete the **Checkpoint** at the end to see how much you've understood and remembered. You can select the units in the order that suits you because they're free-standing and they cross-reference to each other so that you can easily check things out if you need to.

Need a clear and comprehensive German grammar reference book?
The index will show you where everything is. It uses key words in English and German as well as grammar terms, making it easy for you to find what you're looking for quickly.

Want to brush up on your German or do some revision?
The first page of each unit summarises the key points. Reading these and trying your hand at the **Checkpoint** activities will pinpoint any gaps in your knowledge so that you know what might be useful to spend some time on.

Just want to generally improve your German, deepen your understanding and boost your vocabulary?
Dip into the book at random, reminding yourself of the structures, reading the examples, checking out the **Word power** pages and using the **Checkpoints**.

getting started

What is grammar?

When we talk, we do more than just say words randomly; we use them in a specific order and they relate to one another. Grammar is the explanation of how that works: it provides definitions of the structures of a language and how they're used.

Can I communicate without learning grammar?

Yes … if you're happy restricting yourself to phrases from a book or pidgin-type communication. You'll just about be able to make yourself understood but conversation will be a strain and communication hit-and-miss. With relatively little knowledge of grammar you can produce the correct and unambiguous version instead. You'll sound more articulate and it will be a much more constructive and satisfying experience.

How do babies cope without knowing about grammar?

It's true that children learn to talk without ever having heard of a verb or a noun. But if you listen to a toddler, you'll often hear words like *bited*, *eated*, *sheeps* or *mans*, showing that the child has in fact absorbed regular patterns of English and is applying them quite unconsciously – albeit not always correctly. As time goes on, irregularities get ironed out and the child, with no apparent effort, starts saying *bit* and *ate*, *sheep* and *men*.

It takes many months of constant exposure to a language to learn in this way. By the time the average child is starting to form sentences, they will have been hearing their mother tongue for around 4,500 hours over a period of 18 months or so.

Most adults want results more quickly than that. By consciously learning how German is structured and how new words fit within sentences, you shortcut the process considerably. But you'll still experiment and make mistakes, just as children do, because that's part of the learning curve too.

How much grammar will I need?

At the start, you can get by comfortably with the basics. As you carry on with your German, you'll gradually accumulate knowledge and more pieces of the jigsaw will slot into place. There are some aspects of grammar that you might never need or want to know about – as with most things, there's a level that's largely of interest only to the professional or the enthusiast.

Where do I start?

It pays to become familiar with some of the terms used to describe how a language works because it allows you to make sense of statements that you might come across in course books, such as *The indefinite article is not used when …* or *The verb goes at the end of the sentence*.

Focus first on the six main building blocks of a sentence. Read these descriptions, then see if you can pick them out in sentences.

- **Nouns** are the words for living beings, things, places and abstract concepts: *woman, son, doctor, Oliver, dog, table, house, Scotland, time, joy, freedom*.
- **Pronouns** are words used to avoid repeating a noun: *I, me, we, us, you, he/she, him/her, it, they, them*.
- **Articles** are *the* and *a/an*.
- **Adjectives** are words that describe nouns and pronouns: ***good*** *wine*; ***strong red*** *wine*; ***my*** *wine*; *I am* ***tired***; *it was* ***superb***.
- **Adverbs** add information to adjectives, verbs and other adverbs: ***very*** *good wine*; *you speak* ***clearly***; *you speak* ***really*** *clearly*.
- **Verbs** are words like *go, sleep, eat, like, have, be, live, die* that relate to doing and being.

---

1 Have a look at the underlined words and write N by the nouns, V by the verbs and ADJ by the adjectives.

   a Sofia works for a glossy magazine. She organises interviews, hires professional models and photographers and travels all over the world. Her boyfriend is a well-known actor.

   b My father comes from Bonn although he now lives in Düsseldorf because he works at the central office of a large company.

   c They prepared a fantastic meal for us. We ate grilled fish, fresh asparagus and new potatoes, drank a superb German white wine – and the dessert was absolutely incredible.

2 Now pick out the adjectives ADJ and the adverbs ADV.

   a The house was very reasonable but it was rather dilapidated … and the garden was really small and overgrown.

   b We played superbly. It wasn't our fault that the pitch was terribly uneven and the ref deliberately unfair.

How different are German and English?

On the whole, German grammar is similar to English, but there are a few aspects which are rather different. If you're prepared for these, you'll find that you get used to them very quickly.

Different versions of *you*

In English there's only one word for *you*; in German there are three. With people you know really well, you use **du** when talking to one person and **ihr** to more than one. When talking to people you've just met, don't know well or who are older than you, you use **Sie** to one person and also to a group of people.

Gender: masculine, feminine and neuter

Every German noun is either masculine (m), feminine (f) or neuter (nt); this is its **gender**. In German, gender is grammatical, not biological as in English. This means that objects or concepts which are neuter in English (*it*) can be masculine, feminine or neuter in German. Articles (*the, a/an*) have different forms to reflect the gender of the noun.

Capital letter for all nouns

In German, all nouns must be written with a capital letter, regardless of where they occur in a sentence.

Case

In both languages, a noun can be the subject of a sentence or the object. In German, the role a noun plays within a sentence is referred to as its **case**. The concept of case is important in German because words like *the*, *a* or *my* change according to the case of the noun they're with.

Verb endings; I, we, you, s/he, they

In English a verb stays pretty much the same no matter who's carrying it out: *I eat, we eat, you eat, the cats eat, Joe eats*. In German, as well as using *I, you, she* etc., the ending of the verb changes to show who is doing what.

Word order

In most German sentences the main verb has to be the second element. If you start a sentence for instance with an expression of time, then the verb has to come next. *Tomorrow I go to Berlin* is expressed in German as *Tomorrow go I to Berlin*. If there are two verbs in a sentence, the second one usually goes to the end: **Sie kann gut tanzen** literally means *She can well dance*.

What about vocabulary?

Learning a new language is a several-pronged process. Knowledge of grammar has a key place; even a few simple structures go a long way towards making sure you're understood. Knowing how to use verbs and when to include words like **außerdem** *furthermore*, **deshalb** *therefore* or **weil** *because* take you a big step further, letting you express more complex thoughts.

But all these are of limited use without a good stock of words to slot into the structures – and the most obvious source of these is a dictionary.

What sort of dictionary is best?

When choosing your first English/German dictionary, go for a medium-sized one. Too small and it won't give you enough information; too big and it will confuse you with too much. There are also dictionaries online, many of them free, some with apps for your phone.

Why are dictionaries so full of abbreviations?

Some words are straightforward, with just one meaning: *prefer* can only be a verb, *possible* an adjective.

Others are more complex, with the same word belonging in more than one grammatical category. *Mind* can mean what you think with (noun) and to look after (verb). *Book* can mean something to read (noun) and to reserve a place (verb). *Calm* can mean peaceful (adjective), peace (noun) and to soothe (verb).

To make sure you find the right category of word, each has an abbreviation next to it. The most common are:

acc accusative	*adj* adjective	*adv* adverb
art article	*dat* dative	*f* feminine
gen genitive	*m* masculine	*n* noun
nt neuter	*pl* plural	*prep* preposition
pron pronoun	*sing* singular	*v* verb

You may find slight variations in some dictionaries, so it's worth checking with the introduction.

How do I make sure I choose the right translation?

Some words have more than one meaning even within the same grammatical category: the adjective *hard* can mean *solid* and it can mean *difficult*. The noun *habit* can be something a monk wears or it can be something you do on a regular basis. The verb *to press* can mean to iron clothes or to push down on something.

There's often an explanation or a phrase to guide you, but if you've looked up an English word and are still not sure which of the German translations to use, look them all up and see what English translations are given.

hard *adj* **1.** *(not soft)* hart **2.** *(difficult)* schwer; *(complicated)* schwierig; *(hard to endure)* hart: *I know it's ~ for you* Ich weiß, es ist schwer/hart für Sie; *~ luck*: so ein Pech **3.** *(severe, harsh)* hart; *(voice, tone)* schroff: *~ frost* streng; *a ~ man* ein harter Mann

habit *n* **1.** Gewohnheit *f*: *good/bad ~* gute/schlechte Angewohnheit; *it became a ~* es wurde zur Gewohnheit; *out of/by (sheer) ~* aus (reiner) Gewohnheit **2.** *(costume)* Gewand *nt*; *(monk's)* Habit *nt* or *m*; *riding ~* Reitkleid *nt*

press *vt* **1.** *(push, squeeze)* drücken *(to* an + *acc.)*; *(button, doorbell, knob, pedal)* drücken auf *(+ acc.)*; *(grapes, fruit)* (aus)pressen **2.** *(iron clothes)* bügeln **3.** *(urge, persuade)* drängen; *(harass)* bedrängen, unter Druck setzen **4.** *to ~ sb (hard)* jemandem (hart) zusetzen; *be ~ed (for money/time)* in Geldnot sein/unter Zeitdruck stehen

What if I can't find the word I'm looking for?

This is where your knowledge of German grammar comes in. The main points to take into account are that:

- nouns are listed in the nominative case;
- verbs are listed in the infinitive;

and so they might have a different ending from the version you have come across.

If you still have a problem, it probably means that you've come across part of an irregular verb, the most common of which are written out in full on page 134.

How else can I build up a wide vocabulary?

The most obvious source of German outside German-speaking countries is the internet, where you can find information in German on practically anything. Use a dictionary to find the key words relating to your interests then just browse. You'll be surprised at how much German you absorb when words are in a familiar context that interests you.

Don't forget that you already have a huge latent vocabulary simply because, for historical reasons, German and English have a lot of words in common. Some word groups have quite similar vocabulary, others have moved further apart. This is one of the aspects of the **Word power** pages, which show you similarities between both languages. Not only will you find your vocabulary increasing considerably, but you'll also have the knowledge and the confidence to make an educated guess at the meaning of new words.

Is it true that many English words are used in German?

Over the years, German and English have borrowed and absorbed many words from each other, but in more recent times the number of English words imported into German has been much greater than the other way round. These words are often referred to as **Denglisch**, from **Deutsch + Englisch**.

Denglisch includes in particular many words relating to business, IT, sport and fashion, such as **das Marketing**, **die Homepage**, **offline**, **joggen**, **die Sneakers**. The rules of German grammar apply to them, e.g. nouns are written with a capital letter and verbs add appropriate endings. To say *I'm jogging* or *I had lunch* you manipulate the verbs **joggen** and **lunchen** accordingly: **ich jogge**, **ich habe geluncht**.

Some English words have taken on a whole different meaning in German, such as **das Handy** *mobile phone*, **der Oldtimer** *vintage car* and **der Smoking** *tuxedo, dinner jacket*.

Never assume that words you recognise in German sound the same as they do in English. **Handy**, for example, sounds more like *hendy*. Many words that derive from the same root, such as **Schule** and *school*, sound different. Other words, such as *name, Japan* or *orange*, that look and mean the same in both languages, are not pronounced in the same way.

Here are a few words of German origin used in English:

lager	*dachshund*
schnapps	*Dobermann*
spritzer	*Rottweiler*
vermouth	*schnauzer*
beer garden (from **Biergarten**)	*Weimaraner*
frankfurter	*glockenspiel*
hamburger	*lied*
bratwurst	*abseil*
sauerkraut	*kitsch*
muesli	*wanderlust*
pretzel	*rucksack*
aspirin	*angst*
Alzheimer's	*doppelganger*
diesel	*wunderkind*
Fahrenheit	*kindergarten*
hertz	*schadenfreude*
schmaltz	*zeitgeist*

… and some words of English origin regularly used in German:

booten	**Anchorman**
canceln	**Blockbuster**
downloaden	**Contest**
joggen	**Soap**
lunchen	**Public Viewing**
recyceln	**Trailer**
Business	**Coffee to go**
Briefing	**Drink**
Deadline	**Happy Hour**
Feedback	**Sandwich**
Manager	**Snack**
Meeting	**Lifestyle**
Workflow	**Joke**

Sounds and spelling

In English, letters sound different according to which word they're in.
a: c**a**rt, c**a**re, w**a**r, wom**a**n
ea: b**ea**rd, h**ea**rd, m**ea**t, gr**ea**t, thr**ea**t

In German, pronunciation and spelling are much more consistent; the pronunciation of letters doesn't vary from one word to the next. This means that once you're familiar with the way single letters and combinations of letters are said, you'll be in a position to use the new words you come across with confidence.

The German alphabet uses the same 26 letters as the English alphabet, plus four additional letters. Three of these are formed by adding an umlaut – two dots – above the vowels **a**, **o** and **u**: **Äpfel** *apples*, **Österreich** *Austria*, **grün** *green*. These vowels with umlauts are pronounced differently from those without.

The fourth additional letter is ß, which is called **scharfes** *sharp* **s** or **eszett**. The ß is used after a long vowel or diphthong in words such as **Straße** or **heißen**.

The stress in most German words falls on the first syllable, as in **E̲ngland**, **A̲utobahn**, **te̲xten**, **wu̲nderbar**.

However good your knowledge of grammar, however wide your vocabulary, you won't learn to speak German just by reading and writing. You need to listen too – take every opportunity to listen to native German speakers. Even if at first you don't understand a great deal of what they're saying, you can focus on how German sounds. This will really help you to speak it clearly and comprehensibly.

pronunciation

vowels

German vowels are never silent like the *e* in English words such as *make*, *some* or *file*. They sound much as they do in these English words, with the vowel longer in some words than others:

	short	long
a	c**a**t	c**a**r
e	**e**x	ch**a**os
i	**i**n	f**ee**
o	h**o**t	m**o**re
u	p**u**t	c**oo**l

The three umlauts are pronounced roughly as in the following English words, with the longer versions being given greater intensity:

ä	**e**gg
ö	f**u**r
ü	d**eu**ce

diphthongs

A diphthong is a combination of two vowels that together produce a particular sound. There are three main diphthongs in German:

au	c**ow**
ei	b**y**/l**ie**
eu	c**oy**/**oy**ster

A few words such as **Mai** or **Kaiser** contain the diphthong **ai**, which is pronounced exactly like **ei**. Sometimes an umlaut is added to **au**, which is pronounced like **eu**: **Häuser, Mäuse, Fräulein, träumen**.

long and short vowels

A vowel or an umlaut is pronounced long:
- when followed by **h**: **fahren, Ihnen, Höhle**
- when a double vowel occurs: **Haar, Meer, Boot**
  Diphthongs and **ie** usually sound long too: **Haus, die, sieben**

Vowels are normally pronounced short:
- when followed by a double consonant: **nass, Bett, schwimmen, können**
- when followed by two or more consonants: **dick, sechs, Fenster**
- when the vowel comes at the end of a word: **habe, Liebe, Flaschen**

consonants

Most consonants sound very similar in German and English, except for:

	English	
c before ä, e, i	ts (as in puts)	Cäsar, Ceylon, circa
c otherwise (except ch)	k	Café, Computer
j	y (as in yes)	ja, Jacke
s at the beginning of a word or a syllable	z	singen, Sie, Sonne zusammen, gesund
s at the end of a word or end of a syllable	s	alles, besonders Busfahrer
v	f	Vater, viel, Vogel
w	v	wie, Wasser, Wein
z	ts (as in puts)	Zeit, Zimmer, zwei, Herz

These combinations of consonants have a distinctive sound:

ch following a, o or u	roughly like the ch in loch: Buch, Bach
ch following any letter apart from a, o or u	pronounced with the mouth in the position of a tight smile ich, Milch, manche
ph	as in phrase Philosophie, Phrase
sch	sh as in shoe Schuh, schön
sp	shp spät, Spaß
st at the beginning of a word	sht Stadt, Stil
st within a word	st gestern, Fenster
tsch	tch (as in witch) Deutsch, Quatsch

stress

As a general rule, the vast majority of German words are stressed on the first syllable: <u>Deutsch</u>land, <u>Na</u>me, <u>se</u>hen, <u>Su</u>permarkt, <u>lang</u>weilig. But the stress can appear on other syllables as well:

- on the second syllable, for example after words beginning with be-, ge-, er-, ent-, emp-, ver-, and zer-: be<u>son</u>ders, Ver<u>ein</u>, Ent<u>täu</u>schung
- on the second to last syllable in verbs ending in -ieren: telefo<u>nie</u>ren, kommen<u>tie</u>ren, stu<u>die</u>ren
- on the last syllable with some suffixes, including -ei, -ie, -ik, -tät: Bäcke<u>rei</u>, Büche<u>rei</u>, Che<u>mie</u>, Theo<u>rie</u>, Mu<u>sik</u>, Kreativi<u>tät</u>

Foreign words imported into German tend to keep their original stress, e.g. Com<u>pu</u>ter, Ca<u>fé</u>, Ga<u>ra</u>ge, Ho<u>tel</u>.

the German alphabet

The German alphabet uses the same 26 letters as the English alphabet, plus four additional letters: the three umlauts, ä, ö, ü and ß, which is called **scharfes s** or **eszett**.

When spelling words out, the letters of the alphabet sound similar to the English sounds in the middle columns below. The words listed in the right-hand columns are used when clarification is needed, in the same way as the UK uses: *alpha*, *bravo*, *charlie* ... *X-ray*, *yankee*, *zulu*.

a	ah	Anton	n	en	Nordpol
b	beh	Berta	o	oh	Otto
c	tseh	Cäsar	p	peh	Paula
d	deh	Dora	q	kuh	Quelle
e	eh	Emil	r	air	Richard
f	ef	Friedrich	s	ess	Samuel
g	geh	Gustav	t	teh	Theodor
h	hah	Heinrich	u	uh	Ulrich
i	ee	Ida	v	fow	Viktor
j	yot	Julius	w	veh	Wilhelm
k	kah	Kaufmann	x	iks	Xanthippe
l	el	Ludwig	y	ipsilon	Ypsilon
m	em	Martha	z	tsett	Zacharias

ä	a-umlaut	Ärger
ö	o-umlaut	Ökonom
ü	u-umlaut	Übermut
ß	scharfes s or eszett	

In informal text messages, emails etc. it's acceptable to replace ä, ö and ü with **ae**, **oe** and **ue**. You'll also find these spelling variations in some internet domain names: **sueddeutsche.de** instead of **süddeutsche.de**.

spelling things out

Spelling out *Brighton* would sound like this:
beh, air, ee, geh, hah, teh, oh, en

Double is **Doppel-**, so *Liverpool* would be:
el, ee, fow, eh, air, peh, **Doppel**-oh, el

When using **Anton**, **Berta**, etc. the link word is **wie** *as/like*:
Bond: **B wie Berta**, **O wie Otto**, **N wie Nordpol**, **D wie Dora**

punctuation marks

* **Sternchen**	@ **At-Zeichen**
. **Punkt**	/ **Schrägstrich, Slash**
, **Komma**	\ **umgekehrter Schrägstrich**
; **Semikolon**	# **Doppelkreuz**
: **Doppelpunkt**	*ABC upper case* **Großbuchstabe(n)**
- **(Binde-)Strich, Minus**	*abc lower case* **Kleinbuchstabe(n)**
_ **Unterstrich**	*(in brackets)* **in Klammern**
space **Leerzeichen**	*"in inverted commas"* **in Anführungsstrichen/-zeichen**

It's useful to know the German for punctuation marks and keyboard symbols for when you need to spell out, for example, your **E-Mail-Adresse** *email address*.

When spelling out the address of a **Webseite** *website*, you need *www*, which is pronounced **veh veh veh**.

www.bbcactive.com sounds like this:

veh veh veh, **Punkt**, beh, beh, tseh, ah, tseh, teh, ee, fow, eh, **Punkt**, com

German punctuation is similar to English but there are some differences in the way commas are used. In German, a comma is always needed at the beginning of a subordinate clause, i.e. a clause often introduced by words such as **dass** *that*, **weil** *because* or **obwohl** *although* (page 93):

Man sagt, dass Chinesisch schwer ist. *It is said that Chinese is difficult.*

Er trägt Shorts, weil es warm ist. *He is wearing shorts because it's warm.*

capital letters

German uses capital letters much more than English because all nouns, not only proper nouns, i.e. the names of people, companies, places, months, days of the week etc., need to be capitalised. This is regardless of whether they're at the beginning of or within a sentence:

Zum Frühstück trinkt er Kaffee, isst einen Toast mit Honig und liest die Zeitung. *For breakfast he drinks coffee, eats a (piece of) toast with honey and reads the newspaper.*

Auf alle Laptops, Smartphones und Flachbildschirme gibt es zehn Prozent Rabatt. *There's a ten per cent discount on all laptops, smartphones and flat screens.*

- The formal *you* **Sie** and *your* **Ihr** are also written with a capital letter:
  Woher kommen Sie? *Where do you come from?*
  Wie ist Ihr Name? *What's your name?*

  The word for *I* **ich**, however, is not written with a capital unless it starts a sentence:
  Und ich möchte ein Bier. *And I would like a beer.*
  Ich mag Sport, aber ich jogge nicht gern. *I like sport, but I don't like jogging.*

- Whereas in English, adjectives describing nationalities and political or religious groups are written with a capital letter, they take a lower-case letter in German:
  Sie kauft italienischen Wein. *She buys Italian wine.*
  Er ist der sozialistische Kandidat. *He is the Socialist candidate.*
  Es ist ein katholisches Land. *It's a Catholic country.*

When writing in German it may take some time to get used to the concept of using capital letters for all nouns. There have been suggestions that this practice should be abandoned, but they have not been successful and the capitalisation of nouns is still an important feature of German. This actually makes it easier to understand a German text because the capitals tell you which words are nouns.

word power

Many words in English and German come from the same original root but have developed differently over time. Knowing what the differences are makes it possible to make an educated guess at the meaning of many German words. Here are a few examples of how certain letters and letter combinations have changed:

🇬🇧 🇩🇪

ch	k	*child* Kind, *church* Kirche, *chin* Kinn, *cheese* Käse
d	t/tt	*dance* Tanz, *door* Tür, *dream* Traum, *to drink* trinken
f	v	*folk* Volk, *forward* vorwärts, *father* Vater, *full* voll
p	f/ff	*deep* tief, *ape* Affe, *ship* Schiff, *hope* hoffen
p/pp	pf	*pound* Pfund, *pan* Pfanne, *plant* Pflanze, *apple* Apfel
s/sh	sch	*swim* schwimmen, *false* falsch, *shoe* Schuh, *fish* Fisch
t	z	*two* zwei, *ten* zehn, *heart* Herz, *to* zu, *tongue* Zunge
th	d	*this* dies, *three* drei, *bath* Bad, *earth* Erde, *leather* Leder
t/tt	ss	*better* besser, *water* Wasser, *that* dass, *to eat* essen
oo	u	*blood* Blut, *foot* Fuß, *school* Schule, *flood* Flut

If you have some old German books, you might notice that certain words are written differently in them. This is due to new spelling rules, agreed by Germany, Austria and Switzerland in 2007.

One of the key changes is that ß is now only used after a long vowel or diphthong, and ss must be used after a short vowel: *must* **muss** (new)/**muß** (old). Another change is that three consonants or vowels occurring together are not condensed as they used to be: *football league* **Fußballliga** (new)/**Fußballiga** (old). And although German still has its long words made up of more than one noun, combinations of noun + verb and verb + verb are now usually separated: **Rad fahren** *to cycle* (new)/**radfahren** (old); *to go for a walk* **spazieren gehen** (new)/ **spazierengehen** (old).

checkpoint 1

1   ü occurs twice in **Frühstück**. Which is pronounced short and which long? Why is this?

2   In which of these words is the letter **s** pronounced like the English z: **Sand, sie, Thomas, Fantasie, ins?**

3   When spelling words out, what names are used for clarification for the letters **a, c, n** and **o**?

4   How is *www* pronounced?

5   Where does the stress fall in most German words?

6   Where does the stress fall in these words:
   Politik, Musik, probieren, gemacht, Fleischerei?

7   **ich möchte eine tasse tee mit milch und zucker.** Which words in this sentence need a capital letter?

8   Which is the correct spelling: **Herr Peters, kommen sie/Sie aus England? Nein, ich/Ich komme aus Schottland?**

9   Which four letters in the German alphabet are additional to the 26 shared with the English alphabet?

10 According to the new spelling rules, would you write **Schiffahrt** or **Schifffahrt** for *shipping*?

11 Which of these combinations sounds like the *y* in *fry*: **ie** or **ei?**

12 Where should there be a comma in **Ich denke dass London interessant ist** *I think that London is interesting*?

13 What do you think these words are in English: **Bischof, scharf, gut, Ding?**

Once you're comfortable with spelling out your own details, have a go at spelling out the names and email addresses of friends and family.

Numbers, time and date

Numbers aren't particularly difficult to learn in German.

- 1–12 sound similar to the English numbers, for instance **vier** *four*, **sechs** *six*, **sieben** *seven*, **neun** *nine*.
- 13–19 are formed by adding **zehn** *ten*, just like *-teen* in English.
- Numbers over 20 are slightly different as they start with the unit, then **und** and then the tens: 49, **neunundvierzig**, literally translated is *nine-and-forty*. However, once you're used to this pattern, it's straightforward to form higher numbers.

A striking difference between larger numbers in German and English is that in German there are no spaces between words when they're written out:
zweihundertfünfundzwanzig *two hundred and twenty-five*
Don't be fazed by this – in reality you very rarely see large numbers written as words.

A more crucial difference is the punctuation used with numbers.
In German:

- **ein Komma** *comma* is used to indicate a decimal point:
  7,5 **sieben Komma fünf**; 0,7 **null Komma sieben**
- **ein Punkt** *full stop* or a space is used to separate thousands:
  28.000   28 000
  100.000   100 000

Zero is **null** in German.

null 1. nought, zero: *unter* ~ below zero; *über* ~ above zero; *Stunde* ~ zero hour; *bei* ~ *anfangen* to start from scratch **2.** *[sport]* nil: *zwei zu* ~ *gewinnen* to win 2:0. **3.** *[tennis]* love: *dreißig* ~ 30:0. **4.** *[telephone]* zero, O.

cardinal numbers 1-99

1	eins	11	elf
2	zwei	12	zwölf
3	drei	13	dreizehn
4	vier	14	vierzehn
5	fünf	15	fünfzehn
6	sechs	16	sechzehn
7	sieben	17	siebzehn
8	acht	18	achtzehn
9	neun	19	neunzehn
10	zehn		

- **Zehn** *ten* is added to the numbers 13–19.
- The second **s** is dropped from **sechs** in **sechzehn**.
- **Siebzehn** is formed without the **en** used in **sieben**.
- **Zwo** is sometimes used instead of **zwei**, especially on the telephone, to avoid confusion with **drei**.

20	zwanzig	29	neunundzwanzig
21	einundzwanzig	30	dreißig
22	zweiundzwanzig	40	vierzig
23	dreiundzwanzig	50	fünfzig
24	vierundzwanzig	60	sechzig
25	fünfundzwanzig	70	siebzig
26	sechsundzwanzig	80	achtzig
27	siebenundzwanzig	90	neunzig
28	achtundzwanzig		

- 31–99 repeat the pattern 21–29, i.e. the unit + **und** + the tens: *21* is literally *one-and-twenty*, *22 two-and-twenty*, etc: **achtundvierzig** *48*, **sechsundsiebzig** *76*, **neunundneunzig** *99*
- **Eins** drops the **s** in numbers above 20: **einunddreißig** *31*, **einundachtzig** *81*
- **Dreißig** is spelled with **ß** instead of **z**: **neununddreißig** *39*
- The second **s** in **sechs** is dropped to form **sechzig**: **einundsechzig** *61*, **siebenundsechzig** *67*
- The **en** is dropped in **siebzig**: **vierundsiebzig** *74*, **achtundsiebzig** *78*
- **%** is **Prozent**; a **Komma** *comma* is used to indicate a decimal point: **fünfzig Prozent** *50%*; **7,5 Prozent** *7.5%*, said as **sieben Komma fünf Prozent**

100 +

100	(ein)hundert	1 000	(ein)tausend
101	(ein)hunderteins	1 100	(ein)tausendeinhundert
102	(ein)hundertzwei	1 500	(ein)tausendfünfhundert
200	zweihundert	2 000	zweitausend
210	zweihundertzehn	10 000	zehntausend
250	zweihundertfünfzig	100 000	hunderttausend
500	fünfhundert	500 000	fünfhunderttausend
		1 000 000	eine Million
		2 000 000	zwei Millionen
		1 000 000 000	eine Milliarde

- **Ein** is often dropped when referring to numbers from 100–199:
  hundertzehn *110*, **hundertdreiundachtzig** *183*
  Ein, however, is not dropped with thousands:
  zweitausendeinhundertvier *2,104*, **zwölftausendeinhundert** *12,100*

- **und** is not normally added after hundreds or thousands:
  einhundertsiebenundsechzig *167*, **siebentausendzweiundsechzig**
  7,062

- 100 and 1,000 have a plural only when used in general terms: **hunderte von Menschen** *hundreds of people*; **tausende von Besuchern** *thousands of visitors*. **Eine Million** and **eine Milliarde** are always **Millionen** and **Milliarden** in the plural:
  zwei Millionen einhunderttausend *2,100,000*
  sieben Milliarden *7,000,000,000*

- a **Punkt** *full stop* or a space can be used to separate thousands.
  1.000/1 000 *1,000*
  10.000/10 000 *10,000*
  8.000.000/8 000 000 *8,000,000*

Eins *one* is used differently from other German numbers. When used before nouns, its endings reflect the gender and case of the noun, just like the indefinite article *a/an* (page 54):
Er verdient eine Million Euro. *He earns one million euros.*
Sie hat einen Sohn. *She's got one son.*

ordinal numbers

- Ordinal numbers 1–19 are formed by adding **-te** to the cardinal numbers. Slightly irregular forms are **erste** *first*, **dritte** *third*, **siebte** *seventh* and **achte** *eighth*.

1st	**erste (1.)**	8th	**achte (8.)**
2nd	**zweite (2.)**	9th	**neunte (9.)**
3rd	**dritte (3.)**	10th	**zehnte (10.)**
4th	**vierte (4.)**	12th	**zwölfte (12.)**
5th	**fünfte (5.)**	15th	**fünfzehnte (15.)**
6th	**sechste (6.)**	18th	**achtzehnte (18.)**
7th	**siebte (7.)**	19th	**neunzehnte (19.)**

- From 20th onwards, ordinal numbers are formed by adding **-ste** to the cardinal number:

20th	**zwanzigste**	30th	**dreißigste**
21st	**einundzwanzigste**	50th	**fünfzigste**
22nd	**zweiundzwanzigste**	100th	**hundertste**

- Ordinal numbers are used much the same as in English, except that they change their endings as any other adjective (pages 57–62):
  die erste Liebe *the first love*
  am ersten Mai *on the first of May*

- When referring to sovereigns or popes, you use **der** for masculine and **die** for feminine names:

Heinrich der Achte	*Henry VIII*
Königin Elisabeth die Zweite	*Queen Elizabeth II*
Papst Benedikt der Sechzehnte	*Pope Benedict XVI*

Seeing German words on a regular basis helps to embed them in your memory. If you search on the internet for **Jahreskalender** and the relevant year, you'll find downloadable calendars which will provide a daily reminder of the days and the months as well as German public holidays.

time

As in English, there are several ways of telling the time in German:

- the 12-hour clock: **Es ist zehn Minuten nach zwei Uhr** *It's ten minutes past two (o'clock)*; or, more informally, **Es ist zehn nach zwei** *It's ten past two*.
- the 24-hour clock: **zwei Uhr zehn** *2.10*.

  The 12-hour clock uses **vor** *to*, **nach** *past*, **Viertel** *quarter*, **halb** *half*.

  Wie viel Uhr ist es? *What time is it?*

  Wie spät ist es? *What time is it?* (lit. *How late is it?*)

  Es ist … *It's …*
  09.00 **neun Uhr**
  09.05 **fünf nach neun**
  09.10 **zehn nach neun**
  09.15 **fünfzehn nach neun** or **Viertel nach neun**
  09.20 **zwanzig nach neun**
  09.25 **fünfundzwanzig nach neun**
  09.30 **halb zehn** (!)
  09.35 **fünfundzwanzig vor zehn** or **fünf nach halb zehn**
  09.40 **zwanzig vor zehn**
  09.45 **fünfzehn vor zehn** or **Viertel vor zehn**
  09.50 **zehn vor zehn**
  09.55 **fünf vor zehn**

- **Halb** is not used in the same way as the English *half* when referring to time. **Halb** conveys halfway to the next hour, not half past the hour: *6.30* **halb sieben**; *2.30* **halb drei**; *10.30* **halb elf**.
- **Eins** drops the **s** when used with **Uhr**:
  Es ist ein Uhr *It's one o'clock*, but **Es ist eins** *It's one*.

  Um wie viel Uhr …? *(At) what time …?*
  um zwei, um drei … um elf Uhr *at two, at three … at 11 o'clock*
  um Mitternacht *at midnight*

- The use of the 24-hour clock is widespread in Germany, especially for timetables and schedules:

  Es ist sieben Uhr zehn. *It's 7.10.*
  um vierzehn Uhr *at 14.00/2pm*
  zwischen achtzehn und zwanzig Uhr *between 18.00 and 20.00/ 6pm and 8pm*

date: days, months, years

- **Die Wochentage** *the days of the week* are:

Montag	*Monday*
Dienstag	*Tuesday*
Mittwoch	*Wednesday*
Donnerstag	*Thursday*
Freitag	*Friday*
Samstag/Sonnabend	*Saturday*
Sonntag	*Sunday*

> All days in German are masculine. The equivalent to the English *on* is **am**: **Ich sehe dich am Montag.** *I'll see you on Monday.*

- **Die Monate** *the months of the year* in German are also masculine:

Januar	*January*	**Juli**	*July*
Februar	*February*	**August**	*August*
März	*March*	**September**	*September*
April	*April*	**Oktober**	*October*
Mai	*May*	**November**	*November*
Juni	*June*	**Dezember**	*December*

- **Die vier Jahreszeiten** *the four seasons* are:

der Frühling	*spring*	**der Sommer**	*summer*
der Herbst	*autumn*	**der Winter**	*winter*
im Frühling ... im Winter ...		*in the spring ... in winter ...*	

- When referring to years in German there's no word for *in*:
  Das Buch erschien 1989. *The book was published in 1989.*
  Sie ist 2004 geboren. *She was born in 2004.*

- Previous centuries are referred to in hundreds, and years from 2000 onwards start with *two thousand*, not *twenty* as often in English:
  1989 **neunzehnhundertneunundachtzig**
  2012 **zweitausendzwölf**

- With dates, ordinal numbers are used (abbreviated with a full stop):
  der erste (1.) Juni, der dritte (3.) September *1st June, 3rd September*

- **Am** is the equivalent to the English *on*. When using **am**, an **-n** is added to the number:
  am ersten Juni *on the first of June*
  am dritten September *on the third of September*

wann? *when?*
genau um drei Uhr *at three o'clock on the dot*
gegen sechs Uhr *at about six o'clock*
in fünf Minuten *in five minutes' time*
bis um fünf Uhr *until five o'clock*
zwischen neun und zwölf Uhr *between nine and twelve o'clock*

heute *today*
morgens/nachmittags/abends *in the morning/afternoon/evening*
um zehn Uhr morgens *at ten o'clock in the morning*
um drei Uhr nachmittags *at three o'clock in the afternoon*
um zehn Uhr abends *at ten o'clock in the evening*

heute Morgen *this morning*; **heute Abend** *this evening*
heute Nachmittag *this afternoon*

jeden Tag/alle zwei Tage *every day/every two days*
jede Woche/jeden Monat *every week/every month*
einmal pro Woche/Monat *once a week/month*
oft/manchmal/nie *often/sometimes/never*

morgen *tomorrow*
morgen früh *tomorrow morning*
übermorgen *the day after tomorrow*
in zwei Tagen *in two days*
nächste Woche *next week*
nächstes Jahr *next year*

gestern *yesterday*
gestern Morgen/Abend *yesterday morning/evening*
vorgestern *the day before yesterday*
vor zwei Tagen/vor einer Woche *two days/a week ago*
letzte Woche *last week*
letztes Jahr *last year*

in den Sechzigerjahren *in the '60s*
im zwanzigsten Jahrhundert/im einundzwanzigsten Jahrhundert
in the 20th/21st century

checkpoint 2

1   What's the German for *nil*?

2   Is einhundertzweiundsechzig greater or smaller than einhundertsechsundzwanzig?

3   Write down the German for 8, 18, 28 and 88.

4   Now write zwei Millionen dreihundertvierundsiebzigtausend in numbers, punctuating it the German way.

5   What do these mean?
   a Es ist fünf Uhr.   b um sieben Uhr abends
   c nach Mitternacht   d gestern Abend um sieben Uhr
   e um halb sieben   f vor einer Woche
   g Es ist Viertel nach eins.   h nächste Woche
   i genau um ein Uhr   j zwischen vier und sechs Uhr

6   And how do you say these times in German?
   a *It's 11 o'clock.*   b *at 12 midnight*
   c *at 7.30*   d *It's quarter to three.*
   e *It's twenty past four.*   f *tomorrow at ten o'clock*
   g *yesterday at five*   h *on Sunday at 16.00*
   i *every day at seven o'clock*   j *at four o'clock on the dot*

7   What are the German words for *in, on, and at* in these phrases?
   a in winter   b on Monday   c at three o'clock

8   Januar, Februar, ... Which month comes next?

9   New Year's Day in German is der erste Januar. How would you write the dates for Christmas Day and New Year's Eve?

10 What does übermorgen mean?

11 What time is this train expected: einundzwanzig Uhr zweiundvierzig?

12 achtzig, ..., hundert What's missing from the sequence?

13 In German, which century is the year siebzehnhundertsechzig in?

14 Is Herbst or Frühling the German for *spring*?

15 How do you say *75%* in German?

Nouns

Nouns are the words for
- living beings: man, sister, doctor, lion, Sebastian
- things: table, water, night, lesson, sport
- places: country, town, Germany, Berlin
- concepts: beauty, freedom, time, democracy

In German, nouns are always written with a capital letter, regardless of where they are in a sentence: **Deutschland hat viele interessante Städte und schöne Landschaften**. *Germany has many interesting cities and beautiful landscapes.*

Unlike English nouns, every German noun is classified as either masculine (m), feminine (f) or neuter (nt). This is its **gender**, and you need to know a noun's **gender** because words used with it, such as articles and adjectives, have corresponding masculine, feminine and neuter forms. For example: **der Apfel** (m) *the apple*, **die Firma** (f) *the company*, **das Buch** (nt) *the book*.

When you're talking about more than one of something in German, you don't routinely add **-s** to the noun as in English. Instead, there's a range of endings; some nouns also add an umlaut. For example: **die Äpfel** *the apples*, **die Firmen** *the companies*, **die Bücher** *the books*.

In an English–German dictionary, abbreviations to look out for include *n (noun), m (masculine), f (feminine), nt (neuter), sing (singular), pl (plural).* If you look up *car, journey* and *baggage*, this is what you might find:

car *n* Wagen *m*, Auto *nt: by* ~ mit dem Wagen/Auto; ~ *park n* Parkplatz *m*, Parkhaus *nt*; ~ *accident n* Autounfall *m*; ~ *hire n* Autovermietung *f*

journey *n* Reise *f*: *(by car, train etc.) also* Fahrt *f*; *to go on a* ~ eine Reise machen; *Have a good* ~! Gute Reise/Fahrt!

baggage *n* Gepäck *nt:* *hand* ~ *n* Handgepäck *nt*; *excess* ~ *n* Überfracht *f*, Übergepäck *nt*; ~ *room n* Gepäckaufbewahrung *f*; *with bag and* ~ mit Sack und Pack

gender

Understanding about linguistic gender, which has no equivalent in modern English, is key to using German nouns. Gender is not confined to male and female persons; it affects all German nouns, which are classified as masculine, feminine or neuter.

Words used alongside nouns, such as articles (pages 51–56) and possessives (pages 78–79), have masculine, feminine and neuter forms, and the one that corresponds to the noun has to be selected. For example, *the* is

der (m)   **die** (f)   **das** (nt)

people

The gender of most words for people is predictable, with the great majority of nouns for males being masculine and females feminine: **der Mann**, **die Frau**. However, **die Person** is always feminine and **das Opfer** always neuter, regardless of who they refer to: **Die Person/das Opfer heißt Thomas** *The person/the victim is called Thomas*, and the words for *girl*, **das Mädchen** and **das Fräulein**, are both neuter, as are **das Baby** *baby*, **das Kind** *child* and **das Individuum** *individual*.

other nouns

Although the ending of many other nouns is a guide to their gender, there's no foolproof way of predicting that, for example, **das Haus** *house* is neuter, **der Zug** *train* is masculine or that **der Lohn** *wage* is masculine, **die Steuer** *tax* feminine and **das Gehalt** *salary* neuter. The best tactic is to associate a noun with its gender by learning it with **der**, **die** or **das** and to look out for the endings listed on the following pages.

If you make a mistake with the gender of a noun, more often than not you'll be understood anyway. But look out for nouns like these below, which are identical apart from their gender yet have quite different meanings:

der Leiter *leader*   **die Leiter** *ladder*
die Maß *litre of beer*   **das Maß** *measure*
der See *lake*   **die See** *sea*
der Kiefer *jaw*   **die Kiefer** *pine tree*
der Tor *fool*   **das Tor** *gate*

masculine nouns

The nouns for males and male animals are masculine:

der Junge *boy*   **der Sohn** *son*
der Löwe *lion*   **der Bulle** *bull*

With a few exceptions, nouns in the following categories are masculine:

- days of the week, months and seasons: **der Montag** *Monday*, **der Mai** *May*, **der Sommer** *summer*
- makes of cars: **der Audi**, **der BMW**, **der Jaguar**, **der VW**
- alcoholic drinks: **der Champagner**, **der Gin**, **der Whisky**, **der Wein**, **der Wodka**. But *beer* is **das Bier**
- points of the compass: **der Norden** *the north*, **der Süden** *the south*, **der Osten** *the east*, **der Westen** *the west*
- currencies: **der Euro**, **der Dollar**, **der Schweizer Franken**. But *sterling* is **das Britische Pfund**.

Most nouns with these endings are masculine:

-ant	**der Aspirant** *candidate*, **der Brillant** *diamond*, **der Fabrikant** *industrialist*, **der Garant** *guarantor*
-ig	**der Honig** *honey*, **der Käfig** *cage*, **der König** *king*, **der Essig** *vinegar*
-ismus	**der Egoismus** *egoism*, **der Idealismus** *idealism*, **der Materialismus** *materialism*, **der Optimismus** *optimism*
-ling	**der Liebling** *darling/favourite*, **der Schmetterling** *butterfly*, **der Zwilling** *twin*, **der Lehrling** *trainee*
-or	**der Faktor** *factor*, **der Katalysator** *catalyst*, **der Motor** *engine*, **der Reaktor** *reactor*. Exceptions include **das Labor** *laboratory*

weak nouns

About 10% of masculine nouns, most of them referring to male people and animals, are weak nouns: they add **-(e)n** to all forms apart from the nominative singular (for more information on cases, see pages 43–50). They include **Architekt** *architect*, **Junge** *boy*, **Mensch** *person*, **Name**, **Löwe** *lion*, **Tourist** and **Student**:

Der Student kommt aus London. *The student comes from London.*
Wir treffen den Studenten. *We're meeting the student.*
Sie hilft dem Studenten. *She helps the student.*

Herr, also a weak noun, adds **-n** for all the singular forms apart from the nominative, and **-en** for the plural:

Kennst du Herrn Stark? *Do you know Mr Stark?*
Meine Damen und Herren. *Ladies and gentlemen.*

feminine nouns

The nouns for females and female animals are nearly all feminine:

die Frau *woman*   **die Tante** *aunt*
die Löwin *lioness*   **die Henne** *hen*

The following categories are also nearly all feminine:

- motorbikes and ships: **die Yamaha**, **die BMW**, **die Titanic**.
- numerals: **die Eins**, **die Hundert**, **die Million**.
- major rivers: **die Elbe**, **die Donau** *the Danube*, **die Themse** *the Thames*. But *the Rhine* is **der Rhein** and *the Mississippi* is **der Mississipi**.
- names of trees and flowers: **die Eiche** *oak tree*, **die Lärche** *larch*, **die Tulpe** *tulip*

There are more endings associated with feminine nouns than with masculine and neuter nouns.

-e	About 90% of nouns ending in **-e** are feminine: **die Frage** *question*, **die Lampe** *lamp*, **die Tasche** *bag*, **die Tasse** *cup*. Exceptions include **der Name** *name*, **der Käse** *cheese*.
-ei	**die Bäckerei** *bakery*, **die Metzgerei** *butcher's*, **die Türkei** *Turkey*
-heit, -keit	**die Freiheit** *freedom*, **die Krankheit** *illness*, **die Mehrheit** *majority*, **die Möglichkeit** *possibility*, **die Schwierigkeit** *difficulty*
-ie, -ik	**die Astrologie** *astrology*, **die Demokratie** *democracy*, **die Fantasie** *imagination*, **die Musik** *music*, **die Kritik** *criticism*, **die Panik** *panic*
-ion	**die Emigration**, **die Explosion**, **die Nation**, **die Option**, **die Station**, **die Religion**
-schaft	**die Erbschaft** *inheritance*, **die Landschaft** *landscape*, **die Mannschaft** *team*, **die Meisterschaft** *championship*
-tät	**die Kreativität** *creativity*, **die Normalität** *normality*, **die Realität** *reality*, **die Universität** *university*
-ung	**die Hoffnung** *hope*, **die Rechnung** *invoice*, **die Zeitung** *newspaper*
-ur	**die Frisur** *hairstyle*, **die Kultur** *culture*, **die Natur** *nature*

corresponding masculine and feminine nouns

Many masculine nouns referring to people and professions have a feminine equivalent formed by adding **-in**:

der Teenager (m)   die Teenagerin (f)
der Student (m)   die Studentin (f)

A few of the feminine versions also add an umlaut to the final **a**, **o** or **u** of the masculine noun:

der Schwager *brother-in-law*   die Schwägerin *sister-in-law*
der Arzt *doctor*   die Ärztin *female doctor*
der Koch *cook*   die Köchin *cook*

but not:

der Fahrer *driver*   die Fahrerin *driver*
der Pate *godfather*   die Patin *godmother*

Whether or not an umlaut should be added is something that you'll soon get a feeling for.

This use of the **-in** ending is particularly evident in occupations.

der Apotheker   die Apothekerin *pharmacist*
der Designer   die Designerin *designer*
der Ingenieur   die Ingenieurin *engineer*
der Journalist   die Journalistin *journalist*
der Kassierer   die Kassiererin *cashier, check-out assistant*
der Kellner   die Kellnerin *waiter/waitress*
der Kundenberater   die Kundenberaterin *customer advisor*
der Manager   die Managerin *manager/manageress*
der Schauspieler   die Schauspielerin *actor/actress*
der Verkäufer   die Verkäuferin *sales assistant*
der Rechtsanwalt   die Rechtsanwältin *lawyer*
der Zahnarzt   die Zahnärztin *dentist*

However, it isn't possible to add **-in** to all occupations; some behave differently:

Angestellter   Angestellte   *employee*
Kaufmann   Kauffrau   *trader*

If you search on the internet for **Stellenangebote** *job offers* you'll come across many more jobs and professions, such as **Immobilienkauffrau/ -mann** *estate agent*, **IT-Spezialist (m/w)**, **Rezeptionist (m/w)**. The abbreviation **m** refers to **männlich** *male*, and **w** to **weiblich** *female*.

neuter nouns

The following categories of noun are all neuter:

- young people and young animals: **das Baby, das Kind** *child,* **das Kalb** *calf,* **das Lamm** *lamb*
- most countries and towns: **England, Frankreich** *France,* **das Berlin von heute** *today's Berlin*
- names of hotels and cinemas: **das Hilton, das Lumière**
- metals and chemicals: **das Silber** *silver,* **das Gold, das Helium**
- infinitives (see page 117) used as nouns: **das Singen** *singing,* **das Schwimmen** *swimming,* **das Tanzen** *dancing*

The following endings are usually associated with neuter nouns. As with masculine and feminine endings, there are exceptions.

-chen/-lein	**das Brötchen** *roll,* **das Mädchen** *young girl,* **das Märchen** *fairy tale,* **das Fräulein** *young, unmarried woman,* **das Männlein** *little man*
-ing	**das Doping, das Meeting, das Shopping, das Training** (usually words from English)
-ma	**das Asthma, das Dogma, das Klima** *climate,* **das Komma** *comma,* **das Thema** *theme/topic* Exceptions include **die Firma** *company.*
-ment	**das Argument, das Dokument, das Experiment, das Instrument** Exceptions include **der Moment.**
-o	**das Auto** *car,* **das Büro** *office,* **das Kino** *cinema* Exceptions include **der Tango.**
-um	**das Album** *album,* **das Eigentum** *property,* **das Museum** *museum,* **das Visum** *visa,* **das Zentrum** *centre*

compound nouns

- The use of compound nouns is very common in German. These are words that consist of one or more nouns used together and, unlike English, written as one long word. The last noun decides the gender:

  das Auto + der Mechaniker = der Automechaniker *car mechanic*
  der Kaffee + die Pause = die Kaffeepause *coffee break*
  der Computer + das Spiel = das Computerspiel *computer game*

- When joining nouns, an extra **s** is sometimes added. This normally happens when the first word ends in **-heit, -ing, -ion, -keit, -schaft, -tät, -tum** or **-ung**:

  der Liebling + die Gruppe = Lieblingsgruppe *favourite band*
  die Mannschaft + der Sport = Mannschaftssport *team sport*
  die Universität + die Stadt = Universitätsstadt *university town*

- An **s** is also added when the first noun is derived from a verb and ends in **-en**:

  das Leben + die Freude = die Lebensfreude *joy of life*
  das Schlafen + die Zeit = die Schlafenszeit *bedtime*

  The extra **s** can also appear in other combinations such as **der Geburtstag** *birthday*, **der Glücksfall** *stroke of luck*, **die Eintrittskarte** *entrance ticket*.

The *captain of the Danube steamship line* is a classic example of a long compound noun in German that really existed: **Donaudampfschifffahrtsgesellschaftskapitän.**

If, however, a word gets too long and difficult to read, then a hyphen can be used: **das Consulting-Unternehmen** *consulting company*.

adjectival nouns

Adjectival nouns are nouns derived from adjectives:
krank *ill, sick*: **ein Kranker/eine Kranke** *a sick person*
deutsch *German*: **Deutscher/Deutsche** *a German person*
Other examples include **Angestellte(r)** *employee*, **Arbeitslose(r)** *unemployed person*, **Erwachsene(r)** *adult*, **Jugendliche(r)** *young person*, **Verlobte(r)** *fiancée/fiancé*, **Verwandte(r)** *relative*.

These nouns take the same endings as adjectives (pages 57–64).

making nouns plural

In the plural, *the* is **die** for nouns of all three genders.

German nouns don't automatically add -s to form the plural like English nouns. Instead, they add one of several different endings and it's a good idea to learn a new word together with its plural form.

Any good German–English dictionary will indicate the plural ending alongside other basic information such as gender, e.g:

Hund *m*; **~es**, **~e** *dog*

The first ending (**~es**) indicates the genitive case ending (page 48) and the second (**~e**) shows that the plural form is **die Hunde** *dogs*.

There are straightforward rules for the plural of some nouns:

- most masculine nouns add **-e**, or **-e** + umlaut
  der Beruf → die Berufe *jobs*
  der Film → die Filme *films*
  der Tag → die Tage *days*
  der Gast → die Gäste *guests*
  der Schnaps → die Schnäpse *schnapps*
  der Supermarkt → die Supermärkte *supermarkets*

- feminine nouns ending in e add **-n** and most others add **-en**
  die Flasche → die Flaschen *bottles*
  die Handtasche → die Handtaschen *handbags*
  die Sprache → die Sprachen *languages*
  die Bäckerei → die Bäckereien *bakeries*
  die Mehrheit → die Mehrheiten *majorities*
  die Zeitung → die Zeitungen *newspapers*

- for female professions and people, **-nen** is added
  Ärztin → Ärztinnen *female doctors*
  Studentin → Studentinnen *female students*
  Freundin → Freundinnen *female friends*

- some short feminine nouns add **-e** + umlaut
  die Hand → die Hände *hands*
  die Kunst → die Künste *arts*
  die Stadt → die Städte *cities/towns*

- most neuter nouns add **-e** but no umlaut, or **-er** with an umlaut where possible – i.e. on **a**, **au**, **o** or **u**:
  das Haar → die Haare *hairs*
  das Jahr → die Jahre *years*
  das Geschenk → die Geschenke *presents*
  das Kind → die Kinder *children*
  das Buch → die Bücher *books*
  das Haus → die Häuser *houses*

- nouns ending in **-el**, **-en**, **-er**, **-chen** or **-lein** don't add an ending but most add an **umlaut** where possible:
  der Spiegel → die Spiegel *mirrors*
  das Theater → die Theater *theatres*
  der Apfel → die Äpfel *apples*
  die Mutter → die Mütter *mothers*
  der Vater → die Väter *fathers*

- most words imported from French or English simply add **-s**:
  der Club → die Clubs   das Taxi → die Taxis
  das Steak → die Steaks   der Laptop → die Laptops
  das Hobby → die Hobbys   die Party → die Partys
  but: der Computer → die Computer

- some nouns imported from Latin or Greek behave as follows:
  der Organismus → die Organismen *organisms*
  der/das Virus → die Viren *viruses*
  das Museum → die Museen *museums*

- The plural forms of compound nouns always follow the pattern of the final noun in the compound:
  der Zahn+arzt → die Zahnärzte *dentists*
  die Auto+bahn+ausfahrt → die Autobahnausfahrten *motorway exits*

- a few words are normally used only in the plural, including **Eltern** *parents*, **Geschwister** *brothers and sisters*, **Ferien** *holidays*, **Kosten** *costs*, **Lebensmittel** *food*, **Leute** *people*, **Möbel** *furniture*.

A few nouns that are plural in English are singular in German: *glasses* **die Brille** (plural **Brillen** *pairs of glasses*), *scissors* **die Schere** (plural **Scheren** *pairs of scissors*), *trousers* **die Hose** (plural **Hosen** *pairs of trousers*).

word power

Because German and English share common linguistic roots, many words are very similar when you say them, even though the written version may not be the same. This is especially true of words relating to life's fundamentals, as seen, for example, in nouns describing family relationships.

the family
der Vater *father*, die Mutter *mother*
der Sohn *son*, die Tochter *daughter*
der Bruder *brother*, die Schwester *sister*
der Halbbruder *half-brother*, die Halbschwester *half-sister*
der Cousin *male cousin*, die Cousine *female cousin*
der Onkel *uncle*, die Tante *aunt*

Some other words are close enough for the meaning to be clear, particularly when the context is known:
der Großvater *grandfather*, die Großmutter *grandmother*
der Großonkel *great uncle*, die Großtante *great aunt*

Other useful words in the context of the family are:
der Neffe *nephew*, die Nichte *niece*
der Enkelsohn *grandson*, die Enkeltochter *granddaughter*
das Enkelkind *grandchild*
der Schwiegervater *father-in-law*, die Schwiegermutter *mother-in-law*
der Schwager *brother-in-law*, die Schwägerin *sister-in-law*
der Schwiegersohn *son-in-law*
die Schwiegertochter *daughter-in-law*
der Stiefbruder *stepbrother*, die Stiefschwester *stepsister*
der Pate/der Patenonkel *godfather*
die Patin/die Patentante *godmother*
der Pflegevater *foster father*, die Pflegemutter *foster mother*
die Pflegefamilie *foster family*

Some words tend to be used only in the plural:
Hast du Geschwister? *Do you have any brothers and sisters?*
Wo wohnen deine Eltern? *Where do your parents live?*
Meine Großeltern wohnen in Mainz. *My grandparents live in Mainz.*

food and drinks
das Brot *bread*, die Butter *butter*, das Korn *corn*, der Fisch *fish*
die Milch *milk*, das Bier *beer*, der Wein *wine*, das Wasser *water*
der Apfel *apple*, die Karotte *carrots*, das Radieschen *radish*

houses and surroundings
das Haus *house*, das Heim *home*, der Garten *garden*, das Feld *field*
der Stein *stone*, der Pfad *path*, die Tür *door*, der Ofen *oven*
das Bad *bath*, der Raum *room*, der Keller *cellar*, die Küche *kitchen*

parts of the body and illness
die Nase *nose*, das Ohr *ear*, der Mund *mouth*, die Lippe *lip*
der Finger *finger*, die Hand *hand*, der Arm *arm*, das Haar *hair*
die Brust *breast*, die Lunge *lung*, die Leber *liver*, das Herz *heart*
der Mumps *mumps*, das Fieber *fever*, die Masern *measles*

animals
der Wolf *wolf*, der Bär *bear*, der Luchs *lynx*, der Fuchs *fox*
die Kuh *cow*, der Bulle *bull*, das Lamm *lamb*, die Sau *sow*
die Katze *cat*, die Maus *mouse*, die Ratte *rat*, die Henne *hen*
der Falke *falcon*, der Storch *stork*, der Bussard *buzzard*

nature and weather
die Erde *earth*, die Welt *world*, die Natur *nature*
die Sonne *sun*, der Mond *moon*, der Stern *star*, der Planet *planet*
die Pflanze *plant*, das Gras *grass*, das Wetter *weather*
der Wind *wind*, der Sturm *storm*, das Eis *ice*

false friends

Not all nouns mean what they appear to mean:

die Box means *loudspeaker*   *box* is die Schachtel
die Chips means *crisps*   *chips* are die Pommes frites
der Flur means *hall*   *floor* is der Fußboden
das Gymnasium means   *the gym* is die Turnhalle or
grammar school   das Fitnesscenter
das Gift means *poison*   *gift* is das Geschenk
der Mist means *dung*   *mist* is der Dunst
die Rente means *pension*   *rent* is die Miete
die Weste means *waistcoat*   *vest* is das Unterhemd

checkpoint 3

1   Write m, f, or nt in the boxes depending on whether the noun is masculine, feminine or neuter.

Arzt	☐	Ärztin	☐	Montag	☐
Tasche	☐	Schwimmen	☐	Thema	☐
Astrologie	☐	Kultur	☐	September	☐
Kino	☐	Universität	☐	Kind	☐

2   What are these in the plural?

der Beruf	das Theater
der Freund	die Mutter
der Fuß	das Café
die Frage	das Museum
die Sonne	die Stadt
die Zeitung	der Apfel
das Kind	das Land
die Bankerin	der Film
das Geschenk	das Handy
das Haus	die Party

3   Is **Bier** masculine or neuter?

4   What two meanings does **See** have?

5   **Frage, Name, Tasche**: which is the odd one out and why?

6   Does **Studentinnen** mean one male student, one female student, several male students, several female students or a mixed group?

7   Think of a word that's feminine even when it refers to a man.

8   Can you name a) three typical male endings, b) three typical female endings and c) three typical neuter endings for nouns?

9   Which part of a compound noun decides its gender?

10   Can you put these words together: **das Internet + die Firma =** .... ; **die Zeitung + der Artikel =** .... ?

11   How would you say: *Do you know Mr Kahn?*

12   What are the male equivalents of **Schwester** and **Tante**?

13   Given that **Redakteur** is *male editor* and **Redakteurin** *female editor*, what's the female equivalent of **Übersetzer** *translator*?

Cases

Case refers to the role that a noun or pronoun plays in a sentence. In German there are four cases, each one associated with a different role. Once you understand the nature of those four roles, it's easier to implement rules involving case.

1 **Nominative** case. The noun/pronoun is the subject of the sentence, i.e. it carries out the action of the verb:
   The man eats a sandwich. ***He*** eats a sandwich.
2 **Accusative** case. The noun/pronoun is the direct object of the sentence, i.e. it is directly affected by the verb:
   The dog bites **the man**. *The dog bites* **him**.
3 **Dative** case. The noun/pronoun is the indirect object of the sentence, i.e. it is affected, but indirectly:
   She gives a book to **the man**. *She gives (to)* **him** *a book.*
4 **Genitive** case. The noun/pronoun relates to possession:
   This is **the man's** *car. This is* **his** *car.*

In English, case makes a difference only when using the personal pronouns *I/me, we/us, he/him, she/her, they/them*. In German, on the other hand, all words that accompany a noun, i.e. articles (pages 51–56), demonstratives and possessives (pages 73–80), negatives (pages 123–126) and adjectives (pages 57–64), have different forms according to the role of that noun in that particular sentence, i.e. its case.

For instance, when a masculine noun is the subject of a sentence, the definite article (*the*) is **der**: <u>Der</u> **Mann isst ein Sandwich**. But when that same masculine noun is the direct object of a sentence, *the* is **den**: **Der Hund beißt <u>den</u> Mann**.

Certain prepositions and verbs require a following noun/pronoun to be in a specific case. For example, **für** *for* is followed by the accusative: **Ist dieses Glas für den Rotwein?** *Is this glass for the red wine?*; and **helfen** *to help* is followed by the dative: **Helfen Sie mir!** *Help me!*

nominative case: subject

The subject of a sentence carries out the action. It can be a person, thing or idea, in the singular or plural. It's not always at the beginning of the sentence.

Der Junge liest. *The boy is reading.*
Das Fahrrad kostet 200 Euro. *The bike costs 200 euros.*
Ich höre Musik. *I'm listening to music.*
Sie gehen heute ins Kino. *They're going to the cinema today.*
Morgen fährt er nach Berlin. *Tomorrow he's going to Berlin.*

> You can easily identify the subject by asking who or what is doing the action. Who is reading? <u>The boy</u>. What costs 200 euros? <u>The bike</u>.

- When the subject is a personal pronoun, the following forms are used:

ich *I*	wir *we*
du informal *you*	ihr informal *you* plural
Sie formal *you*	Sie formal *you* plural
er *he*, sie *she*, es *it*	sie *they*

- When the subject is a noun, words used with it, such as articles and possessives, have different forms, depending on the gender:

	masculine	feminine	neuter	plural
definite article	der	die	das	die
indefinite article	ein	eine	ein	–
possessive	mein	meine	mein	meine
negative	kein	keine	kein	keine

- The indefinite articles (*a, an*), possessives and the negative **kein** all follow the same pattern: no endings with masculine and neuter nouns; **-e** added with feminine and plural nouns.

- The nominative is the case used after the verbs **sein** *to be*, **scheinen** *to seem* and **werden** *to become*:
  Das ist mein Mann. *This is my husband.*
  Das scheint ein guter Deal zu sein. *This seems to be a good deal.*
  Morgen wird ein schöner Tag. *Tomorrow is going to be a lovely day.*

accusative case: direct object

As well as a subject, most sentences have a direct object. This is the person or thing at the receiving end of the action:

Der Mann trinkt <u>einen Kaffee</u>. *The man drinks <u>a coffee</u>.*
Peter kauft <u>ein Handy</u>. *Peter is buying <u>a mobile</u>.*
Ich lese <u>eine Zeitung</u>. *I'm reading <u>a newspaper</u>.*
Die Leute sehen <u>einen Film</u>. *The people are watching <u>a film</u>.*

You can identify the direct object by asking at whom or at what the action is directed. What does the man drink? <u>A coffee.</u>

- When the object is a personal pronoun, the following forms are used:

mich *me*	**uns** *us*
dich informal *you*	**euch** informal *you* plural
Sie formal *you*	**Sie** formal *you* plural
ihn *him*, **sie** *her*, **es** *it*	**sie** *them*

Siehst du <u>mich</u>? *Do you see me?* **Magst du <u>ihn</u>?** *Do you like him?*

- When the object is a noun, words used with it, such as articles, possessives and the negative **kein**, need to be in the accusative. Except for the masculine forms, these are all identical to the nominative:

	masculine	feminine	neuter	plural
definite article	**den**	**die**	**das**	**die**
indefinite article	**einen**	**eine**	**eine**	-
possessive	**meinen**	**meine**	**meine**	**meine**
negative	**keinen**	**keine**	**kein**	**keine**

Ich nehme <u>den</u> Eiskaffee. *I'll have the iced coffee.*
Sehen Sie <u>meinen</u> Mann? *Do you see <u>my</u> husband?*
Sie hat <u>keinen</u> Sohn. *She doesn't have a son.* (Lit. *She has <u>no</u> son.*)

- The accusative is needed after certain prepositions (pages 102–103), including:
bis *until*, **durch** *through*, **für** *for*, **gegen** *against/around*, **ohne** *without*, **um** *around/at*:
Er ist für <u>den</u> Plan. *He's in favour of the plan.*
Die Uhr ist für <u>meine</u> Schwester. *The watch is for my sister.*
Er geht um <u>das</u> Haus herum. *He goes around the house.*

dative case: indirect object

In addition to a direct object, sentences can have an indirect object, i.e. a person or thing to/for whom or to which something is done.

Sie kauft <u>dem Mann</u> einen Kaffee. *She buys <u>(for) the man</u> a coffee.*
Er gibt <u>der Frau</u> eine Zeitung. *He gives <u>(to) the woman</u> a newspaper.*
Peter kauft <u>dem Kind</u> ein Handy. *Peter buys <u>(for) the child</u> a mobile.*
Sie erzählen <u>den Kindern</u> eine Geschichte. *They tell <u>(to) the children</u> a story.*

You can identify the indirect object by asking to/for whom or what the action is being done. For whom does she buy the coffee? <u>For the man.</u>

- When the indirect object is a personal pronoun, the following forms are used:

mir *(to) me*	**uns** *(to) us*
dir informal *(to) you*	**euch** informal *(to) you* plural
Ihnen formal *(to) you*	**Ihnen** formal *(to) you* plural
ihm *(to) him*, **ihr** *(to) her*, **ihm** *(to) it*	**ihnen** *(to) them*

- Articles, possessives and the negative **kein** linked to the indirect object change. Look out for the **-em**, **-er** and **-en** pattern:

	masculine	feminine	neuter	plural
definite article	**dem**	**der**	**dem**	**den**
indefinite article	**einem**	**einer**	**einem**	-
possessive	**meinem**	**meiner**	**meinem**	**meinen**
negative	**keinem**	**keiner**	**keinem**	**keinen**

- For most plural nouns in the dative case **-n** is added:
  die Kinder → den Kinder<u>n</u>; **die Computer → den Computer<u>n</u>**.
  But if the basic plural forms end in **-n** or **-s**, no addition is made:
  die Menschen → den Menschen; **die Partys → den Partys**.

- The dative is also needed after certain prepositions, including:
  aus *from/out of*, **außer** *apart from*, **bei** *at/near*, **gegenüber** *opposite*, **mit** *with/by*, **nach** *after/to*, **seit** *since/for*, **von** *from*, **zu** *to* (pages 100–104):
  Er fährt mit <u>dem</u> Bus. *He goes by bus.*
  Sie wohnt bei <u>ihrer</u> Mutter. *She lives with her mother.*
  Tim studiert seit <u>einem</u> Jahr. *Tim has been studying for one year.*

the dative case after verbs

Although most verbs in German are followed by the accusative case, some are followed by the dative, e.g: **antworten** *to answer*, **begegnen** *to meet, encounter,* **danken** *to thank*, **drohen** *to threaten*, **folgen** *to follow*, **gehören** *to belong to*, **gratulieren** *to congratulate*, **helfen** *to help*, **schaden** *to harm*, **trauen** *to trust*, **zuhören** *to listen to*:

Bitte antworte <u>mir</u>. *Please answer me.*

Sie danken <u>der</u> Frau. *They thank the woman.*

Er gratuliert <u>dem</u> Sieger. *He congratulates the winner.*

Das Auto gehört <u>den</u> Nachbarn. *The car belongs to the neighbours.*

Bitte helfen Sie <u>mir</u>. *Please help me.*

Das schadet <u>dem</u> Motor. *This harms the engine.*

Sie traut <u>dem</u> Chef nicht. *She doesn't trust the boss.*

● Quite a few verbs are frequently used with both a direct and indirect object, including **bringen** *to bring*, **geben** *to give*, **empfehlen** *to recommend*, **erzählen** *to tell, recount* **kaufen** *to buy*, **sagen** *to say*, **schenken** *to give as a present*, **schulden** *to owe*, **zeigen** *to show*:

Können Sie uns ein gutes Restaurant empfehlen? *Can you recommend a good restaurant to us?*

Sie erzählt den Kindern eine Geschichte. *She's telling the children a story.*

Kaufst du mir ein Eis? *Are you going to buy me an ice cream?*

Du schuldest mir zehn Euro. *You owe me ten euros.*

Lars zeigt ihnen seine neue Wohnung. *Lars is showing them his new flat.*

the dative case in expressions

There are a number of common expressions in which the dative case is used:

Wie geht es dir/Ihnen? *How are you?* (Lit. *How does it go for you?*)

Mir geht es gut. *I am well.* (Lit. *It goes well for me.*)

Mir ist kalt/warm. *I am cold/warm.*

Es tut mir leid. *I am sorry (about this).*

Das ist mir egal. *That's all the same to me.*

Gefällt dir/Ihnen das T-Shirt? *Do you like the T-shirt?*

Verzeihen Sie mir, bitte. *Forgive me/Excuse me, please.*

Können Sie mir sagen, wie viel Uhr es ist? *Can you tell me what the time is?*

genitive case: possessive

Nouns can also indicate possession or ownership, corresponding to the English 's or the preposition *of*:

Das ist der Kaffee <u>meines Mannes</u>. *This is <u>my husband's</u> coffee.*
Das ist die Zeitung <u>meiner Frau</u>. *This is <u>my wife's</u> newspaper.*
Das ist das Handy <u>meines Kindes</u>. *This is <u>my child's</u> mobile.*
Das ist das Ende <u>des Filmes</u>. *That's the end <u>of the film</u>.*

 You can identify the possessive form by asking whose ... it is/
they are. Whose coffee is it? <u>My husband's</u>.

- When linked to a noun that indicates possession, the masculine and neuter forms of the articles, possessives and the negative **kein** end in **-es** and the feminine and plural versions in **-er**:

	masculine	feminine	neuter	plural
definite article	des Mannes	der Frau	des Kindes	der Kinder
indefinite article	eines Mannes	einer Frau	eines Kindes	–
possessive	meines Mannes	meiner Frau	meines Kindes	meiner Kinder
negative	keines Mannes	keiner Frau	keines Kindes	keiner Kinder

- Masculine and neuter nouns normally change in the genitive: one-syllable nouns usually add **-es**: **des Mannes, des Kindes**; longer nouns normally only add **-s**: **des Bruders, des Computers**. Feminine and plural nouns are not affected by this.

- The genitive case is used after a few prepositions, including **statt** *instead of*, **trotz** *in spite of*, **während** *during*, **wegen** *due to* (page 105).

- It's common in German to add **-s** to names to indicate ownership. However, unlike in English, there is normally no apostrophe:
  Das ist Peters Auto. *This is Peter's car.*
  Beyoncés letzter Song. *Beyoncé's last song.*

- The use of the genitive forms is decreasing in modern German. In spoken and sometimes in written German it is replaced with **von** + dative:
  das Auto meines Bruders → das Auto von meinem Bruder

word power

Although the use of the genitive is in decline, there are still many structures and areas in which it frequently appears.

expressions
Am Anfang der Geschichte … *At the beginning of the story* …
In der Mitte des Spiels … *In the middle of the game/match* …
Am Ende des Filmes … *At the end of the film* …
Auf der Spitze des Berges … *At the top of the mountain* …
Eines Morgens/eines Abends … *One morning/one evening* …
Eines schönen Tages … *One fine day* …
Meines Erachtens … *In my estimation* …

festivities and special events
Der Tag der Deutschen Einheit *The Day of German Unity*
Tag der Arbeit *May Day*
Welttag des Buches *World Book Day*

the arts and sports
Museum der modernen Kunst *Museum of Modern Art*
Die größten Hits der Neunziger *The biggest hits of the '90s*
Die beste Band aller Zeiten *The best band of all times*
Fifa-Fußballspieler des Jahres *FIFA footballer of the year*

street names, historical events and prizes
Straße des 17. Juni *17th June Street* (in Berlin)
Platz der Republik *Square of the Republic* (in Berlin)
die Geschichte der Deutschen *the history of the Germans*
der Fall der Mauer *the fall of the wall*
der Friedenspreis des Deutschen Buchhandels *the peace prize of the German Book Trade*

professional titles and roles
die Präsidentin des Filmfestivals *the president of the film festival*
der Vorsitzende des Aufsichtsrates *the chairperson of the board*
der Sprecher des Ministeriums *the spokesperson for the ministry*

with some verbs
Es bedurfte nur eines Wortes. *Just one word was needed.* (Lit. *It needed only one word.*)
Sie enthielt sich jeden Kommentars. *She made no comment.*
Er schämte sich seiner Vergesslichkeit. *He was ashamed of his forgetfulness.*

checkpoint 4

1   Identify the subjects and the objects (direct and/or indirect) in these English sentences:

   a   *She's driving the car really slowly.*

   b   *My friend bought my son a present.*

2   What are the words for *the* in the nominative case for the three genders and the plural? Which of these words change when used with a direct object?

3   Add the missing endings: **Sie hat ein____ Schwester und ein____ Bruder.**

4   *The* is dem, der, dem when linked to an indirect object noun (the dative case). What are these indirect object forms for *a*?

5   Identify the subject, direct object and/or indirect object:

   a   **Er liest ein Sportmagazin.**

   b   **Sie schenkt den Kindern ein Eis.**

   c   **Morgen besuche ich eine Freundin.**

   d   **Er schenkt dem Nachbarn eine Flasche Wein.**

6   What letter do you add to most plural nouns in the dative case?

7   Think of three verbs which are followed by the dative case.

8   Complete: **Ich helfe d____ Mann. Er hilft d____ Frau. Ich helfe d____ Kind.**

9   Which preposition is the odd one out: **für, gegen, mit, ohne**?

10   How do you answer? **Wie geht es dir?** ____ **geht es gut.**

11   Add des or der: **der Name** ____ **Computers; die Adresse** ____ **Frau.**

12   How do you say *This is Peter's house* in German? Do you need an apostrophe?

Articles: the, a

An article is used with a noun to show whether you're talking about something which is specific or defined: **the** house, **the** houses, or something which is not: **a** house. In grammatical terms:

- *the* is the definite article
- *a/an* are indefinite articles

There are a few differences in the way articles are used in English and in German. German uses the definite article more than English does – for instance with several countries: **der Irak**, **die Schweiz** and with means of transport such as **mit dem Auto** *by car*; but doesn't use the indefinite article in a sentence like **Er ist Arzt** *He's a doctor*.

More strikingly, whereas *the* and *a/an* are the only options in English, in German there's a range of words to learn because an article takes account of the gender (pages 32–36), the case (pages 43–50) and the number (singular or plural) of the noun that it relates to. This is not as daunting as it sounds since articles are normally learnt in stages and so you build your knowledge gradually.

The starting point for the definite article is to remember that **der** is used with masculine nouns, **die** with feminine nouns, **das** with neuter nouns and **die** with all plural nouns. For the indefinite article, **ein** is used with a masculine or a neuter noun, and **eine** with a feminine noun.

It's useful to focus on the similarities between the definite and indefinite articles. In the accusative, only the masculine form is different from the nominative; in the dative, the masculine and neuter versions end in **-em** and the feminine in **-er**; and in the genitive there is also a clear pattern: **des – eines** for masculine and neuter and **der – einer** for feminine nouns.

the: der, die, das etc.

English has one word for *the*; German has six:
der, die, das, den, dem, des.

Which one you use depends on three things:
- the gender of the noun that's linked to the article;
- the case of the noun, i.e. its function in the sentence;
- whether that noun is singular or plural.

nominative

When the noun with the article is the subject of the sentence, the words for *the* are **der** (masculine), **die** (feminine), **das** (neuter) in the singular, and **die** for all plural nouns:

<u>Der</u> Mann heißt Marco. *The man is called Marco.*
<u>Die</u> Frau kommt aus Berlin. *The woman comes from Berlin.*
<u>Das</u> Kind ist acht Jahre alt. *The child is eight years old.*
<u>Die</u> Kinder spielen Baseball. *The children are playing baseball.*

accusative

When the noun is a direct object, the masculine singular **der** changes to **den** but none of the other articles change:

Sie sieht <u>den</u> Mann. *She sees the man.*
Wir kennen <u>die</u> Frau. *We know the woman.*
Sie mögen <u>das</u> Kind. *They like the child.*
Sie können <u>die</u> Kinder hören. *They can hear the children.*

dative

When the noun is an indirect object, in the singular **dem** is used for masculine and neuter nouns, **der** for a feminine noun, and **den** is used for all plural nouns:

Sie gibt <u>dem</u> Mann ein Buch. *She gives the man a book.*
Er zeigt <u>der</u> Frau das T-Shirt. *He shows the woman the T-shirt.*
Er erzählt <u>dem</u> Kind eine Geschichte. *He tells the child a story.*
Sie kaufen <u>den</u> Kindern ein Computerspiel. *They buy the children a computer game.*

genitive

When talking about possession and the article equates to *of the*, **des** is used with masculine and neuter nouns, and **der** with feminine and plural nouns:

das Smartphone <u>des</u> Vaters *the father's smartphone*
das Auto <u>der</u> Frau *the woman's car*
das Computerspiel <u>des</u> Kindes *the child's computer game*
die Fragen <u>der</u> Kinder *the children's questions*

... and when to use them

Like *the* in English, **der, die, das** etc. are used before a noun referring to a specific person or thing. In German they're also needed:

- with masculine and feminine countries:
  der Irak, der Iran, der Kongo, der Sudan
  die Schweiz, die Türkei, die Slowakei, die Tschechische Republik
  die Vereinigten Staaten, die Arabischen Emirate
  ... but not usually with neuter countries such as **Frankreich** *France*.

- with street names and names of parks and squares:
  Sie wohnt in der Goethestraße. *She lives in Goethestraße.*
  Der Hyde Park ist ziemlich groß. *Hyde Park is quite big.*
  Das ist der Trafalgar Square. *That's Trafalgar Square.*

- with names of lakes and mountains:
  Der Bodensee ist schön. *Lake Constance is beautiful.*
  Er besteigt den Mount Everest. *He is climbing Mount Everest.*

- for institutions such as schools and universities:
  Nadja geht in die Grundschule. *Nadja goes to primary school.*
  Carsten studiert an der Universität. *Carsten studies at university.*

- for months and seasons:
  Der Januar hat 31 Tage. *January has 31 days.*
  Der Frühling ist die schönste Jahreszeit. *Spring is the most beautiful time of the year.*

- with meals:
  Nach dem Frühstück joggt sie. *After breakfast she goes jogging.*
  Das Mittagessen ist serviert. *Lunch is served.*
  Wer macht das Abendessen? *Who is making dinner?*

- with means of transport:
  Er fährt mit dem Fahrrad. *He goes by bike.*
  Fährst du mit der U-Bahn? *Do you take the tube?*
  Oliver fährt mit dem Auto. *Oliver goes by car.*

- with many infinitives (see pages 117–118) when used as nouns:
  Das Leben ist schön. *Life is beautiful.*
  Ich habe Angst vor dem Fliegen. *I'm afraid of flying.*
  Sie will mit dem Rauchen aufhören. *She wants to give up smoking.*

However, when saying that someone plays an instrument, there's no equivalent to *the* in German:
Tina spielt Gitarre und Piano. *Tina plays the guitar and the piano.*

a: ein, eine, einen etc.

English has two forms of the indefinite article: *a* and *an*, depending on whether the related noun starts with a consonant or a vowel. This is not an issue in German, which has six forms: **ein**, **eine**, **einen**, **einem**, **einer** and **eines**. Which one you use depends on:

- the gender of the noun that's related to the article;
- the role of that noun in the sentence, i.e. its case.

nominative

When the article is used with the subject of the sentence, the words for *a* are **ein** with masculine and neuter nouns and **eine** with feminine nouns:

Ein Mann steigt in sein Auto. *A man gets into his car.*
Eine Frau aus Wales wohnt hier. *A woman from Wales lives here.*
Ein Kind braucht viel Zuwendung. *A child needs a lot of attention.*

accusative

As with *the*, only the masculine form is different from the nominative; **ein** becomes **einen**. The feminine **eine** and neuter **ein** are the same:

Wir sahen **einen** Mann. *We saw a man.*
Sie trifft **eine** Frau aus Wales. *She is meeting a woman from Wales.*
Sie adoptiert **ein** Kind. *She is adopting a child.*

dative

Also similar to the definite article, the masculine and neuter forms of *a/an* are **einem** with a noun which is an indirect object, while the feminine form is **einer**:

Er gibt **einem** Mann das Geld. *He gives the money to a man.*
Er gibt **einer** Frau die Blumen. *He gives the flowers to a woman.*
Sie kauft **einem** Kind ein Eis. *She buys an ice cream for a child.*

genitive

When indicating possession and the article equates to *of a/an*, **eines** is used with masculine and neuter nouns and **einer** with feminine nouns:

die Verantwortung **eines** Vaters *a father's responsibilities* (lit. *the responsibilities of a father*)
das Geheimnis **einer** Frau *a woman's secret*
die Fantasie **eines** Kindes *a child's imagination*

... and when to use them

Indefinite articles in German are used in pretty much the same circumstances as *a/an* in English, i.e. before a noun that isn't referring to a specific person or thing.

However, unlike in English, they're not used with nouns denoting:

- nationality and affiliation to a city or province:
  Er ist Australier. *He's an Australian.*
  Ich bin Berliner. *I'm a Berliner.*
  Sie ist Bayerin. *She's a Bavarian.*

- occupation, religion and marital status:
  Sie ist Studentin. *She's a student.*
  Lukas ist Rechtsanwalt. *Lukas is a lawyer.*
  Mein Onkel ist Koch. *My uncle is a chef.*
  Anna ist Katholikin. *Anna is a Catholic.*
  Er ist Witwer. *He's a widower.*

  However, **ein, eine, einen** etc. are used if an adjective is introduced:
  Er ist ein typischer Australier. *He's a typical Australian.*
  Mein Onkel ist ein guter Koch. *My uncle is a good chef.*
  Lukas ist ein teurer Rechtsanwalt. *Lukas is an expensive lawyer.*

articles overview

definite *the*

	masculine	feminine	neuter	plural
nominative	der Mann	die Frau	das Kind	die Kinder
accusative	den Mann	die Frau	das Kind	die Kinder
dative	dem Mann	der Frau	dem Kind	den Kindern
genitive	des Mannes	der Frau	des Kindes	der Kinder

indefinite *a/an*

	masculine	feminine	neuter
nominative	ein Mann	eine Frau	ein Kind
accusative	einen Mann	eine Frau	ein Kind
dative	einem Mann	einer Frau	einem Kind
genitive	eines Mannes	einer Frau	eines Kindes

checkpoint 5

1   Choose **der**, **die**, or **das** for these nouns. If in doubt about what gender they are, check with pages 32–36.

Mann	Frau	Kaffee
Kind	Türkei	Baby
Freiheit	Bruder	Junge
Brötchen	Zeitung	Universität

2   Decide if it's more appropriate to use the indefinite or definite article:

a   Berlin ist eine/die Hauptstadt von Deutschland.

b   München ist eine/die Stadt in Süddeutschland.

c   Wie heißt ein/der Mann von Angela?

d   Carsten hat ein/das Problem mit seinem Smartphone.

e   Ist das ein/der Computer von Petra?

f   Sein oder Nichtsein, das ist hier eine/die Frage.

3   Put **einen**, **eine** or **ein** in front of these nouns.

a   Er ist .... netter Junge.

b   Er trifft .... Kollegin aus den USA.

c   Sie trinkt .... Kaffee und isst .... Brötchen.

d   Mesut kauft .... Zeitung.

e   Thomas braucht .... neuen Computer.

f   Petra hat zwei Kinder – .... Tochter und .... Sohn.

4   The singular forms for *the* when linked to an indirect object are **dem**, **der** and **dem**. What are the equivalent forms for *a*?

5   How do you say *He lives in Schillerstraße* in German?

6   How would you ask a new acquaintance (using **Sie**):

a   if he's a Berliner?

b   if he's a student?

c   if he plays the piano?

d   if he goes by car?

Adjectives

Adjectives are words that describe nouns or pronouns.

- We have a **small** garden.
- The film was **superb**.
- She is **beautiful**.
- Take the **second** turning.
- I prefer **German** beer.

As in English, an adjective in German can either immediately precede a noun or come later in the sentence. In German, the position of the adjective makes a big difference.

If an adjective appears after a noun it doesn't change from the basic form you find in a dictionary:
Der Garten ist klein.
If, however, it precedes a noun it requires an ending:
Wir haben einen kleinen Garten.

The ending needs to reflect the gender of the noun, the case and the number (singular or plural). The ending also depends on whether the adjective is linked to the definite article (*the*), the indefinite article (*a*) or if it appears without an article.

This sounds more complicated than it actually is. In practice, many endings are the same and there are patterns you can apply. After the definite articles for instance, all adjectives end only in **-e** or **-en**.

The dictionary abbreviations for *adjective* are *adj* in English and German (the full word is **Adjektiv**).

If you look up *clear*, this is what you might find:

clear *adj* **1.** *water*, *soup*, *sky*, *weather etc*. klar **2.** *is that ~?* alles klar?
3. *a ~ profit* ein Reingewinn *m* **4.** *conscience* rein: *a ~ conscience* ein reines Gewissen

adjectives after nouns

Adjectives don't change when they appear after the noun they describe. This is often the case in connection with **sein** *to be* and **werden** *to become*:

Helena ist nett. *Helena is nice.*
Das Sandwich war teuer. *The sandwich was expensive.*
Es wird dunkel. *It's getting dark.*
Er war heute ein bisschen gereizt. *He was a bit tetchy today.*
London ist multikulturell. *London is multicultural.*
Ich werde schnell müde. *I get tired quickly.*

Here are some adjectives and their opposites in their basic dictionary form:

alt *old*	**neu** *new*
arm *poor*	**reich** *rich*
billig *cheap*	**teuer** *expensive*
dick *fat*	**dünn** *thin*
dunkel *dark*	**hell** *light*
früh *early*	**spät** *late*
gut *good*	**schlecht** *bad*
glücklich *happy*	**traurig** *sad*
hart *hard*	**weich** *soft*
hässlich *ugly*	**schön** *beautiful*
interessant *interesting*	**langweilig** *boring*
klein *small*	**groß** *big*
langsam *slow*	**schnell** *fast*
laut *loud*	**leise** *quiet*
schwer *heavy*	**leicht** *light*
süß *sweet*	**sauer** *sour*
warm *warm*	**kalt** *cold*

... and some colours:

blau *blue*, **braun** *brown*, **gelb** *yellow*, **grau** *grey*, **grün** *green*, **lila** *purple*, **rosa** *pink*, **rot** *red*, **schwarz** *black*, **weiß** *white*

Learning words in sets is more effective than learning them individually. This doesn't only mean learning words relating to a particular topic or situation but, for example, learning an adjective together with its opposite (**gut/schlecht**, **groß/klein**, **neu/alt**) or a word with a similar meaning (**ausgezeichnet/exzellent**).

Create your own associations. If you were asked to think of a partner for **weiß** *white*, would you choose **schwarz** *black* or **rot** *red* (wine connection)? Both? Or another word altogether?

adjective endings after the

If an adjective follows a definite article, there are only two possible endings:
-e or -en; -en is taken by all dative, genitive and plural forms and appears
after **den** in the masculine accusative:

	masculine	feminine	neuter	plural
nominative	-e	-e	-e	-en
accusative	-en	-e	-e	-en
dative	-en	-en	-en	-en
genitive	-en	-en	-en	-en

nominative

Der grüne Rock ist elegant. *The green skirt is elegant.*
Die blaue Jacke war teuer. *The blue jacket was expensive.*
Das neue T-Shirt ist aus Paris. *The new T-shirt is from Paris.*
Die neuen Schuhe sind schön. *The new shoes are nice.*

accusative

Sie trägt den grünen Rock. *She's wearing the green skirt.*
Kaufst du die blaue Jacke? *Are you buying the blue jacket?*
Ich mag das neue T-Shirt. *I like the new shirt.*
Sie trägt die neuen Schuhe. *She's wearing the new shoes.*

dative

Sie trägt ihre neue Bluse … *She is wearing her new blouse …*
… mit dem grünen Rock. *… with the green skirt.*
… mit der blauen Jacke. *… with the blue jacket.*
… mit dem neuen T-Shirt. *… with the new T-shirt.*
… mit den neuen Schuhen. *… with the new shoes.*

genitive

Trotz des grünen Rockes … *Despite the green skirt …*
Wegen der blauen Jacke … *Because of the blue jacket …*
Wegen des neuen T-Shirt … *Because of the new T-shirt …*
Trotz der neuen Schuhe … *Despite the new shoes …*

The same pattern of endings also applies after **dieser** *this*, *these* and **jeder**
each, *every* and after **alle** *all* and **welcher** *which*, *what* (pages 73–76).
Dieser grüne Rock ist teuer. *This green skirt is expensive.*
Ich nehme diesen grünen Rock. *I'll take this green skirt.*

adjective endings after a

If an adjective follows the indefinite article, the singular endings in the nominative and accusative case reflect the gender of the noun. The indefinite article has no plural.

	masculine	feminine	neuter
nominative	-er	-e	-es
accusative	-en	-e	-es
dative	-en	-en	-en
genitive	-en	-en	-en

nominative
Er ist ein guter Arzt. *He is a good doctor.*
Das ist eine neue Band. *This is a new band.*
Das war ein tolles Konzert. *That was a great concert.*

accusative
Er hat einen guten Arzt. *He has got a good doctor.*
Sie sucht eine neue Band. *She is looking for a new band.*
Sie hört ein tolles Konzert. *She is listening to a great concert.*

dative
Sprechen Sie mit einem guten Arzt. *Talk to a good doctor.*
Sie spielt in einer neuen Band. *She plays in a new band.*
Sie war auf einem tollen Konzert. *She was at a great concert.*

genitive
der Rat eines guten Arztes *the advice of a good doctor*
der Erfolg einer neuen Band *the success of a new band*
trotz eines tollen Konzertes *despite a great concert*

Adjectives following possessives **mein**, **dein** etc. (pages 78–79) and the negative **kein** take the same singular endings as those following an indefinite article:
Er ist kein guter Arzt. *He is not a good doctor.*
Sprich mit deinem neuen Arzt. *Talk to your new doctor.*

All plural endings with the possessives or **kein** are **-en**:
Das sind meine guten Freunde. *These are my good friends.*
Sie hat keine guten Freunde. *She doesn't have good friends.*
mit seinen guten Freunden *with his good friends*
wegen seiner guten Freunde *because of his good friends*

adjectives with no article

Adjectives not preceded by an article, a possessive or the negative **kein** take on endings similar to those of the definite article.

	masculine	feminine	neuter	plural
nominative	-er	-e	-es	-e
accusative	-en	-e	-es	-e
dative	-em	-er	-em	-en
genitive	-en	-er	-en	-er

nominative

Starker Kaffee hält dich wach. *Strong coffee keeps you awake.*
Frische Luft ist gesund. *Fresh air is healthy.*
Deutsches Bier schmeckt gut. *German beer tastes good.*
Spanische Oliven sind lecker. *Spanish olives are yummy.*

accusative

Er trinkt gern starken Kaffee. *He likes drinking strong coffee.*
Sie liebt frische Luft. *She loves fresh air.*
Er mag deutsches Bier. *He likes German beer.*
Sie bestellen spanische Oliven. *They order Spanish olives.*

dative

Er hält sich mit starkem Kaffee wach. *He keeps awake with strong coffee.*
Bewegung an frischer Luft ist gut für den Körper. *Exercise in fresh air is good for the body.*
eine gute Auswahl an deutschem Bier *a good selection of German beer*
Sie essen Fisch mit spanischen Oliven. *They eat fish with Spanish olives.*

genitive

mit der Hilfe starken Kaffees *with the help of strong coffee*
ein Hauch frischer Luft *a breath of fresh air*
der Export deutschen Bieres *the export of German beer*
der Preis spanischer Oliven *the price of Spanish olives*

For greetings and good wishes, the accusative is normally used because the notion of *I wish you ...* is implied but not expressed:
Guten Morgen *Good morning*; **Guten Tag** *Good day*; **Guten Abend** *Good evening*; **Gute Nacht** *Good night*; **Gute Besserung** *Get well*; **Herzlichen Glückwunsch** *Congratulations*

more on adjective endings

- Adjectives like **sauer** *sour* and **teuer** *expensive* drop the **-e** before the final **-r**:
  Sie aß einen sauren Apfel. *She ate a sour apple.*
  Er fährt ein teures Auto. *He drives an expensive car.*

- **Dunkel** *dark* omits the **e-** before the **-l**:
  Es war eine dunkle Nacht. *It was a dark night.*

- **Hoch** *high* loses the **-c**:
  Sie bauen einen hohen Zaun. *They're building a high fence.*

- Adjectives ending in **-a**, such as **lila** *purple*, **rosa** *pink* and **prima** *great*, don't take endings:
  Er trägt ein rosa Hemd. *He's wearing a pink shirt.*
  Sie mag ihren lila Rock. *She likes her purple skirt.*
  Wir hatten einen prima Abend. *We had a great evening.*

- Adjectives constructed from names of towns end in **-er** and don't change their endings:
  Der Kölner Dom ist berühmt. *Cologne cathedral is well known.*
  Sie besuchte den Kölner Dom. *She visited Cologne cathedral.*
  Das ist der Berliner Hauptbahnhof. *That's Berlin main train station.*
  Er arbeitet für eine Berliner Agentur. *He works for an agency in Berlin.*

- When more than one adjective is used before a noun, all the adjectives normally take the same ending:
  Es war ein heißer, sonniger Tag. *It was a hot, sunny day.*
  München hat viele schöne, aber teure Geschäfte. *Munich has many nice, but expensive, shops.*

- If a number of items is listed, a preposition, for instance **mit**, determines the case not only of the first item but also the following items:
  Sie trägt eine weiße Bluse <u>mit</u> <u>einer</u> blauen Jacke und <u>einem</u> roten, modischen Hut. *She's wearing a white blouse with a blue jacket and a red, fashionable hat.*

word **power**

There are hundreds of adjectives which are similar in English and German because they come from the same language root. It's often straightforward to guess their meaning, e.g:

akut *acute*, **alt** *old*, **bitter** *bitter*, **blau** *blue*, **falsch** *false*, **fein** *fine*, **fett** *fat*, **grün** *green*, **gut** *good*, **hart** *hard*, **jung** *young*, **kalt** *cold*, **komplex** *complex*, **mild** *mild*, **lang** *long*, **laut** *loud*, **reich** *rich*, **rot** *red*, **sauer** *sour*, **warm** *warm*, **weiß** *white*

There are also adjectives which have corresponding endings in both English and German:

🇬🇧	🇩🇪	
-al	-al	**digital, final, föderal, ideal, sozial, spezial, real, zentral**
-ic(al)	-isch	**astronomisch, erotisch, diplomatisch, fantastisch, geografisch, islamisch, klassisch, ökologisch, ökonomisch, periodisch, politisch, realistisch, romantisch, typisch, tragisch**
-ive	-iv	**aggressiv, aktiv, alternativ, kommunikativ, exzessiv, impulsiv, informativ, intensiv, kreativ, massiv, negativ, offensiv, positiv**

false friends

brav means *well-behaved*	*brave* is **tapfer, mutig**
delikat means *exquisite*	*delicate* is **zart, heikel**
devot means *obsequious*	*devoted* is **hingebungsvoll**
dezent means *discreet*	*decent* is **anständig**
familiär means *family-related*	*familiar* is **bekannt**
mondän means *fashionable*	*mundane* is **weltlich, banal**
ordinär means *vulgar*	*ordinary* is **normal**
rentabel means *profitable*	*rentable* is **mietbar**
sensibel means *sensitive*	*sensible* is **vernünftig**
seriös means *respectable*	*serious* is **ernst, ernsthaft**
sympathisch means *likeable*	*sympathetic* is **mitfühlend**
unsympathisch means *unlikeable*	*unsympathetic* is **mit wenig Mitgefühl**

checkpoint 6

1   After the definite article there are only two endings for
    adjectives in German. What are they?

2   Complete:
    a Der grün...... Rock ist schön.
    b Das blau...... Hemd hat 20 Euro gekostet.
    c Die braun...... Schuhe waren billig.

3   Find adjectives in this unit with the opposite meaning to these:
    a altmodisch   b schlecht
    c alt   d billig
    e ungesund   f sauer
    g schwach   h hell

4   Complete the endings:
    a Er ist ein gut...... Designer.
    b London ist eine schön...... Stadt.
    c Ich brauche einen neu...... Computer.
    d Ich fahre mit meinem alt...... Auto nach Italien.
    e Er geht mit seiner neu...... Freundin ins Kino.

5   Carsten likes German beer, but doesn't like German wine.
    How would he say this?
    Ich mag .... Bier, aber keinen .... Wein.

6   What does this mean: Er ist sehr unsympathisch?

7   How would you say: This is an expensive car?

8   The main train station in Frankfurt is called Frankfurter
    Hauptbahnhof and the airport Frankfurter Flughafen.
    What are these two places called in Hamburg?

9   Complete:
    a Gut...... Abend.   b Gut...... Nacht.
    c Gut...... Tag.   d Herzlich...... Glückwunsch.

10 How would you say in German:
    a She's buying the blue jacket and the white skirt?
    b He's wearing a white jacket with a blue T-Shirt and
       white shoes?

Adverbs and comparisons

Adverbs are words that:

- say how, when or where something happens or is:
  They cooked it **perfectly**.
  He's talking **quickly**.
  I'm working **tomorrow**; I start **early**.
  We live **here/over there**.

- add an extra dimension to adjectives and other adverbs:
  They cooked it **absolutely** perfectly.
  He's talking **extremely** quickly, **rather** quickly for me.
  I'm **really** tired, **too** tired to work.
  Our house is **very** small.

- add an extra dimension to a whole sentence:
  Unfortunately we have to leave.
  They would be here **otherwise**.

There are two main differences between English and German adverbs.

1 Almost all German adjectives can also be used as adverbs; there's normally no equivalent to the English **-ly** ending: **schnell** *quick, quickly*.

2 German adverbs don't go between the subject and its verb. In a sentence like *Anna often works*, the order is *Anna works often*.

Making comparisons in German is straightforward, with **-er** being added to an adjective or adverb: **schneller** *quicker, more quickly*. There's also an equivalent of the English **-est** ending for superlatives: **am schnellsten** *quickest, most quickly*.

The dictionary abbreviations for *adverb* are *adv* in both English and German (the full word is **Adverb**). If you look up **gut**, this is what you might find:

gut 1. *adj* good, fine: *in Englisch ~ sein* to be good at English; *-en Abend!* good evening **2.** *adv* well: *~ spielen* to play well; *~ gemacht!* well done!; *es kann ~ sein* that may well be

word power

Unlike in English, most German adjectives can also be used as adverbs, usually with no equivalent -ly ending:

Sie ist <u>schnell</u>. *She is quick.* (adjective)
Sie spricht <u>schnell</u>. *She talks quickly.* (adverb)

Here are a few more examples of adverbs derived from adjectives:
Die Mannschaft spielte brilliant. *The team played brilliantly.*
Er spricht klar. *He speaks clearly.*
Sie verletzte sich schwer. *She hurt herself badly.*
Er kocht gut. *He cooks well.*
Die Demonstration verlief friedlich. *The demonstration proceeded peacefully.*

There are also hundreds of adverbs in German which are not based on adjectives. They can refer to time, place, manner or degree and sometimes help to connect sentences.

- Adverbs referring to time and the sequence of events include:

morgens *in the morning*	**zuerst** *(at) first*
mittags *at lunchtime*	**zuletzt** *last, finally*
abends *in the evening*	**dann** *then*
nachts *in the night*	**danach** *after (that)*
heute *today*	**anschließend** *afterwards*
gestern *yesterday*	**schließlich** *finally*
morgen *tomorrow*	**vorher** *before*
früh *early*	**nachher** *after(wards)*
spät *late*	**nie** *never*
jetzt *now*	**selten** *seldom*
sofort *immediately*	**manchmal** *sometimes*
bald *soon*	**oft** *often*
erstens *firstly*	**meistens** *mostly*
zweitens *secondly*	**immer** *always*

- Adverbs referring to place and direction include:

hier *here*	**unten** *under, below*
da *there, here*	**oben** *above*
dort *(over) there*	**herein** *in, into*
außen *outside*	**hinaus** *out*
innen *inside*	**links** *left*
weit *far (away)*	**rechts** *right*
nah *close (by)*	**geradeaus** *straight on*

- Adverbs which quantify an adjective or another adverb include:

sehr *very*	**viel** *a lot*
so *so*	**wirklich** *really*
zu *too*	**absolut** *absolutely*
zirka *about, circa*	**extrem** *extremely*
ungefähr *approximately*	**besonders** *especially*
fast *almost*	**ganz** *quite*
genau *exactly*	**kaum** *hardly*
relativ *relatively*	**völlig** *completely*
ziemlich *fairly*	

- Other frequently used adverbs describe manner and include:

glücklicherweise *fortunately*	**wahrscheinlich** *probably*
leider *unfortunately*	**hoffentlich** *hopefully*
sicherlich *surely*	**vielleicht** *maybe, perhaps*
bestimmt *certainly*	**überraschend** *surprisingly*

- Adverbs can also indicate a reason or cause of an action:

deshalb *therefore*	**daher** *that's why, hence*
deswegen *therefore*	**trotzdem** *nevertheless*
darum *that's why*	

  ... deshalb konnte sie nicht kommen. *... therefore she couldn't come.*

  Er ist durstig, darum trinkt er eine Cola. *He's thirsty, that's why he's drinking a cola.*

- Another common adverb is **gern**, which is used to say what you like doing:

  Sie liest gern. *She likes reading.*

  Ich gehe gern shoppen. *I like going shopping.*

  Treibst du gern Sport? *Do you like doing sports?*

There are a number of adverbs in German ending in **-lich**. When derived from nouns such as **friedlich** *peaceful(ly)*, **ängstlich** *fearful(ly)* or **herzlich** *warm(ly), sincere(ly)* they can usually also be used as adjectives.

Others such as **hoffentlich** *hopefully*, **schließlich** *finally*, **sicherlich** *surely* or **wirklich** *really* only exist as adverbs.

Words ending in **-weise** such as **ärgerlicherweise** *annoyingly* or **glücklicherweise** *fortunately* can also only be used as adverbs.

position of adverbs

Adverbs in German are used in a very similar way to English and often appear in the same position.

- Adverbs derived from adjectives normally follow the verb:
  Sie tanzten <u>schön</u>. *They danced <u>beautifully</u>.*
  Er isst <u>gut</u>. *He eats <u>well</u>.*

- Quantifying adverbs such as **sehr**, **wirklich**, **absolut** and **zu** usually come before the adjective or adverb they describe:
  Er isst <u>sehr</u> gut. *He eats <u>very</u> well.*
  Ich bin <u>wirklich</u> müde. *I'm <u>really</u> tired.*
  Du hast <u>absolut</u> recht. *You're <u>absolutely</u> right.*
  Das ist viel <u>zu</u> teuer. *That's much <u>too</u> expensive.*

- Adverbs relating to time, place and direction can be used in various positions:
  Komm <u>jetzt</u>! *Come <u>now</u>!*
  Wie <u>oft</u> gehst du ins Kino? *How <u>often</u> do you go to the cinema?*
  <u>Hier</u> ist das Hotel. *<u>Here</u> is the hotel.*
  Es ist kalt <u>draußen</u>. *It's cold <u>outside</u>.*

- However, an adverb cannot go between the subject and the verb in German. The adverb often follows the verb, but it can also start the sentence. The verb normally remains in second position:
  Anna arbeitet <u>oft</u>. *Anna <u>often</u> works.*
  Er geht <u>nie</u> ins Fitnessstudio. *He <u>never</u> goes to the gym.*
  <u>Morgen</u> fahren sie in den Urlaub. *<u>Tomorrow</u> they're going on holiday.*

- Also, when an adverb of time and place appear together in a sentence, the time adverb usually comes first:
  Ich bin <u>morgen</u> wieder hier. *I am back here again <u>tomorrow</u>.*
  Er geht <u>jetzt</u> nach draußen. *He is going outside <u>now</u>.*

  More on word order on pages 89–94.

Adverbs are usually added extras in the sense that a sentence will often work without them. But they bring colour and depth to what you say, making it well worth the effort of using them – particularly since they're used in a very similar way in English and German. It's largely a matter of acquiring the vocabulary and remembering not to put them between the subject and verb.

comparisons

When making comparisons, both with adverbs and adjectives, **-er** is normally added to the basic form. This corresponds to the English pattern: *smaller, cheaper, nicer, bigger*, but in German it also works with longer adjectives:

klein → **kleiner** *small* → *smaller*
nett → **netter** *nice(ly)* → *nicer/more nicely*
effizient → **effizienter** *efficient(ly)* → *more efficient(ly)*
langweilig → **langweiliger** *boring(ly)* → *more boring(ly)*
interessant → **interessanter** *interesting(ly)* → *more interesting(ly)*

- Most adjectives and adverbs of one syllable and containing **a**, **o** or **u** add an umlaut:
  alt → **älter** *old* → *older*
  groß → **größer** *big* → *bigger*
  jung → **jünger** *young* → *younger*
  lang → **länger** *long* → *longer*
  warm → **wärmer** *warm(ly)* → *warmer/more warmly*
  Exceptions are: **flach** → **flacher** *flat(ly)* → *flatter/more flatly*; **klar** → **klarer** *clear(ly)* → *clearer/more clearly*; **bunt** → **bunter** *colourful(ly)* → *more colourful(ly)*

- A few adjectives and adverbs have irregular forms:
  gut → **besser** *good, well* → *better*
  viel → **mehr** *a lot* → *more*
  gern → **lieber** used with a verb to express liking and preference

- There are spelling variations for **hoch** → **höher** *high* → *higher*, **dunkel** → **dunkler** *dark* → *darker*, **teuer** → **teurer** *expensive* → *more expensive*

Than is **als**:
Martha ist jünger als Marco. *Martha is younger than Marco.*
Wein ist teurer als Bier. *Wine is more expensive than beer.*
Es ist länger als ich dachte. *It's longer than I thought.*
Das Team arbeitet effizienter als vorher. *The team works more efficiently than before.*

To say *as … as*, you use **so … wie**:
Sie ist so groß wie ihre Schwester. *She is as tall as her sister.*
Es ist so kalt wie gestern. *It's as cold as yesterday.*
Der Film ist nicht so gut wie das Buch. *The film is not as good as the book.*

superlatives

The superlative of adjectives and adverbs is normally formed by adding -sten. In addition, it is usually preceded by **am**:

klein → **am kleinsten** *small* → *smallest*
schnell → **am schnellsten** *quick(ly)* → *quickest/most quickly*
langweilig → **am langweiligsten** *boring* → *most boring*
sympathisch → **am sympathischsten** *likeable* → *most likeable*

- As with comparisons, most adjectives and adverbs with one syllable and containing **a**, **o** or **u** add an umlaut:
  lang → **am längsten** *long* → *longest*
  jung → **am jüngsten** *young* → *youngest*
  warm → **am wärmsten** *warm(ly)* → *warmest/most warm(ly)*
  Exceptions include: **flach** → **am flachsten** *flat(ly)* → *flattest/most flatly*; **klar** → **am klarsten** *clear(ly)* → *clearest/most clearly*; **bunt** → **am buntesten** *colourful(ly)* → *most colourful(ly)*

- The superlative forms for **gut**, **viel** and **gern** are:
  gut → **am besten** *good, well* → *best*
  viel → **am meisten** *a lot* → *most*
  gern → **am liebsten** used with a verb to express liking and strongest preference

- If the basic form ends in **-d**, **-t**, **-s** or **-z**, an extra **e** is used before **-sten**:
  wild → **am wildesten** *wild(ly)* → *wildest/most wild(ly)*
  interessant → **am interessantesten** *interesting(ly)* → *most interesting(ly)*
  nass → **am nassesten** *wet* → *wettest*
  kurz → **am kürzesten** *short* → *shortest*

- **groß** *big* only adds **-ten**: **am größten** *biggest*

- **hoch** *high*, **dunkel** *dark* and **teuer** *expensive*, which have slight spelling variations in the comparative, follow a regular pattern in the superlative: **am höchsten**, **am dunkelsten**, **am teuersten**

Leons Zimmer ist am kleinsten. *Leon's room is the smallest.*
Diese Pizza schmeckt am besten. *This pizza tastes best.*
Annas Kleid war am teuersten. *Anna's dress was the most expensive one.*
Am liebsten mag sie grünen Tee. *She likes green tea best.*
Hamburg ist größer als München, aber Berlin ist am größten.
Hamburg is bigger than Munich, but Berlin is the biggest.

comparative and superlative adjectives before a noun

When a comparative or superlative adjective comes directly before a noun, it behaves like any other adjective and takes the appropriate ending.

● The comparative can be used after various accompanying words, including articles and possessives:
Er hat noch einen älteren Bruder. *He also has an older brother.*
Das ist meine jüngere Schwester. *This is my younger sister.*
Ich nehme das billigere Ticket. *I'll take the cheaper ticket.*
Sie möchte den dunkleren Rock. *She would like the darker skirt.*

● The superlative is mainly used with the definite article and possessives:
die schnellste Frau der Welt *the quickest woman on earth*
Was ist das größte Land? *Which is the biggest country?*
Er kauft den teuersten Anzug. *He's buying the most expensive suit.*
Sie spricht mit ihrer besten Freundin. *She's talking to her best friend.*

more and less/fewer

The equivalents to *more* and *less/fewer* in German are **mehr** and **weniger**. They are used with both verbs and nouns and don't add endings when used to compare items:
Sie haben mehr Zeit als wir. *They have more time than us.*
Wein kostet mehr als Bier. *Wine costs more than beer.*
Claudia verdient weniger Geld als ihre Kollegin. *Claudia earns less money than her colleague.*
Britta hat weniger Kinder als ihre Schwester. *Britta has fewer children than her sister.*

There are a few frequently used adverbs which derive from the superlative and which are worth committing to memory, including:
Ich möchte Ihnen herzlichst danken. *I should like to thank you most warmly/sincerely.*
Das kostet höchstens zwei Euro. *That costs at most two euros.*
Der Film dauert mindestens drei Stunden. *The film lasts at least three hours.*
Du könntest ihr wenigstens schreiben. *You could at least write to her.*

checkpoint 7

1 How would you say in German:
   a *He cooks badly?*
   b *She dances very well?*
   c *They speak quickly?*

2 Find the opposites of these adverbs. They're all in this unit.
   a früh *early*
   b oben *above*
   c links *left*
   d ungefähr *approximately*
   e selten *seldom*
   f immer *always*
   g vorher *before*
   h nah *close (by)*
   i dort *there*
   j zuerst *first(ly)*

3 Put the adverbs in brackets in the correct place in these sentences:
   a Ich bin müde. (wirklich)
   b Er geht einkaufen. (nie)
   c Sie spielen Badminton. (gern)
   d Das ist zu teuer. (viel)

4 Fill in the comparative and superlative forms of these words:

billig		am billigsten
warm	wärmer	
hoch		
interessant		
rund		
kommerziell		
	lieber	
gut		

5 Translate:
   a *London is bigger than Berlin.*
   b *I'd rather drink coffee than tea.*
   c *Barcelona is as interesting as Paris.*
   d *The pizza tastes as good as in Italy.*
   e *Rebecca is older than Leon. But Valentin is the oldest.*

6 Add the appropriate ending:
   a Er heiratet eine jünger___ Frau.
   b Sie kauft einen schneller___ Computer.
   c Ich möchte ein größer___ Zimmer, bitte.
   d Wir hatten den kältest___ Winter seit 1996.
   e Der Mount Everest ist der höchst___ Berg der Welt.

Demonstratives, indefinites and possessives

These three categories can either be adjectives used with a noun, or pronouns taking the place of a noun. In general they agree – in gender, number and case – with the noun they're describing or replacing.

Demonstratives are words like *this*, *that one*, *those*, used to point out specific things.
- adjectives: *I'm going to buy this house, not that bungalow;*
- pronouns: *I'm going to buy this (one), not that (one).*

The most important demonstrative in German is **dieser**, which translates both *this* and *that*, *this one* and *that one*: the word *one* has no German equivalent here. Unlike English, German definite articles (**der**, **die**, **das**, etc.) are also used as demonstratives in informal speech.

Indefinites refer to things that are not closely identified: <u>*Some*</u> *houses are very expensive*.
They include **jeder** *each/every/everyone*, **einige** *some/some people*, **alle** *all*, **viele** *many/many people*.
Indefinite adjectives and pronouns take the same endings as **dieser** and **der**.

Man *one/they/you* is used to refer to people in a general sense: **100 Dinge, die man wissen muss**. *100 things you need to know.*

Possessives denote ownership or possession:
- adjectives: *my, our, your, his, her, its, their;*
- pronouns: *mine, ours, yours, his, hers, theirs.*

German possessives take a range of endings to agree with the noun they describe or replace. These endings are very similar to the endings for the indefinite article **ein**.

demonstrative adjectives: this/that

- **Dieser**, which translates *this, that, these, those*, needs to agree in gender, case and number (singular or plural) with the noun that follows it. Its endings closely mirror those of the definite article *the*:

	masculine	feminine	neuter	plural
nominative	dieser	diese	dieses	diese
accusative	diesen	diese	dieses	diese
dative	diesem	dieser	diesem	diesen
genitive	dieses	dieser	dieses	dieser

Dieser Mantel kostet 200 €. *This/That coat costs 200 euros.*
Diese Kirche ist neu. *This/That church is new.*
Diese Teile kommen aus China. *These parts come from China.*
Meistens kommt er zu spät. Dieses Mal war er pünktlich. *Usually he's late. This time he was on time.*

- Unlike English, the definite article can also be used as a demonstrative in German. It's mainly used in spoken language and normally in an informal context:
Ich möchte <u>den</u> Kaffee. *I'd like this/that coffee.*
Was kostet <u>die</u> Dose Bier? *What does this/that can of beer cost?*
Kennst du <u>das</u> Kind? *Do you know this/that child?*

- For clarification, **hier** *here* and **da/dort** *there/over there* are frequently used alongside **dieser** and **der**:
Meinst du das Buch hier? *Do you mean this book here?*
Siehst du den Mann dort? *Do you see that man there?*
Bist du mit diesen Schuhen hier wandern gegangen? *Did you go hiking with these shoes here?*

- **Jener** *that* can also be used in more formal contexts and with **dieser** to make a contrast between one thing and another. It takes the same endings as **dieser/der**:
An jenem besonderen Tag … *On that particular day …*
Möchtest du diesen Ring oder jenen Ring? *Would you like this ring or that ring?*

demonstrative pronouns: this/that one

The demonstratives **dieser**, **der** and **jener** can also be used as pronouns, i.e. taking the place of a noun, meaning *this (one), that (one), these (ones), those (ones)*:

Welchen Fernseher möchten Sie? Ich nehme diesen. *Which TV would you like? I'll take this one.*

Geben Sie mir diese, bitte. *Give me those, please.*

Willst du dieses T-Shirt oder das? *Do you want this T-shirt or that one?*

Ich mag diesen Film, nicht jenen. *I like this film, not that one.*

- Demonstrative pronouns have the same forms as the adjectives (see opposite), except for the dative plural, where **den** changes to **denen**:
  Arbeitest du bei <u>den</u> Leuten? – Ja, ich arbeite bei denen. *Do you work for those people? – Yes, I work for those (people).*
  Denen gebe ich nichts. *I won't give a penny to those (people).*

- the genitive masculine and neuter form **des** becomes **dessen**, the singular feminine **derer** and the plural **deren**. These forms are rarely used in modern German and only appear in formal contexts:
  Im täglichen Leben bedarf man <u>dessen</u> nicht. *In daily life you have no need of that.*

- **hier** *here*, **da/dort** *there/over there* are often used with demonstrative pronouns:
  Ich nehme den hier. *I'll take this one here.*
  Meinst du dieses hier oder das da? *You mean this one here or that one over there?*
  Das Restaurant hier ist besser als das dort. *This restaurant here is better than that one over there.*

To say *This is …* or *These are …* when introducing people in German you can either use **das** or **dies**:
Das ist meine Frau. *This is my wife.*
Das ist mein Bruder Florian. *This is my brother Florian.*
Das sind meine Kinder. *These are my children.*
Dies ist mein Mann. *This is my husband.*
Dies ist meine Tante Mia. *This is my aunt Mia.*
Dies sind meine Freunde. *These are my friends.*

indefinite adjectives: every, some, any

- Unlike *this* and *that*, indefinites don't refer to a specific person or object. The most widely used indefinite adjectives are **jeder** *each/every/any*, **einige** *some*, **alle** *all* and **viele** *many*. They're used with a noun, function in a similar way to articles and take the same endings as **der/dieser** (page 74):

- **Jeder** *each, every, any* can only be used in the singular:
  Jeder Besucher bekommt einen Gutschein. *Every visitor gets a voucher.*
  Der Film fängt jede Minute an. *The film will start any minute.*

- **Einige** *some*, **manche** *some* and **alle** *all* normally accompany plural nouns:
  Einige Teile waren kaputt. *Some parts were broken.*
  Er sprach mit einigen Leuten. *He talked to some people.*
  Manche Leute essen viel. *Some people eat a lot.*
  Sie komponiert alle Lieder selbst. *She composes all her own songs.*
  Trotz aller Probleme … *Despite all problems …*

- **Viele** can also be used as an indefinite:
  Viele Köche verderben den Brei. *(Too) many cooks spoil the broth.*
  Er hat bei vielen Vereinen gespielt. *He played for many clubs.*
  Vielen Leuten gefällt das neue Design. *Many people like the new design.*

use of *some/any*
There's no need to translate the English *some* and *any* when they're unstressed, i.e. when they have no real emphasis in the sentence.
Haben Sie Tomaten? *Do you have any tomatoes?*
Ich habe Kaffee gekauft. *I've bought some coffee.*

When *some* is stressed, **einige** is often used:
Einige Studenten haben Probleme. *Some students are having (some) problems.*
Jeder can be used for the stressed form of *any*:
Das versteht jedes Kind! *Any child understands that!*

indefinite pronouns

Indefinite pronouns are words like *everything* or *something*, which refer to people, things or ideas that are not closely defined. They're used in much the same way in English and German, but in German their endings need to reflect the grammatical role the pronoun has in the sentence.

- **jeder** *everyone* can only be used in the singular. It follows the pattern of **dieser** (page 74):
  Jeder hat die gleichen Rechte. *Everyone has the same rights.*
  Er gab jedem ein Geschenk. *He gave a present to everyone.*

- **jemand** *someone* and **niemand** *no one* are masculine, so in the accusative and dative they take the **-en** and **-em** endings respectively.
  In an informal context these endings are often dropped:
  Kann jemand bitte kommen? *Can someone please come?*
  Niemand war zu Hause. *No one was at home.*
  Hast du jemand(en) gesehen? *Did you see anyone?*
  Ich habe mit niemand(em) gesprochen. *I've spoken to no one.*

- **einige** *some*, **manche** *some,* **alle** *all*, **viele** *many* take the plural endings of **dieser**:
  Einige sprechen Englisch. *Some speak English.*
  Manche kapieren es nie. *Some never get it.*
  Er hat sich mit allen gut verstanden. *He got on well with everyone.*
  Das neue Gerät hat über 50 Funktionen, aber viele nutzt man nie.
  The new appliance has more than 50 functions but many (of them) are never used.

- **alles** *everything*, **etwas** *something*, **nichts** *nothing, anything* don't change:
  Alles wird gut. *Everything is going to be fine.*
  Mach doch etwas! *Do something!*
  Sie glaubt an nichts. *She doesn't believe in anything.*

- **man** *one* refers to *people/they* or *you* in a general sense:
  Man kann nicht alles wissen. *One can't know everything.*
  Man sagt, Paris ist romantisch. *They say that Paris is romantic.*

  It is also used where the passive would be used in English: **Hier spricht man Deutsch.** *German is spoken here.* (See page 83 for more on **man**).

possessive adjectives

The possessive adjectives in English, indicating ownership or belonging, are *my*, *our*, *your*, *his*, *her*, *its*, *their*. German has more because of the various words for *you*:

mein *my*   **unser** *our*
dein *your* (du)   **euer** *your* (ihr, plural)
Ihr *your* (Sie)   **Ihr** *your* (Sie, plural)
sein *his/its* **ihr** *her/its* **ihr** *their*

The ending of a possessive adjective has to agree in gender, number and case with the noun that follows it, i.e. the adjective agrees with what is owned, not with the owner. The endings follow the pattern of **ein** and **kein**.

	masculine	feminine	neuter	plural
nominative	mein	meine	mein	meine
accusative	meinen	meine	mein	meine
dative	meinem	meiner	meinem	meinen
genitive	meines	meiner	meines	meiner

Kennst du meine Schwester Tina? *Do you know my sister Tina?*
Leon spielt mit meinem Sohn. *Leon is playing with my son.*
Sie wohnt bei meinen Eltern. *She lives with my parents.*

The above endings for **mein** are the same for all the other persons.
Wie ist dein Name? *What's your name?*
Geben Sie mir Ihre Adresse, bitte. *Give me your address, please.*
Das ist seine Schwester. *This is his sister.*
Clara fährt mit ihrem Auto. *Clare is driving her car.*
Wo sind unsere Taschen? *Where are our bags?*
Ist das euer Haus? *Is this your house?*
Sie feiern ihren Sieg. *They celebrate their victory.*

There's a slight spelling variation for **euer**, which drops its second **e** if an adjective ending is added:
Gebt mir eure Adresse, bitte. *Give me your address, please.*
Sind das eure Taschen? *Are these your bags?*

Ihr/ihr used as a possessive can mean *your*, *her*, *its* or *their* – but this is rarely a problem as the context will usually make it clear who it refers to. When it refers to the formal **Sie** (singular and plural) it's written with a capital **I** but when it refers to *her* or to *they*, it's written with a small **i**.

possessive pronouns

Possessive pronouns, i.e. *mine*, *yours*, *theirs*, etc. are used without a noun, but they still have to agree in number and gender with the noun they replace. They have the same form as the possessive adjectives apart from the nominative masculine (**meiner**) and the neuter nominative and accusative forms (**meins**):

	masculine	feminine	neuter	plural
nominative	meiner	meine	meins	meine
accusative	meinen	meine	meins	meine
dative	meinem	meiner	meinem	meinen
genitive	meines	meiner	meines	meiner

- The above endings are also added to the basic forms of the other possessive pronouns, **deiner, Ihrer, seiner, ihrer, unserer, eurer, ihrer**.

- **Euer** drops the second e with masculine and feminine nouns and in the plural: **eure, eurer, euren**.

- The possessive pronouns are mainly used in the nominative:
  Ist das dein Hund? Ja, der Hund ist meiner. *Is this your dog? Yes, the dog is mine.*
  Ist das ihre Uhr? Ja, das ist ihre. *Is this her watch? Yes, it's hers.*
  Dieses Geschenk – ist das deins? *This present – is it yours?*
  Sind das eure Schuhe? Nein, das sind nicht unsere. *Are these your shoes? No, these aren't ours.*

- However, they can also appear in other cases:
  Sie vergaß ihren Schirm. Darum nimmt sie seinen. *She forgot her umbrella. That's why she's taking his.* (accusative)
  Fahren wir mit meinem Auto oder mit deinem? *Shall we take my car or yours?* (dative)
  Wir gedenken ihrer. *We remember them.* (genitive, very formal)

> As an alternative structure to **Das ist meins, deins, seins**, etc., German speakers frequently use **gehören** (lit. *to belong to*):
> **Ist das dein Hund? Ja, der Hund gehört mir.** *Is this your dog? Yes, the dog belongs to me.*
> **Ist das ihre Uhr? Ja, die Uhr gehört ihr.** *Is it her watch? Yes, the watch belongs to her.*

checkpoint 8

1   How would you say the following using the correct form of **dieser**?
   a *I'd like this book here.*   b *Who is that woman there?*
   c *These cars come from Japan.*

2   What are the two ways of saying *This is my sister*?

3   Choose the correct demonstrative pronoun:
   a **Nimmst du das Parfum hier oder** ....? **(diesen, dieses)**
   b **Magst du diese Hose oder** .... **dort? (die, das)**
   c **Das Restaurant hier ist billiger als** .... **dort. (jene, jenes)**
   d **Meinen Sie diese Lampe hier oder** .... **dort? (jene, jenes)**

4   How would you say the following in German?
   a *Each jacket costs 50 euros.*   b *Some people are nice.*
   c *They are all at home.*   d *No one is here.*
   e *Everything is too expensive.*

5   If you wanted to say *I bought some tea* in German, why would you
   not translate *some*?

6   **Alles** is the opposite of **nichts**: **niemand** is the opposite
   of ....

7   Underline the correct possessive:
   a **Das ist Sophias Mann. Das ist sein/ihr Mann.**
   b **Das ist die Schwester von Leon. Das ist seine/ihre
      Schwester.**
   c **Kennst du den Onkel von Tina? Ja, ich kenne seinen/ihren
      Onkel.**
   d **Anna hat ein neues Auto. Komm, wir fahren mit seinem/
      ihrem Auto.**
   e **Sind das eure Fotos? Nein, das sind nicht eure/unsere Fotos.**

8   How would you say *It is believed that …* (Lit. *One believes that …*)?

9   Answer the questions using the possessive pronoun in brackets.
   a **Ist das dein Buch? Ja, das ist** .... (*mine*).
   b **Gehört die Tasche Claudia? Ja, das ist** .... (*hers*).
   c **Ist dies das Smartphone von Tim? Ja, das ist** .... (*his*).
   d **Sind das eure Schuhe? Ja, das sind** .... (*ours*).
   e **Spielen wir mit meinem oder deinem Ball? Mit** .... (*yours*).

Personal pronouns

A pronoun is a word which replaces a noun to avoid repeating it:
The plumber called – **he**'s going to be late.
Have you seen **the children**? I can't find **them**.
Where's **my key**? I've lost **it**!

The main pronoun groups are:
- demonstrative, e.g. *this one, those* (page 75)
- possessive, e.g. *mine, yours, theirs* (page 79)
- relative, e.g. *who, which, what* (pages 95–96)
- interrogative, e.g. *what, which* (pages 128–129)
- personal, e.g. *I, she, we, us, them*

Personal pronouns can be:
- the subject of a verb (nominative case): *I, we, you, he, she, they*
- the direct object of a verb (accusative case): *me, us, you, him, her, them*
- the indirect object of a verb (dative case): *(to/for) me, (to/for) us, (to/for) you, (to/for) him, (to/for) her, (to/for) them.*

There are rules governing the order in which object pronouns appear after the verb in German. When the verb is followed by two personal pronouns, the standard rule is that the direct object pronoun comes before the indirect object pronoun:
Wo ist mein Handy? Ich habe es dir schon gegeben! *Where's my mobile? I have already given it to you!*

While there appears to be a large number of personal pronouns in German, in reality there's a parallel with English where most of the subject pronouns are also different from the direct object pronouns.

subject pronouns (nominative)

The subject pronouns (nominative case) are:

ich *I*	wir *we*
du *you* (informal)	ihr *you* (informal)
Sie *you* (formal)	Sie *you* (formal)
er *he*, sie *she*, es *it*	sie *they*

- The formal **Sie** is always written with a capital letter, while **ich** is written with a capital letter only when it starts a sentence.

- There are three words for *you*:
  du (informal singular): to a friend or family member, a child, a pet or someone you might call by their first name.

  Sie (formal singular and plural): to someone older than you, or someone you don't know so well. It can also be used to address a group of people in a more formal situation.

  ihr (informal plural): to more than one person you say **du** to. It's often used in less formal situations, even with people you don't know well.

- In German, the pronouns **er**, **sie** and **es** indicate the grammatical gender of the nouns they replace, regardless of whether they represent people, animals or things. This is different from English, where *he* and *she* generally refer to male and female people and *it* refers to animals and things:
  Der Kaffee ist stark. Er ist stark. *The coffee is strong. It (He) is strong.*
  Die Reise war schön. Sie war schön. *The trip was nice. It (She) was nice.*
  Das Radio ist kaputt. Es ist kaputt. *The radio is broken. It's broken.*

- Subject pronouns are often at the beginning of the sentence:
  Sie wohnen nicht hier. *They don't live here.*
  Wir gehen morgen ins Theater. *We're going to the theatre tomorrow.*

  But, because in German the verb has to be the second element in a main clause, the subject pronoun at times appears after the verb:
  Hier wohnen sie nicht. *They don't live here.*
  Morgen gehen wir ins Theater. *Tomorrow we're going to the theatre.*

- To emphasise the subject pronoun you can add **selbst/selber**:
  Ich mache das selber. *I'll do it myself.*
  Habt ihr selbst keine Ideen? *Do you have any ideas yourselves?*

- You'll often hear subject pronouns in phrases like these:
  Ich bin es. *It's me.*
  Wer, ich? *Who, me?*
  Er ist es! *It's him!* **Sie ist es nicht!** *It's not her!*
  Wir auch. *So are we./So did we./So have we.*
  Ich auch nicht. *Me neither./Nor me./Nor do I.*

man: undefined subject

When the subject of a verb is no one in particular, **man** is often used. The English equivalent is *one, you, we, they, people*, but **man** has a less formal feel to it than *one*. The verb with **man** has the same ending as with *he/she/it*.
Darf man hier parken? *Are you allowed to park here?*
Man kann online oder im Geschäft kaufen. *You can buy online or in-store.*
Hier darf man nicht fotografieren. *You can't take photos here.*

Sometimes when English speakers use *one*, what they really mean is *I*. **Man** is used in this way in German, too, especially when you're on rather delicate ground:
Darf man fragen, wie alt Sie sind? *Might one (I) ask how old you are?*

The accusative and dative forms of **man** are **einen** and **einem**:
Das macht einen nur sprachlos. *That just makes one speechless.*
Man ist arbeitslos und keiner hilft einem. *You're without a job and no one helps you.*

German often uses **man** when English prefers a passive construction:
Das macht man einfach nicht! *That just isn't done!*
Hier spricht man Deutsch. *German is spoken here.*
Man glaubt, dass er jetzt in London wohnt. *It is believed that he now lives in London.*

Grammatically, nouns like **das Kind** *the child* should be referred to by the neuter pronoun **es**: **Wo ist mein Kind? Ich finde <u>es</u> nicht.** *Where's my child? I can't find him/her.*
But these days, the feeling that a child must in real life be male or female often leads to the pronouns **sie** and **er** being used instead of **es**:
Suchst du dein Kind? <u>Sie</u> ist da drüben. *Are you looking for your child? She's over there.*

direct object pronouns (accusative)

The direct object pronouns are:

mich *me*	uns *us*
dich *you*	euch *you*
Sie *you*	Sie *you*
ihn *him*, sie *her*, es *it*	sie *them*

- They're used as the direct object of most German verbs, i.e. the accusative case:
  Anna kennt mich. *Anna knows me.*
  Ich liebe dich. *I love you.*
  Die Kinder sahen ihn. *The children saw him.*
  Er besucht uns morgen. *He's going to visit us tomorrow.*
  Wir haben euch gehört. *We heard you.*
  Ich habe sie eingeladen. *I have invited them.* (This could also mean *I have invited her*; the context normally makes the meaning clear.)

- Direct object pronouns can replace a noun functioning as the direct object:
  Kennst du Tim? Ja, ich kenne ihn. *Do you know Tim? Yes, I know him.*
  Magst du das Buch? Ja, ich mag es. *Do you like the book? Yes, I like it.*
  Die CDs – hast du sie gesehen? *The CDs – have you seen them?*

- **Ihn** *him* and **sie** *her* are used for masculine and feminine objects and ideas, even though the English translation is *it*.
  Willst du den Film sehen? Ja, ich will ihn sehen. *Do you want to watch the film? Yes, I want to watch it (him).*
  Kauft ihr die Jacke? Ja, wir kaufen sie. *Are you going to buy the jacket? Yes, we're going to buy it (her).*

- Direct object pronouns are automatically required after certain prepositions, including **bis** *until, by*, **durch** *through*, **für** *for*, **gegen** *against*, **ohne** *without*, **um** *at, around*:
  Für euch ist es zu einfach. *For you it's too easy.*
  Ich bin nicht gegen Sie. *I'm not against you.*
  Die Mannschaft muss ohne ihn spielen. *The team has to play without him.*

There's a list of these prepositions on page 102.

indirect object pronouns (dative)

- The indirect object pronouns are:

mir *(to/for) me*	uns *(to/for) us*
dir *(to/for) you*	euch *(to/for) you*
Ihnen *(to/for) you*	Ihnen *(to/for) you*
ihm *(to/for) him*, ihr *(to/for) her*, ihm *(to/for) it*	ihnen *(to/for) them*

- English often doesn't differentiate between direct and indirect pronouns but in German it's necessary to know the difference. The above are in the dative case, often replacing a noun functioning as the indirect object, i.e. a person or thing to whom/to which something is given/done etc:
  Sie kauft Nico einen Kaffee. Sie kauft <u>ihm</u> einen Kaffee. *She is buying Nico a coffee. She is buying (for) him a coffee.*
  Er schickt Anke eine SMS. Er schickt <u>ihr</u> eine SMS. *He is sending Anke a text. He is sending (to) her a text.*
  Was schenken wir den Kindern? Was schenken wir <u>ihnen</u>? *What shall we give the children (as a present)? What shall we give (to) them?*

- The dative case is automatically required after certain verbs, including **antworten** *to answer*, **danken** *to thank*, **folgen** *to follow*, **gehören** *to belong to*, **gefallen** *to be pleasing, like*, **gratulieren** *to congratulate*, **helfen** *to help*, **schaden** *to harm*, **verzeihen** *to excuse*:
  Antworte <u>mir</u>, bitte. *Answer me, please.*
  Verzeihen Sie <u>mir</u>, bitte. *Forgive me/Excuse me, please.*
  Ich danke <u>euch</u> herzlichst. *I thank you (pl) most warmly.*
  Gefällt <u>Ihnen</u> die Pizza? *Do you like the pizza?*
  Können Sie <u>uns</u> bitte helfen? *Can you please help us?*

- Indirect object pronouns are also required after certain prepositions, including **aus** *from, out*, **außer** *apart from*, **bei** *at, near*, **gegenüber** *opposite*, **mit** *with, by*, **nach** *after, to*, **seit** *since, for*, **von** *from*, **zu** *to* (page 100):
  Kann ich das bei <u>dir</u> zu Hause lassen? *Can I leave this at your place?*
  Er wohnt mit <u>ihr</u>. *He lives with her.*
  Nach <u>Ihnen</u>, bitte. *After you.*
  Was hast du von <u>ihnen</u> bekommen? *What did you get from them?*

- They also feature in expressions such as **Wie geht es <u>dir/Ihnen</u>?** *How are you?* or **<u>Mir</u> ist kalt.** *I am cold.*

position of object pronouns

As a general rule, object pronouns normally follow the first verb in a main clause.

Das Publikum liebte ihn. *The audience loved him.*
Ich kann dich nicht hören. *I can't hear you.*
Ich habe ihm Ihre Nachricht gegeben. *I have given him your message.*

- When there are two object pronouns in a sentence, the accusative comes before the dative:
  Das ist ein tolles T-Shirt! Kaufst du <u>es mir</u>, bitte? *That's a great T-shirt! Will you buy it for me, please?*
  Ich brauche meine Kamera. Ich kann <u>sie dir</u> nicht leihen. *I need my camera. I can't lend it to you.*

- When one of the objects is not a pronoun but a noun, the pronoun comes before the noun, regardless of the cases the noun and pronoun are in:
  Das Geschenk? Ich habe <u>es</u> Petra gegeben. *The present? I've given it to Petra.* (accusative)
  Die Schokolade? Ich habe <u>sie</u> Oliver geschenkt. *The chocolate? I've given it to Oliver.* (accusative)
  Tina schreibt <u>ihm</u> eine SMS. *Tina is texting him.* (dative)
  Zeig <u>ihnen</u> das neue Haus! *Show them the new house.* (dative)

- Usually a pronoun – accusative or dative – immediately follows a preposition:
  Für <u>dich</u> habe ich immer Zeit. *I've always got time for you.*
  Wollen Sie mit <u>uns</u> ins Kino gehen? *Would you like to go to the cinema with us?*

You will often come across object pronouns in verb + preposition constructions:
Ich denke an dich. *I'm thinking of you.*
Er wartet auf sie. *He's waiting for her.*
Ich kann mich gut an ihn erinnern. *I can remember him well.*
Hat sich Jörg bei dir entschuldigt? *Did Jörg apologise to you?*
Sprechen Sie mit mir. *Talk to me.*
Er hat nach dir gefragt. *He asked after you.*

There's a list of verbs like these on pages 185–190.

reflexive pronouns

- Reflexive pronouns are object pronouns which are an integral part of reflexive verbs: **sich erinnern** *to remember*, **sich verletzen** *to hurt oneself* (pages 119–120). Their essential meaning is *self*, which is rarely translated into English. Most reflexive verbs have a direct object pronoun (accusative) but there are quite a few that have an indirect object pronoun (dative): **sich etwas überlegen** *to think about something*, **sich etwas vorstellen** *to imagine something*. Accusative and dative reflexive pronouns are identical except for the *me* and *you* (**du**) forms:

- Direct object reflexive pronouns (accusative case):

mich *myself*	**uns** *ourselves*
dich *yourself*	**euch** *yourselves*
sich *yourself*	**sich** *yourselves*
sich *himself, herself, itself*	**sich** *themselves*

Ich erinnere <u>mich</u> nicht. *I don't remember.*
Hast du <u>dich</u> entschieden? *Have you decided?*
Setzen Sie <u>sich</u>. *Take a seat.*
Wir interessieren <u>uns</u> für Kunst. *We're interested in art.*
Beeilt <u>euch</u>! *Hurry up!*

- Indirect object reflexive pronouns (dative case):

mir *to/for myself*	**uns** *to/for ourselves*
dir *to/for yourself*	**euch** *to/for yourselves*
sich *to/for yourself*	**sich** *to/for yourselves*
sich *to/for himself, herself, itself*	**sich** *to/for themselves*

Das muss ich <u>mir</u> überlegen. *I'll have to think about that.*
Stell <u>dir</u> vor! *Just imagine!*
Das hat sie <u>sich</u> gemerkt. *She remembered that.*
Wir sehen <u>uns</u> die Stadt an. *We're taking a look at the town.*
Wascht <u>euch</u> die Hände! *Wash your hands!*

- Some verbs can be used either with the accusative or the dative reflexive pronoun, depending whether there is an object or not:
  Ich ziehe <u>mich</u> an. *I'm getting dressed.*
  Ich ziehe <u>mir</u> meinen neuen Mantel an. *I'm putting my new coat on.*
  Hast du <u>dich</u> gewaschen? *Have you washed (yourself)?*
  Hast du <u>dir</u> die Hände gewaschen? *Have you washed your hands?*

For more on reflexive verbs, see page 119.

checkpoint 9

1   Would you use **du**, **Sie** or **ihr** to address these people?
   a a six-year-old child   b your doctor
   c two friends   d a new client of your company
   e your dog   f a group of fellow students

2   Replace the subject of each sentence with a pronoun:
   a **Louise kommt aus Liverpool.**
   b **Die Kinder spielen im Park.**
   c **Die Pizza kostet 10,99 Euro.**
   d **Das Auto hat einen Elektromotor.**
   e **Die Blumen sind sehr frisch.**

3   To emphasise that you've made something yourself, what could you add to **Das habe ich gemacht**?

4   Using **man**, how would you say in German *You're not allowed to park here*?

5   Indicate whether the underlined pronouns are direct object (do) or indirect object (io) pronouns.
   a **Michael kennt <u>mich</u> gut.** ( )
   b **Er hat <u>mir</u> eine Mail geschickt.** ( )
   c **Ich bezahle den Wein. – Nein, *ich* bezahle <u>ihn</u>.** ( )
   d **Was schenkst du deiner Mutter? – Ich schenke <u>ihr</u> Blumen.** ( )
   e **Gibst du Ines die EC-Karte? – Ich habe <u>sie</u> <u>ihr</u> schon gegeben.**
      ( ) ( )

6   The direct and indirect object pronouns of **ich** are **mich** and **mir**. What are the object pronouns for **du**, **Sie**, **er** and **sie** (*she*)?

7   Fill the gaps with the correct object pronouns.
   a **Kennst du Florian? – Ja, ich kenne** .... **gut.**
   b **Kommt Hanna zur Party? – Ja, ich habe** .... **eingeladen.**
   c **Hast du eine E-Mail-Adresse? – Ja, ich gebe** ....
   d **Hat Max das Handy? – Ja, ich habe** .... **gegeben.**
   e **Aisha möchte diese Schuhe. – Ich kaufe** ....

8   How would you say these in German?
   a *It's me.*
   b *German is spoken here.*
   c *Angela is playing with him.*
   d *Nico is sending them an email.*
   e *Can you help me, please?* (**Sie**)
   f *I love you.* (**du**)

Sentence structure

The more German you learn, the more you'll progress from simple, short phrases to longer sentences which express your needs and opinions in more detail. The two main things to consider when constructing more complex sentences are word order and how to join together the various parts of the sentence. An important part of a sentence's structure is the **clause**. A clause is a meaningful sequence of words that includes a verb. A **main clause** does not need any extra information to make sense: *Although the sun is shining, it's cold*. A **subordinate clause**, however, does not make sense on its own: ***Although the sun is shining**, it's cold*.

- Word order is different in English and German, particularly the position of the verb, which often comes at the end of the clause or sentence. There are precise word-order rules, but there is also more leeway to be flexible than in English.

- To join together the various elements of what you want to say, you can use conjunctions – words like *and*, *but*, *since*, *so, however*. You also need words that save you having to repeat nouns or phrases when you're giving additional information about them: words like **der**, **die** and **das** which, as well as meaning *the*, can also mean *who, that* or *which*.

Progressing isn't simply about more and more grammatical rules. If you listen to native speakers of any language, you'll find that they use expressions like *well then, see what I mean, actually, and so on,* which bring a sense of continuity to what they say and take it beyond the strictly functional. When you learn a new language, it's an effort at first to remember to use these words and phrases as well as everything else – but when you get used to them you'll find not only that they make you sound more fluent but also that they give you useful thinking time when you're stuck for a word.

word order

English and German word order is similar in very short, simple sentences, but there are striking differences in longer and more complex sentences.

- In main clauses that are statements – not questions – the verb is always the second idea. That isn't necessarily the second word; an idea can be a combination of words that make up a single element:
  Es <u>gibt</u> keine guten Geschäfte in dieser Stadt. *There aren't any good shops in this town.*
  Mein Bruder und ich <u>fahren</u> morgen nach Berlin. *My brother and I are going to Berlin tomorrow.*

  If the clause begins with something other than the subject, the verb nevertheless remains the second idea (there is no comma between the first and the second idea):
  In dieser Stadt gibt es keine guten Geschäfte.
  Morgen fahren mein Bruder und ich nach Berlin.

- Modals (see pages 172–176) and some other verbs send the infinitive (see pages 117–118) of a second verb to the end of the clause:
  Wir konnten nur zwei Tage bleiben. *We could only stay two days.*
  Hier darf man nicht rauchen. *You're not allowed to smoke here.*
  Ich sah ihn kommen. *I saw him coming.*

- In compound tenses the auxiliary verb is the second idea, while the past participle or infinitive is placed at the end of the clause:
  Lukas wird Mathematik an der Uni studieren. *Lukas is going to study mathematics at university.*
  Meine Eltern sind zwei Wochen bei uns geblieben. *My parents stayed two weeks with us.*

- The main part of the present and simple past/imperfect tenses of separable verbs is the second idea, and the separable prefix is placed at the end of the main clause:
  Der Zug kommt/kam pünktlich an. *The train arrives/arrived on time.*
  In compound tenses the separable prefix joins up with the main verb to form the infinitive or past participle:
  Der Zug ist pünktlich angekommen. *The train arrived on time.*
  Hoffentlich wird der Zug pünktlich ankommen. *Hopefully the train will arrive on time.*

questions and commands

- For questions introduced by a question word, the verb that agrees with the subject is the second idea. German does not have an equivalent of *do* or *did*:
  Was hast du gesagt? *What did you say?*
  Wie lange könnt ihr bleiben? *How long can you stay?*
- In questions where the expected answer is *yes* or *no*, the main verb is first, and the subject second:
  Ist der Arzt schon angekommen? *Has the doctor arrived yet?*
  Möchtest du ein Glas Wein? *Would you like a glass of wine?*
- The verb is also in first place in commands:
  Gib mir das Buch! *Give me the book.* **Gehen Sie sofort!** *Go immediately!*

direct and indirect objects

- When there are two nouns, the indirect object precedes the direct:
  Er gab dem Studenten das Buch. *He gave the student the book.*
  Alternatively, the sentence can begin with one of the objects:
  Das Buch gab er dem Studenten./Dem Studenten gab er das Buch.
- For two pronouns, the direct object pronoun precedes the indirect:
  Ich habe es ihm geschickt. *I've sent it to him.*
- For a noun plus pronoun, the pronoun precedes the noun:
  Er hat es meinem Bruder gegeben. *He gave it to my brother.*
  Ich habe ihm ein Paket geschickt. *I sent him a parcel.*

Although strict guidelines apply to the position of the verb, there is more flexibility in German word order than in English. In English, normal word order is subject – verb – object, and changing the word order changes the meaning. In German the endings show whether a word is the subject or object, not word order:
Den Postboten biss der Hund. *The dog bit the postman.*
Den Postboten is the accusative case, i.e. the object, and **der Hund** is the nominative, i.e the subject.

position of adverbs

- Broadly speaking, the order of adverbs or adverbial phrases is time – manner – place:
  Ich fahre morgen mit dem Zug nach Köln. *I'm going to Cologne by train tomorrow.* (English prefers place before time.)
  Dürfen deine Kinder alleine draußen spielen? *Are your children allowed to play outside alone?* (manner, place)
  Ich trainiere abends im Fitnessstudio. *I train in the gym in the evenings.* (time, place)
  When there are several adverbial phrases, German likes to begin the clause with one of them:
  Morgen fahre ich mit dem Zug nach Köln.
  Abends trainiere ich im Fitnessstudio.

- The more general adverbial phrase of time or place comes before the more specific:
  Sie kommt jeden Nachmittag um vier Uhr. *She comes every afternoon at four o'clock.*
  Ich sitze im Garten hinter dem Gebüsch. *I'm sitting behind the bushes in the garden.*

- Adverbs and adverbial phrases come after pronouns that stand alone but precede prepositional phrases, nouns and adjectives:
  Ich habe ihn gestern gesehen. *I saw him yesterday.*
  Ich habe gestern mit ihm gesprochen. *I spoke to him yesterday.*
  Er hat neulich sein Auto verkauft. *He's recently sold his car.*
  Er sah gestern krank aus. *He looked ill yesterday.*
  However, German will often begin with the adverb: **Gestern habe ich …**

Interjections such as **ach** *oh*, **pfui** *ugh*, **nanu** *what* (surprise), **tja** *oh well*, and **ja** *yes*, **nein** *no* and some other phrases including **das heißt** *that is to say*, **im Gegenteil** *on the contrary*, **mit anderen Worten** *in other words*, **weißt du/wissen Sie?** *do you know?* do not affect word order because they are separated from the rest of the sentence:
Im Gegenteil, ich habe es gemacht. *On the contrary, I did it.*
Ach, das ist wahr. *Oh, that's true.*
Nein, das glaube ich nicht. *No, I don't believe it.*

joining words

- Clauses can be joined by words such as *and, but, since, because, while, although* etc. These are called conjunctions.

- A small number of conjunctions (called co-ordinating conjunctions) link clauses without affecting word order at all. The key co-ordinating conjunctions are: **aber** *but*, **denn** *for, because*, **oder** *or*, **sondern** *but … instead* and **und** *and*:

  Er konnte nicht kommen, denn er war zu müde. *He couldn't come because he was too tired.*

  Kommst du oder kommst du nicht? *Are you coming or aren't you?*

  Die Sonne scheint, aber mir ist kalt. *The sun is shining but I'm cold.*

  Ich bin früh aufgestanden und dann habe ich gefrühstückt. *I got up early and then I had breakfast.*

- Many more conjunctions (called subordinating conjunctions) send the main verb of the clause they introduce (called the subordinate clause) to the end. They are preceded by a comma. Common subordinating conjunctions are:

als *when*	**als ob** *as if*	**bevor** *before*
bis *until*	**da** *since* (= *because*)	**damit** *so that*
dass *that*	**erst als/wenn** *not until, only when*	**falls** *in case*
indem *while, by*	**nachdem** *after*	**ob** *if, whether*
obwohl *although*	**seit(dem)** *since* (time)	**sobald** *as soon as*
solange *as long as*	**während** *while, whereas*	**weil** *because*
wenn *if, whenever*		

  Ich weiß nicht, ob er schon angekommen ist. *I don't know if he's arrived yet.*

  Sie frühstückt immer, bevor sie zur Arbeit geht. *She always has breakfast before she goes to work.*

- If the subordinate clause begins the sentence, the verb and subject in the main clause are reversed:

  Während er in London wohnte, ging er oft ins Theater. *While he was living in London, he often went to the theatre.*

  Wenn du willst, können wir gehen. *If you want, we can go.*

  Erst als sie seine Stimme hörte, erkannte sie ihn. *Only when she heard his voice did she recognise him./She didn't recognise him until she heard his voice.*

- Question words that introduce indirect questions also send the verb to the end:

  Wissen Sie, wie lange sie bleiben werden? *Do you know how long they will stay?*

  Erinnerst du dich daran, wo du es gelesen hast? *Do you remember where you read it?*

- Other joining words (called adverbial conjunctions) are followed by an reversal of verb and subject. The most common are:

außerdem *besides, moreover*	**dagegen** *on the other hand*
daher/darum/deshalb/deswegen *so, therefore, for that reason*	**dennoch** *however, nevertheless*
kaum *hardly, no sooner*	**sonst** *otherwise, or else*
trotzdem *anyway, nevertheless*	

Er muss dringend zum Zahnarzt gehen, sonst werden seine Zahnschmerzen noch schlimmer. *He must go to the dentist's urgently, otherwise his toothache will get worse.*

Unsere Wohnung ist sehr teuer, deshalb möchten wir umziehen. *Our flat is very expensive, so we'd like to move.*

checkpoint 10

1 Rearrange these words and phrases to form sentences. Begin with the subject:
   a morgen | kommt | um neun Uhr | sie
   b hat | Blumen | gekauft | mir | mein Bruder
   c nach Hamburg | wir | mit dem Zug | gefahren | am Montag | sind

2 Join these two sentences: **Er geht ins Kino** and **Ich bleibe zu Hause** with the conjunctions a) **aber** b) **obwohl** and c) **deswegen** to make the sentences:
   a He's going to the cinema but I'm staying at home.
   b He's going to the cinema although I'm staying at home.
   c He's going to the cinema therefore I'm staying at home.

3 Which of these conjunctions does <u>not</u> send the verb to the end of the clause: **damit, solange, sonst, während, wenn?**

who, whom, whose, which, that

These words save you having to repeat a noun or a phrase when you're giving additional information about it. Grammatically they're known as relative pronouns. They cannot be omitted in German as they are in English, e.g. *the man (that) I saw*. Like subordinating conjunctions, they send the verb to the end of the relative clause. These clauses are separated from the rest of the sentence by commas.

- Relative pronouns have gender, case and number endings. They agree in gender and number with the noun they refer to, but their case is determined by the role they play in the clause:

  der Mann, der gestern ankam *the man who/that arrived yesterday*
  der Mann, den ich gestern gesehen habe *the man (whom) I saw yesterday*
  Der Mann, dessen Frau krank ist, kann nicht kommen. *The man whose wife is ill can't come.*
  der Mann, dem sie das Buch gab *the man to whom she gave the book*

- The relative pronoun has the following forms:

	masculine	feminine	neuter	plural
nominative	der	die	das	die
accusative	den	die	das	die
dative	dem	der	dem	denen
genitive	dessen	deren	dessen	deren

  Note that, apart from all genitive forms and the dative plural, the relative pronouns are identical to the definite article (see page 52).

- There is an alternative to the **der**, **die**, **das** relative pronoun – **welcher**, which is identical to the question word **welcher** *which*. It is seen mostly in formal written texts. It has no genitive form.

	masculine	feminine	neuter	plural
nominative	welcher	welche	welches	welche
accusative	welchen	welche	welches	welche
dative	welchem	welcher	welchem	welchen

- Relative pronouns can be used with prepositions. They are never shortened as some prepositions with the definite article can be (**zum, im** etc.):

  die Leute, mit denen er vor zwanzig Jahren arbeitete *the people who he worked with/with whom he worked 20 years ago*

  Angelika, bei deren Eltern wir wohnten, ist unsere Nachbarin. *Angelika, whose parents we stayed with, is our neighbour.*

  Das Konzert, zu dem wir gingen, hatte schon angefangen. *The concert to which we were going had already started.* (NB **zu dem** not **zum**)

- When referring to something abstract or indefinite, the preposition combines with **wo-** (**wor-** before vowels):

  Er gibt den Kindern alles, worum sie bitten. *He gives the children everything they ask for.*

  das Letzte, woran ich mich erinnere *the last thing I remember*

was, wo

Was *that, which, what* exists only in the neuter form and is used:

- after indefinite words such as **alles** *everything*, **etwas** *something*, **nichts** *nothing*, **viel(es)** *a lot* and **wenig(es)** *a little*:

  Sie versteht alles, was wir sagen. *She understands everything (that) we say.*

  Es gibt nicht viel, was er nicht weiß. *There's not much that he doesn't know.*

- after **das** *that*, and neuter adjectives used as nouns:

  Das, was wir lernen, ist sehr interessant. *What* (lit. *that which*) *we're learning is very interesting.*

  Das war das Beste, was ich tun konnte. *That was the best I could do.*

- to refer back to a whole clause:

  Wir fahren ans Meer, was immer Spaß macht. *We're going to the seaside, which is always fun.*

  Er kommt immer spät, was mich ärgert. *He's always late, which annoys me.*

Wo *where* can replace a relative pronoun plus **in**:

die Stadt, in der/wo er wohnt *the town in which/where he lives*

die Firma, in der/wo ich arbeite *the company where I work*

making conversation flow

Words that help the flow of conversation and indicate the speaker's attitude, such as *really* or *well*, are very common in German. They are difficult to translate exactly, so it is best to focus on the context they're used in.

Also can convey *Well/Right then* … or *So* … at the start of a sentence. Other words used in the same way are **nun**, **na** and **na ja**.

Eben conveys acceptance, a sense of *That's just how it is*. Other expressions used in the same way are **nun einmal** and, in south Germany and Austria, **halt**.

Eigentlich is like the English *actually, really*. It can tone down a question.

Denn also makes questions seem less abrupt, while **mal** softens or tones down a command.

Wohl indicates probability, like *I suppose* in English.

Doch is used to express disagreement, impatience or surprise, or for emphasis.

Schon has lots of different meanings. It can be used to express agreement or to show impatience.

opinions

When giving your opinion, you can start with **ich denke** or **ich meine** *I think* or **ich bin der Meinung, dass** *I think (am of the opinion) that*.

As you get into your stride, you can punctuate what you're saying with **erstens** *firstly*, then **zweitens** *secondly* and summarise with **kurz** or **kurzum** *in short*.

And you can show that you're coming to a conclusion with **also** *so, therefore* or **zum Schluss** *in conclusion*.

To give both sides of an argument, you can say **einerseits** *on the one hand* and **andererseits** *on the other hand*.

Was denkst du?/Was meinen Sie?/Was ist Ihre Meinung? *What do you think?/What's your opinion?* bring others into the discussion.

To agree with someone, you can say **Das stimmt** *That's right* or **Ich bin damit einverstanden** *I agree*. Germans are often quite direct when they disagree and are likely to say **Das stimmt nicht** *That's not correct* or **Ich bin nicht damit einverstanden** *I don't agree*.

checkpoint 11

1 Which of these would you use:

Das stimmt.

Ich bin der Meinung, dass ...

Also, ...

Zum Schluss ...

andererseits

Was meinst du?

    a when you're about to give the other side of the argument?
    b when asking someone for their opinion?
    c when coming to a conclusion?
    d when offering your opinion?
    e to say you agree with what has been said?
    Which one is left over and what does it mean?

2 Put the correct relative pronoun from the box in the gap.

der	die	den	dem	deren	denen

    a die Frau, mit .... er sprach
    b der Film, ... wir letzte Woche gesehen haben
    c die Leute, von .... sie sprach
    d Frau Schmidt, ... du sehr gut kennst
    e Frau Schmidt, ... Sohn du sehr gut kennst
    f der Student, ... die Lehrerin das Buch gab

3 Do you need was or wo in the gap?
    Wir wohnen im Haus, ... mein Großvater geboren
    wurde.

4 Which of these would you use if you were sure of your facts:
    ich denke, ich weiß, ich meine?

5 Is Ich bin damit einverstanden closer in meaning to Das
    stimmt or Das stimmt nicht?

6 Which two of these mean the same as na ja: nun, nein, nicht
    wahr, also?

7 What is Das ist eben so in English?

Prepositions

Prepositions are words like *at, in, on, of, with, to, between*:
I'm **at** home.
He's going **to** Germany **with** her.
It's **in** the office, **by** the phone.

The main difference between the use of prepositions in English and German is that in German prepositions require a certain case. Articles, possessives, pronouns and other words following prepositions therefore need to take the appropriate case endings.

Most prepositions, such as **mit**, **von** and **zu** take the dative; some prepositions, such as **für** or **gegen**, take the accusative; while the genitive nowadays tends to be used only with a few prepositions, such as **trotz** and **während**.

There are also some prepositions such as **in** and **auf** which can take either the accusative or the dative case, depending on whether the verb indicates movement or focuses on position.

This may seem highly complicated but you'll probably find that you develop a feeling for which case sounds right. And if you do make a mistake, it will rarely lead to a breakdown in meaning.

Some German and English prepositions correspond directly, such as **mit** *with*, **ohne** *without*, **hinter** *behind*, **während** *during*, **seit** *since*. But this is by no means always the case. For example:

- **nach** can mean *after*, as in **nach dem Frühstück** *after breakfast*, but also *to*, as in **nach Frankreich** *to France*.
- **zu** can mean *to* as in **zum Bahnhof** *to the station*, but it can be used as in **zum Frühstück** *for breakfast* or **zu Fuß** *on foot*.

It's therefore often more effective to associate a preposition with the way it's used rather than look for a straight translation.

prepositions + dative

The most common prepositions followed by the dative case are:

- **ab** *from (onwards)*
  Sie lernen Englisch ab dem ersten Schuljahr. *They learn English from the first school year.*
  Ab diesem Flughafen gibt es wenige Flüge. *There are few flights from this airport.*

- **aus** *from, out of, made of*
  Sie kommt aus Frankreich. *She comes from France.*
  Er lief aus dem Haus. *He ran out of the house.*
  Der Tisch ist aus Plastik. *The table is made of plastic.*

- **außer** *apart from, besides, out of (order, control, breath etc.)*
  Außer einem Sandwich hatte er nichts gegessen. *Apart from a sandwich, he had not eaten a thing.*
  Außer dir kann hier niemand Englisch sprechen. *Besides you, no one here can speak English.*
  Der Fahrstuhl ist außer Betrieb. *The lift is out of order.*
  Sie war außer Atem. *She was out of breath.*

- **bei** *by (near to), at (someone's home), for (work for a specific company)*
  Potsdam liegt bei Berlin. *Potsdam is near to Berlin.*
  Ich habe bei Freunden übernachtet. *I spent the night with friends* (i.e. *at their home*).
  Ich arbeite bei BMW. *I work for BMW.*

- **gegenüber** *opposite, compared to*
  Der Ein-Euroladen liegt gegenüber dem Kino. *The one-euro shop is opposite the cinema.*
  Die Preise stiegen um 3% gegenüber dem Vorjahr. *Prices rose by 3% compared to the previous year.*
  Gegenüber can also appear after a prepositional phrase:
  Der Ein-Euroladen liegt dem Kino gegenüber.

- **mit** *with, by* (means of transport), *at* (age)
  Sie geht mit ihrem Freund ins Konzert. *She's going to a concert with her boyfriend.*
  Er fährt mit dem Auto. *He's going by car.*
  Marion hat mit 20 geheiratet. *Marion got married at 20.*

- **nach** *to* (towns and all neuter countries used with no article), *after, past* (with time), *according to*
  Wir fahren nach England. *We'll go to England.*
  Nach dem Frühstück las sie ihre E-Mails. *After breakfast she read her emails.*
  Es ist fünf nach zehn. *It's five past ten.*
  Es verlief alles nach Plan. *It all went according to plan.*

- **seit** *since, for* (referring to a period of time)
  Ich kenne ihn seit meiner Kindheit. *I've known him since (my) childhood.*
  Er lebt seit drei Jahren in London. *He has been living in London for three years.*
  Seit is normally used with the present tense in German.

- **von** *from, by, of*
  Ist das Geschenk von dir? *Is this present from you?*
  Diese Musik ist von Bach. *This music is by Bach.*
  Er ist ein alter Freund von mir. *He is an old friend of mine.*

- **zu** *to* (place or person)
  Wie komme ich zum Supermarkt? *How do I get to the supermarket?*
  Ich gehe zu Mats. *I am going to (see) Mats.*
  Zu also appears in a number of set expressions, such as **zum Frühstück** *for breakfast*, **zu Fuß** *on foot*, **zu Hause** *at home*.

Bei, von and **zu** combine with **dem** to form **beim, vom** and **zum.**
Zu combines with **der** to form **zur**:
bei + dem: Ich war beim Zahnarzt. *I was at the dentist's.*
von + dem: Kommt er vom Arzt? *Is he coming from the doctor's?*
zu + dem: Ich gehe zum Museum. *I'm going to the museum.*
zu + der: Geht er schon zur Schule? *Does he go to school yet?*

prepositions + accusative

The most common prepositions followed by the accusative case are:

- **bis** *until, by*, *as far as*
  Bis nächste Woche! *Until next week!*
  Die Arbeit muss bis nächsten Montag fertig sein. *The work has to be finished by next Monday.*
  Klara fährt nur bis Köln. *Klara is only going as far as Cologne.*

  When **bis** is used with another preposition, such as **um** or **zu**, the second determines the case ending: **Gehen Sie bis zu dem Haus.** *Go as far as the house.* (**zu** + dative)

- **durch** *through, by (means of)*
  Wir gingen durch den Wald. *We went through the forest.*
  Er verriet sich durch seinen Akzent. *He betrayed himself by his accent.*

- **für** *for*
  Ich fahre für zwei Tage weg. *I'm going away for two days.*
  Hier findest du einige Tipps für deinen Garten. *Here you'll find a few tips for your garden.*

- **gegen** *against, around* (with numbers), *about* (with time)
  Ich bin gegen den neuen Plan. *I'm against the new plan.*
  Wir erwarten gegen 100 Leute. *We expect about 100 people.*
  Sie ist gegen sechs Uhr zu Hause. *She'll be at home at around six.*

- **ohne** *without*
  Wir gehen nicht ohne dich. *We won't go without you.*
  Ich nehme den Kaffee ohne Milch. *I'll take the coffee without milk.*

- **um** *at* (clock, times), *around*
  Der Zug kommt um 14.32 Uhr an. *The train arrives at 2.32pm.*
  Das Geschäft ist um die Ecke. *The shop is around the corner.*

Durch, für and **um** followed by **das** often contract to **durchs, fürs** and **ums**:
Er sah durchs Fenster. *He looked through the window.*
Danke fürs Essen. *Thanks for the meal.*
Er geht ums Haus herum. *He goes around the house.*
This does not happen when **das** is being used as a demonstrative, pointing out a specific person or item.
Er ist um das Haus da vorne herumgegangen. *He went around that house over there.*

prepositions + accusative or dative

There is a group of prepositions which can take either the accusative or the dative case. These are called **Wechselpräpositionen** *variable prepositions*.

- The accusative case is used when the preposition is linked to a verb indicating movement to or into a location, or a change of position. It answers the question **wohin?** *where (to)?*:
  Wir gehen in die Kneipe. *We are going to the pub.*
  Er legt das Buch auf den Tisch. *He puts the book on the table.*

- The dative is used when the verb focuses on position or limited movement within a location. It answers the question **wo?** *where?*:
  Wir blieben bis elf in der Kneipe. *We stayed in the pub until 11.*
  Das Buch liegt auf dem Tisch. *The book is (lying) on the table.*

For each of the following prepositions, the examples illustrate first the use of the accusative case and then that of the dative case.

- **an** *on(to), on, to, at*
  Ich hänge das Poster an die Wand. *I'm hanging the poster on(to) the wall.*
  Wir fahren ans (= an das) Meer. *We're going to the seaside.*
  Das Poster hängt an der Wand. *The poster is hanging on the wall.*
  Wir planen ein Picknick am (= an dem) Meer. *We're planning a picnic at the seaside.*

- **auf** *on (top of), to*
  Er stellt die Vase auf den Tisch. *He puts the vase on the table.*
  Die Vase steht auf dem Tisch. *The vase is on the table.*

- **hinter** *behind*
  Sie legt den Stift hinter den Laptop. *She puts the pen behind the laptop.*
  Der Stift liegt hinter dem Laptop. *The pen is behind the laptop.*

- **in** *in(to), in*
  Lea geht ins (= in das) Fitnesscenter. *Lea goes into the gym.*
  Jonas wartet im (= in dem) Fitnesscenter. *Jonas is waiting in the gym.*

- neben *by, next to, beside*
  Stell dich neben die Tür. *Go and stand by the door.*
  Er steht neben der Tür. *He is standing by the door.*

- über *above, over*
  Ich hänge die Lampe über das Bett. *I'm hanging the lamp above the bed.*
  Sie klettert über den Zaun. *She climbs over the fence.*
  Die Lampe hängt über dem Bett. *The lamp is hanging above the bed.*
  Das T-Shirt hängt über dem Zaun. *The T-shirt is hanging over the fence.*

- unter *under*
  Er stellt die Kiste unter das Sofa. *He puts the box under the sofa.*
  Die Kiste ist unter dem Sofa. *The box is under the sofa.*

- vor *in front of, before (time)*
  Fahr das Auto vor das Haus. *Drive the car in front of the house.*
  Das Auto steht vor dem Haus. *The car is (standing) in front of the house.*
  When **vor** is used to express time it usually takes the dative: **vor dem Mittagessen** *before lunch.*

- zwischen *between*
  Stell die Lampe zwischen den Laptop und den Drucker. *Put the lamp between the laptop and the printer.*
  Die Lampe steht zwischen dem Laptop und dem Drucker. *The lamp is standing between the laptop and the printer.*

An and **in** followed by the masculine and neuter forms of *the* are normally contracted: **an das → ans; an dem → am;**
in das → ins; in dem → im:
Am ersten Mai. *On the first of May.*
Er wohnt im Ausland. *He lives abroad.*

The following can also be contracted; however, these are normally only used in informal speech or set phrases:
auf das → aufs; hinter das → hinters; hinter dem → hinterm; unter das → unters; unter dem → unterm; über das → übers; über dem → überm; vor das → vors; vor dem → vorm
Hand aufs Herz. *Hand on heart.*
Leg es unters Bett. *Put it under the bed.*

prepositions + genitive

The most common prepositions followed by the genitive case include:

- **(an)statt** *instead of*
  Anstatt eines Rotweins möchte ich ein Mineralwasser. *Instead of a red wine, I'd like a mineral water.*

- **außerhalb** *outside (of)*
  Ich wohne etwas außerhalb der Stadt. *I live a bit outside of town.*

- **innerhalb** *within, inside (of)*
  Sie machte ihr Diplom innerhalb eines Jahres. *She finished her diploma within a year.*
  Innerhalb des Hotelgeländes gibt es auch ein Schwimmbad. *Inside the hotel area there's also a swimming pool.*

- **trotz** *in spite of, despite*
  Er spielte trotz seiner Verletzung. *He played in spite of his injury.*
  Trotz des Wirtschaftsbooms gibt es viele Arbeitslose. *Despite the economic boom, there are many people unemployed.*

- **während** *during*
  Er arbeitete während der Ferien. *He worked during the holiday.*

- **wegen** *on account of, because of*
  Wegen des Winterwetters kam es zu Verspätungen. *Because of the winter weather there were delays.*

In contemporary German the use of the genitive is decreasing. In less formal situations it's now quite common to use the dative with **(an)statt**, **trotz**, **während** and **wegen** instead of the genitive:
Anstatt einem Rotwein möchte ich ein Mineralwasser.
Er arbeitete während den Ferien.
Trotz dem Wirtschaftsboom gibt es viele Arbeitslose.
Wegen dem Winterwetter kam es zu Verspätungen.

Innerhalb and **außerhalb** are sometimes followed by **von** + dative:
Ich wohne etwas außerhalb von der Stadt.
Sie machte ihr Diplom innerhalb von einem Jahr.

prepositions in set phrases

When prepositions are used in set phrases, they often take on different meanings and may not correspond to their English equivalent.

It's therefore a good idea to familiarise yourself with commonly used expressions referring to location, means of transport, festivities etc:

Ich bin zu Hause. *I'm at home.*
Wir gehen nach Hause. *We're going home.*
Sie gehen zu Fuß. *They go on foot.*
Ich fahre mit dem Rad/mit dem Auto. *I go by bike/by car.*
Sie fährt mit der U-Bahn. *She goes by tube/underground.*

zu Ostern; zu Weihnachten *at Easter; at Christmas*
zum Geburtstag *for/on your birthday*

zum Frühstück; zum Mittagessen *for breakfast; for lunch*
zum Abendessen *for dinner*

Sie fahren ins Ausland. *They're going abroad.*
Er fährt nach Berlin. *He's going to Berlin.*
Sie ist im/auf Urlaub. *She's on holiday.*

zum Beispiel *for example*

Variable prepositions are frequently used in expressions which don't refer to movement or position. As a general guideline, **auf** and **über** are followed by the accusative case, while the other prepositions take the dative:

auf keinen Fall *on no account*
ein Artikel über neue Technologien *an article about new technologies*
am Wochenende; am Montag *at the weekend; on Monday*
am Morgen *in the morning*
in diesem Fall *in this case*
im Durchschnitt *on average*
unter keinen Umständen *under no circumstances*
unter anderem *among other things*
vor langer Zeit *a long time ago*

prepositions + pronouns

To replace a noun or noun phrase following a preposition there are two different approaches:

- Personal pronouns, such as *me, you, her, him, us, them*, are used after prepositions when talking about people:
  Wir fahren mit unseren Freunden. → **Wir fahren <u>mit ihnen</u>.** *We're going with them.*
  Wir werden bei meinem Sohn wohnen. → **Wir werden <u>bei ihm</u> wohnen.** *We shall stay with him.*

- However, when talking about a thing or a concept, the prefix **da-** (**dar-** for a preposition beginning with a vowel) is added to the preposition:
  Bist du für den Plan? → **Ja, ich bin <u>dafür</u>.** (and not **für ihn**)
  Are you for the plan? Yes, I am for it.
  Hast du die Kiste unter das Bett gestellt? Ja, ich habe die Kiste <u>darunter</u> gestellt (and not **unter es**). *Did you put the box under the bed? Yes I've put the box under it.*

  See also Verbs followed by prepositions, pages 185–190.

summary table: prepositions and cases

The following are the most commonly used prepositions and the cases they take.

accusative	dative	accusative or dative	genitive
bis	ab	an	(an)statt
durch	aus	auf	außerhalb
für	außer	hinter	innerhalb
gegen	bei	in	trotz
ohne	gegenüber	neben	während
um	mit	über	wegen
	nach	unter	
	seit	vor	
	von	zwischen	
	zu		

word **power**

Verbs, adjectives and nouns can all be followed by prepositions. Here are some examples of adjectives and nouns, and you'll find a whole section on verbs with prepositions on pages 185–190.

adjectives + prepositions

an   **reich an** (+ dat.) *rich in*
       Australien ist reich an Mineralien. *Australia is rich in minerals.*

auf   **böse auf** (+ acc.) *angry at/with*
       Felix war böse auf seinen Chef. *Felix was angry with his boss.*
       eifersüchtig auf (+ acc.) *jealous of*
       Marcus war eifersüchtig auf das neue Baby. *Marcus was jealous of the new baby.*
       stolz auf (+ acc.) *proud of*
       Moritz ist stolz auf seinen Sohn. *Moritz is proud of his son.*

für   **typisch für** (+ acc.) *typical of*
       Das ist ja typisch für Jan! *That's typical of Jan!*

mit **verheiratet mit** (+ dat.) *married to*
       Max ist mit einer Französin verheiratet. *Max is married to a French woman.*
       verwandt mit (+ dat.) *related to*
       Silke ist mit meinem Freund verwandt. *Silke is related to my boyfriend.*
       vertraut mit (+ dat.) *familiar with*
       Ich bin mit diesem Problem vertraut. *I am familiar with this problem.*

von **abhängig von** (+ dat.) *dependent on*
       Er ist finanziell von seinen Eltern abhängig. *He is financially dependent on his parents.*
       überzeugt von (+ dat.) *convinced by, of*
       Wir sind von den Reformen nicht überzeugt. *We're not convinced by the reforms.*

zu   **bereit zu** (+ dat.) *ready for*
       Ich bin bereit zu allem. *I'm ready for anything.*
       fähig zu (+ dat.) *capable of*
       Ich bin zu fast allem fähig. *I'm capable of almost anything.*

nouns + prepositions

an   **Interesse an** (+ dat.) *interest in*
          Sie haben großes Interesse an diesem Thema. *They have*
          great interest in this topic.

auf   **Hoffnung auf** (+ acc.) *hope of/for*
          Es gibt immer noch Hoffnung auf ein glückliches Ende.
          There is still hope of a happy ending.
          Rücksicht auf (+ acc.) *consideration for*
          Nehmt Rücksicht auf die Umwelt! *Show consideration for*
          the environment!
          Wunsch auf (+ acc.) *wish for*
          Wir haben den Wunsch auf ein Kind. *We wish for a child.*

für   **Beispiel für** (+ acc.) *example of*
          Er ist kein gutes Beispiel für einen Sportler. *He's not a*
          good example of a sportsman.

über   **Ärger über** (+ acc.) *frustration with, anger at*
          Der Ärger über die Banken nimmt zu. *Anger at the banks is*
          increasing.

von   **Abhängigkeit von** (+ dat.) *dependency on*
          Die steigende Abhängigkeit von Energieimporten ist
          beunruhigend. *The increasing dependency on energy imports*
          is worrying.

vor   **Angst vor** (+ dat.) *fear of*
          Mein Kind hat keine Angst vor Hunden. *My child has no*
          fear of dogs.

Because in many instances the preposition to be used is unpredictable, it's not really possible to guess – the best strategy by far is to learn the adjective or noun together with its preposition.

checkpoint 12

1   Accusative, dative, genitive? Which case is being used after the preposition in each of these sentences?

   a   Das Kino ist <u>um die</u> Ecke.

   b   Max kam <u>trotz des</u> schlechten Wetters.

   c   Ich ging <u>in den</u> Laden.

   d   Die Kinder liefen <u>aus den</u> Häusern.

   e   Vielen Dank <u>für das</u> nette Geschenk.

   f   Ich wohne <u>bei der</u> Familie Frey.

2   Which preposition is the odd one out?
   bis, durch, für, gegen, nach, ohne, um

3   How would you say *He has been living in London for five years*?

4   Provide the correct dative endings.

   a   Fährst du mit d____ Auto zur Arbeit?

   b   Ich komme mit mein____ Partnerin.

   c   Sie wohnt bei ihr____ Eltern.

   d   Unser Hotel liegt direkt gegenüber d____ Kino.

5   Underline the correct form.

   a   Er geht oft ins/im Café. Sie isst sehr gern ins/im Café.

   b   Häng das Bild an die/an der Wand! Das Bild hängt an die/an der Wand.

6   Choose a contracted form from the box.

   | zum   beim   ans   zur   aufs |

   a   Fährst du mit dem Bus _____ Schule?

   b   Setz dich _____ Sofa.

   c   Wie komme ich bitte _____ Bahnhof?

   d   Morgen fahren wir _____ Meer.

   e   Ich war heute _____ Arzt.

7   How would you say the following in German?

   a   *She's going home.*

   b   *She's at home.*

   c   *They're on holiday.*

   d   *She is coming despite the bad weather.*

Verbs: overview

Verbs are the words we use to say
- what people and things are: *be*, *exist*, *have*
- what happens to them: *live, die, become, change, break*
- what they do physically: *breathe, eat, run, wait, arrive*
… and mentally: *like, believe, decide, respect, dream, analyse*.

In a dictionary you find the **infinitive** of a verb. In English this is the basic form of the word: *(to) arrive, (to) decide, (to) finish*.

The vast majority of German infinitives end in **-en: finden, kommen**. A much smaller group ends in **-eln** or **-ern: lächeln** *to smile*, **wandern** *to hike*; and there are two one-offs, **tun** *to do* and **sein** *to be*.

When you remove **-n** or **-en**, you're left with the stem of the verb: **komm, wander, lächel**. Endings can now be added to this stem to convey precise information about:

a   how the verb is being used = **mood**
b   when it's happening: past, present or future = **tense**
c   who/what is doing it = **person**.

Adding endings in this way is called 'conjugating' the verb.

Many verbs in German begin with prefixes. Prefixes can be separable or inseparable. Separable prefixes become separated from the main body of the verb in some tenses and move to the end of a main clause e.g. **ankommen** (made up of the separable prefix **an** + **kommen**) *to arrive*. Inseparable prefixes never become separated from the main body of the verb e.g. **verstehen** (made up of the inseparable prefix **ver** + **stehen**) *to understand*.

A group of verbs called reflexive verbs always has the reflexive pronoun **sich** in front of the infinitive: **sich freuen** *to be pleased*, **sich entspannen** *to relax*, **sich amüsieren** *to enjoy oneself*. These verbs have the same endings as non-reflexive verbs.

moods and tenses

Mood refers to how the verb is being used.

Infinitive	the name of the verb, i.e. the basic dictionary form: *(to) work.*
Indicative	indicating that facts are being talked about: *I work, they were working, he doesn't work, do you work?*
Subjunctive	conveying that the verb is not fact but is subject to opinion, speculation, attitude or emotion: *if you were to work, should I ever work, if only I'd worked.*
Imperative	giving an instruction: *Work! Let's work!*

Tense refers to when the verb is happening: in the past, present or future. Tenses have names, e.g. present, perfect, imperfect.

English and German have
a two simple, i.e. one-word, tenses:
    present: *I work* **ich arbeite**
    simple past/imperfect: *I worked* **ich arbeitete**
b several compound tenses which use extra words with the basic verb:
    future: *I will work* **ich werde arbeiten**
    pluperfect: *I had worked* **ich hatte gearbeitet**
    In German compound tenses, the second element, i.e. the infinitive or past participle, comes at the end of the clause.

German does not have continuous tenses, i.e. *I am working, I was working.*

There are just two sets of verb endings in German – those for the present tense and those for the simple past/imperfect – and there are similarities between them. Modal verbs (page 172–176) and a handful of irregular verbs don't follow the usual pattern in the present tense, and the endings in the simple past tense are not the same for all verbs. Otherwise it's all quite straightforward.

When you know the various key components of a German verb you can form any person of any tense or mood. These are given in most dictionaries; an entry might appear as **trinken (trank, getrunken)**. **Trinken** *to drink* is the infinitive, **trank** the **ich** form of the simple past/imperfect and **getrunken** the past participle. When a verb undergoes a stem change in the **er/sie** form of the present tense, e.g. **helfen** *to help,* this too is included: **helfen (hilft, half, geholfen)**.

infinitive	kaufen *to buy*
stem	kauf
perfect infinitive	gekauft haben *to have bought*

indicative

present	ich kaufe	*I buy, I'm buying*
simple past/imperfect	ich kaufte	*I bought, I was buying*
future	ich werde ... kaufen	*I will/shall buy*
perfect	ich habe ... gekauft	*I have bought, I bought*
pluperfect	ich hatte ... gekauft	*I had bought*
future perfect	ich werde ... gekauft haben	*I will have bought*

conditional

conditional	ich würde ... kaufen	*I would buy*
conditional perfect	ich würde ... gekauft haben	*I would have bought*

subjunctive

present	ich kaufe	*(if) I were to buy*
simple past/imperfect	ich kaufte	*(if only) I bought*
perfect	ich habe ... gekauft	*(if only) I bought*
pluperfect	ich hätte ... gekauft	*(if only) I had bought*

imperative Kauf(e)! Kauft! Kaufen Sie! *Buy!* Kaufen wir! *Let's buy*

Verbs also have **participles**:

present participle	kaufend	*buying*
past participle	gekauft	*bought*

person

The person of a verb refers to who/what is making the verb happen.

A verb has three persons in the singular and three in the plural, and this is the order in which verbs are set out in this book:

1st person singular	**ich** *I*
2nd person singular	**du** *you*, **Sie** *you*
3rd person singular	**er**, **sie**, **es** *he*, *she*, *it*
1st person plural	**wir** *we*
2nd person plural	**ihr** *you*, **Sie** *you*
3rd person plural	**sie** *they*

Each of the persons requires the verb with it to have a particular ending – but these don't usually vary hugely across the various moods and tenses.

In English there's only one word for *you,* while German has three:

du: someone you call by their first name;

ihr: two or more people you call by their first names;

Sie: one or more people you don't know well; someone older or more senior than you. **Sie** is always written with a capital letter when it means *you* and takes the same endings as **sie** *they*, i.e. the third person plural.

Each of these words for *you* is classed as a different person and is therefore linked to a different verb ending. For instance, the verb **wohnen** *to live* is different in the question *Where do you live?* depending on who you're talking to:

Wo wohnst du?

Wo wohnt ihr?

Wo wohnen Sie?

It can be tricky to know whether to call someone **du** or **Sie**. On the whole, it is best to assume that you will use **Sie**. Leave it to the other person to suggest that you **duzen** *say 'du' to each other*.

weak and strong verbs

Most German verbs are either 'weak' or 'strong', and this distinction is important when it comes to conjugating the verb. You cannot tell to which group a verb belongs from the infinitive alone.

Weak verbs are characterised by the letter **-t-** in the simple past/imperfect tense and as the last letter of the past participle. There are thousands of weak verbs which follow the same, regular pattern, but there are also irregular weak verbs, whose stems undergo changes in the simple past/imperfect tense and past participle. Verb endings for all weak verbs follow the same pattern.

regular weak verbs

infinitive	simple past/imperfect	past participle
fragen *to ask*	**fragte**	**gefragt**
arbeiten *to work*	**arbeitete**	**gearbeitet**
erinnern *to remind*	**erinnerte**	**erinnert**

irregular weak verbs

infinitive	simple past/imperfect	past participle
brennen *to burn*	**brannte**	**gebrannt**
bringen *to bring*	**brachte**	**gebracht**
denken *to think*	**dachte**	**gedacht**

Strong verbs are characterised by the letters **-en** at the end of the past participle and a change of stem in the simple past and/or past participle. They don't follow a predictable pattern and have to be learnt individually.

infinitive	simple past/imperfect	past participle
trinken *to drink*	**trank**	**getrunken**
schlafen *to sleep*	**schlief**	**geschlafen**
verstehen *to understand*	**verstand**	**verstanden**

irregular verbs

There are a few verbs which do not fit neatly into the weak/strong categories and whose endings do not follow the usual pattern. These include the six modal verbs (**dürfen**, **können**, **mögen**, **müssen**, **sollen** and **wollen**), **wissen** *to know*, **haben** *to have* and **sein** *to be*.

separable and inseparable verbs

Verbs beginning with a separable prefix are known as **separable verbs**. The prefix of a separable verb is stressed when pronounced. The commonest separable prefixes are: **ab-, an-, auf-, aus-, bei-, ein-, fort-, heim-, her-, hin-, mit-, nach-, nieder-, vor-, weg-, zu-, zurück-, zusammen-**.

Separable prefixes separate from the main body of the verb in simple tenses in main clauses. In past participles the **ge-** is placed between the prefix and the main body of the verb. The **zu** accompanying an infinitive is placed between the prefix and the main body of the verb.

Ich stehe um sieben Uhr auf. *I get up at seven o'clock.*

Er ist gestern zurückgefahren. *He went back yesterday.*

Vergiss nicht mich anzurufen. *Don't forget to ring me.*

Verbs beginning with an inseparable prefix are known as **inseparable verbs**. The prefix of an inseparable verb is not stressed when pronounced (with the exception of <u>miss</u>verstehen). The inseparable prefixes are: **be-, emp-, ent-, er-, ge-, miss-, ver-, zer-**.

Inseparable verbs never separate into two parts. They do not add **ge-** to form the past participle.

Ich verstehe Sie nicht. *I don't understand you.*

Hast du meine E-Mail erhalten? *Did you receive my email?*

Ich habe vor, mich heute Abend zu entspannen. *I intend to relax this evening.*

A few prefixes can be either separable or inseparable: **durch-, hinter-, über-, um-, unter-, wider-, wieder-**. The prefixes are stressed when separable, but not when inseparable. Broadly speaking, the meaning of separable verbs in this group is often closer to the literal meaning of the prefix + main verb, whereas the prefix on the inseparable verbs is used figuratively.

Wiederholen Sie das bitte! *Repeat that please.* (stress on <u>holen</u>)

Wann sehen wir uns wieder? *When will we see each other again?* (stress on <u>wieder</u>)

Mein Freund umarmte mich. *My friend embraced me.*

Wir stiegen in Berlin um. *We changed (trains) in Berlin.*

Verbs such as **angewöhnen** *to get used to* or **anvertrauen** *to entrust*, which start with a separable prefix followed by an inseparable prefix, are separable but don't add **ge-** in the past participle:

Er hat mir all sein Geld anvertraut. *He entrusted me with all his money.*

the infinitive

The infinitive is the form of a verb that you find in a dictionary, ending in -en, or -n: **gehen** *to go*, **pendeln** *to commute*. It corresponds to the basic form of the English verb (*to* …) and often translates the *-ing* form as well.

It is placed at the end of the phrase or clause, but before any past participle:

Fußball spielen *to play football*

Er will Fußball draußen spielen. *He wants to play football outside.*

Ich habe ihn Fußball spielen gesehen. *I saw him playing football.*

The infinitive is used with the verb **werden** to form the future tense and conditional sentences:

Ich werde Sie morgen anrufen. *I'll phone you tomorrow.*

Ich würde lieber am Montag kommen. *I'd rather come on Monday.*

Most German infinitives are preceded by **zu** when there's a conjugated verb earlier in the sentence. **Zu** comes immediately before simple and inseparable verbs, and between the prefix and main body of separable verbs:

Jeden Tag versuche ich, zehn neue Wörter zu lernen. *I try to learn ten new words every day.*

Ich beabsichtige, meine Tante bald zu besuchen. *I intend to visit my aunt soon.*

Ich hoffe, Sie bald wiederzusehen. *I hope to see you again soon.*

Only a handful of verbs do not take **zu**. These are:

- the six modal verbs: **dürfen, können, mögen, müssen, sollen** and **wollen** (pages 172–176):

  Ich will ins Kino gehen. *I want to go to the cinema.*

  Du solltest so früh wie möglich ankommen. *You should arrive as early as possible.*

- verbs of perception: **hören** *to hear*, **sehen** *to see*, **fühlen** *to feel*, **spüren** *to feel*:

  Siehst du ihn kommen? *Can you see him coming?*

  Sie hörte die Kinder lachen. *She heard the children laughing.*

- **gehen, fahren** and other verbs of motion, also **schicken** *to send*:

  Ich gehe heute schwimmen. *I'm going swimming today.*

  Kommst du mit einkaufen? *Are you coming shopping with me?*

  Sie schickte die Kinder schlafen. *She sent the children to bed* (lit. *to sleep*).

- verbs following **lassen** *to let*:
  Lass uns alles vergessen. *Let's forget everything.*
  Ich lasse mir die Haare wachsen. *I'm letting my hair grow.*

- verbs following **bleiben** *to remain*, if describing position:
  Er blieb stehen. *He remained standing.*
  But **zu** is needed in other contexts:
  Es bleibt zu hoffen, dass ... *It is to be hoped that ...* (idiom)
  Es bleibt noch viel zu tun. *There's still a lot to do.*

  The infinitive is also used:

- after **um ... zu** *(in order) to*, **ohne ... zu** *without ... -ing*, and **anstatt ... zu** *instead of ... -ing*:
  Er ist nach Hause gegangen, ... *He went home ...*
  ... um seine Hausaufgaben zu machen. *... (in order) to do his homework.*
  ... ohne jemandem Bescheid zu sagen. *... without telling anyone.*
  ... anstatt zur Arbeit zu gehen. *... instead of going to work.*
  In order can be omitted before *to* in English, but **um** cannot be omitted in German in this context.

- when giving written instructions:
  Nicht stören. *Do not disturb.*
  Zucker, Butter und Eier vermischen. *Mix the sugar, butter and eggs together.*

- to form a noun, usually denoting the action of the verb and often translated by the English *-ing* form. Nouns formed from infinitives are written with a capital letter, are neuter in gender and no longer have to be placed at the end of the sentence.
  Das Rauchen ist in öffentlichen Gebäuden verboten. *Smoking is forbidden in public buildings.*
  Sie können beim Einkaufen Geld sparen. *You can save money when shopping.*

reflexive verbs

Reflexive verbs have **sich** before the infinitive. They can be weak, strong, separable or inseparable:

sich abgewöhnen *to give up, get out of the habit of**
sich anziehen *to get dressed***
sich ärgern *to be annoyed*
sich ausziehen *to get undressed***
sich beeilen *to hurry*
sich befinden *to be located*
sich beschäftigen *to occupy oneself*
sich duschen *to have a shower*
sich erinnern (an) *to remember*
sich erkälten *to catch a cold*
sich entspannen *to relax*
sich freuen (über) *to be glad* (**sich freuen auf** *to look forward to*)
sich gewöhnen (an) *to get used (to)*
sich interessieren (für) *to be interested (in)*
sich leisten *to afford**
sich merken *to remember, note**
sich setzen *to sit down*
sich umziehen *to change one's clothes*
sich unterhalten *to talk, chat*
sich verabschieden *to say goodbye*
sich vornehmen *to plan**
sich vorstellen *to imagine*, to introduce oneself***
sich waschen *to get washed***

* These take a dative reflexive pronoun. The rest usually take an accusative reflexive pronoun. The difference is seen only in the **ich** and **du** forms.
** Some verbs can be used either with the accusative or dative reflexive pronoun, depending on whether there is an object or not (see page 87).

Sich means *oneself, himself, herself, itself, themselves* and *yourself/ves* (**Sie**). To say *myself, yourself* (**du**), *ourselves, yourselves* (**ihr**), you replace **sich** with **mich/mir**, **dich/dir**, **uns** or **euch** (pages 84–85).
The two elements of the reflexive infinitive don't necessarily stay together.
Möchten Sie sich setzen? *Would you like to sit down?*
Das kann ich mir nicht vorstellen. *I can't imagine.*
Fällt es dir schwer, dich daran zu erinnern? *Do you find it hard to remember that?*

... and various tenses

sich duschen *to have a shower* (sich is accusative)
sich merken *to remember* (sich is dative)

present	ich dusche mich	ich merke mir
	du duschst dich	du merkst dir
	er, sie, es duscht sich	er, sie, es merkt sich
	wir duschen uns	wir merken uns
	ihr duscht euch	ihr merkt euch
	sie duschen sich	sie merken sich
	Sie duschen sich	Sie merken sich
simple past	ich duschte mich	ich merkte mir

In the future tense and conditional sentences, the infinitive is placed at the end of the clause. In other compound tenses, reflexive verbs use **haben** and the past participle is placed at the end of the clause, unless there is an infinitive, in which case that comes at the end:

future	ich werde mich ... duschen	ich werde mir ... merken
conditional	ich würde mich ... duschen	ich würde mir ... merken
perfect	ich habe mich ... geduscht	ich habe mir ... gemerkt
	du hast dich ... geduscht	du hast dir ... gemerkt
	er, sie hat sich ... geduscht	er hat sich ... gemerkt
	wir haben uns ... geduscht	wir haben uns ... gemerkt
	ihr habt euch ... geduscht	ihr habt euch ... gemerkt
	sie haben sich ... geduscht	sie haben sich ... gemerkt
	Sie haben sich ... geduscht	Sie haben sich ... gemerkt
pluperfect	ich hatte mich ... geduscht	ich hatte mir ... gemerkt
future perfect	ich werde mich ... geduscht haben	ich werde mir ... gemerkt haben
conditional perfect	ich würde mich ... geduscht haben or	ich würde mir ... gemerkt haben or
	ich hätte mich ... geduscht	ich hätte mir ... gemerkt

word **power**

Many verbs in German are the same as their English equivalent with the addition of **-en**. They are, however, usually pronounced differently: **bringen**, **fallen**, **filmen**, **finden**, **packen**, **senden**, **singen**, **sinken**, **stinken**, **warnen**.

The meaning of many other German verbs can be guessed, particularly those belonging to the **-ieren** group. These are all weak verbs (except for **frieren** *to freeze* and **verlieren** *to lose*): **fotografieren**, **probieren** *to try*, **reparieren**, **reservieren**, **servieren**, **studieren**.

All verbs ending in **-eln** and **-ern** are also weak.

- **-eln**: **behandeln** *to treat*, **bügeln** *to iron*, **bummeln** *to stroll*, **entwickeln** *to develop*, **handeln** *to act*, **klingeln** *to ring*, **lächeln** *to smile*, **mangeln** *to lack*, **pendeln** *to commute*, **regeln** *to regulate*, **sammeln** *to collect*, **schütteln** *to shake*, **wechseln** *to change*, **zweifeln** *to doubt*

- **-ern**: **ändern** *to change*, **ärgern** *to annoy*, **äußern** *to express*, **behindern** *to impede*, **bewundern** *to admire*, **donnern** *to thunder*, **erinnern** *to remind*, **sich erinnern** *to remember*, **feiern** *to celebrate*, **flüstern** *to whisper*, **klettern** *to climb*, **liefern** *to deliver*, **verändern** *to change*, **verbessern** *to improve*, **zögern** *to hesitate*

false friends

bekommen means *to receive*	*to become* is **werden**
blenden means *to dazzle*	*to blend* is **mischen**
hissen means *to hoist*	*to hiss* is **zischen**
konkurrieren means *to compete*	*to concur* is **übereinstimmen**
picken means *to peck*	*to pick* is **auswählen** (= *choose*), **pflücken** (of flowers and fruit)
realisieren means *to realise* (a dream/project)	*to realise (become aware)* is **erkennen**
spenden means *to donate*	*to spend* is **ausgeben**
tasten means *to feel one's way*	*to taste* is **schmecken**, **probieren**
winken means *to wave*	*to wink* is **(zu)zwinkern**

checkpoint 13

1   Two of these words are not verbs. Can you identify them?*
    know, negotiate, applaud, arrival, disintegrate, play, depend, deep, realise, depart

2   Which of these words can be a verb and a noun in English?
    disturb, describe, deny, distribute, deliver, dream

3   Ignoring the one-offs **sein** and **tun**, if a German infinitive does not end in **-en**, what two sequences of three letters might it end in?

4   Does mood or tense refer to the time something takes place?

5   In English, who's doing something when a verb is in the first person singular? And the third person plural?

6   Which verb ending do you need for **Sie** *you*?

7   What letter does the past participle of weak verbs end in?

8   Are these prefixes separable or inseparable? a) **er-** b) **ver-** c) **an-**

9   **Beeinflussen** *to influence* starts with two prefixes; **be-** is an inseparable prefix and **ein-** is a separable prefix. Is **beeinflussen** a separable or inseparable verb?

10 What little word often comes in a sentence before a second verb in the infinitive?

11 If **analysieren** is *to analyse*, what do you think *to organise* is?

12 Given that the prefix **wieder-** means *again*, and the prefix **miss-** is equivalent to the English *mis-*, what do the verbs **wiederkommen** and **missverstehen** mean?

*If ever you're not sure, remember that you can put *to* in front of a verb and *the* in front of a noun.

Negatives and questions

There are two words particularly associated with negatives in German: **kein** and **nicht**.

- **Kein** negates a noun preceded by **ein**, and has parallel endings to **ein**:
  Ich habe einen Hund. *I have got a dog.*
  Ich habe keinen Hund. *I haven't got a dog (I have no dog).*

- **Nicht** is used in other circumstances, such as with adjectives, adverbs or nouns prefaced by a definite article or possessive adjective:
  Ich arbeite heute nicht. *I'm not working today.*
  Das Wetter ist nicht gut. *The weather's not good.*
  Fahr nicht so schnell! *Don't drive so fast!*
  Das ist nicht unsere Lehrerin. *That's not our teacher.*

German doesn't use *do, does* and *did* to ask questions. Instead it reverses the order of the subject and verb:
Sie wohnt in Berlin. *She lives in Berlin.*
Wohnt sie in Berlin? *Does she live in Berlin?*
Wo wohnt sie? *Where does she live?*

Question words such as **wann** *when* and **wo** *where* behave very like their English equivalents. They go at or near the beginning of the question, before the verb:
Wo hast du ihn gesehen? *Where did you see him?*
Seit wann arbeitest du hier? *How long have you been working here?* (Lit. *Since when are you working here?*)

Most question words don't change, but **wer** *who* has case endings and **welcher** *which* has gender, case and number (singular or plural) endings to agree with its noun:
Für wen ist dieser Bericht? *Who is this report for?*
Welches Auto kaufst du? *Which car are you buying?*

negatives: nicht

Nicht is used to translate *not*, except when it refers to a noun preceded by **ein** or by no article.

- It very often goes at the end of a clause:
  Ich verstehe Sie nicht. *I don't understand you.*
  Ich kaufe das Auto nicht. *I'm not buying the car.*
  Wir kommen heute nicht. *We're not coming today.*

  ... except when that clause contains a separable prefix, infinitive or past participle, which all go after **nicht**:
  Ich werde das Auto nicht kaufen. *I won't buy the car.*
  Er hat mir das Geld nicht gegeben. *He didn't give me the money.*
  Wir kommen heute nicht zurück. *We're not coming back today.*

- **Nicht** goes before adjectives, adverbs of manner and place, non-specific adverbs of time and prepositional phrases:
  Sie ist nicht freundlich. *She is not friendly.*
  Er spielt nicht gern Fußball. *He doesn't like playing football.*
  Wir werden nicht hier bleiben. *We won't stay here.*
  Ich fliege nicht oft. *I don't fly often.*
  Er kommt nicht aus Spanien. *He doesn't come from Spain.*

  If a sentence begins with the adverb, **nicht** doesn't move with it:
  Heute kommen wir nicht zurück.

Changing the position of **nicht** changes the emphasis:
Ich fahre morgen nicht. *I'm not going tomorrow.*
Ich fahre nicht morgen, sondern übermorgen. *I'm not going tomorrow, but the day after (instead).*
Nicht alle Studenten haben die Prüfung bestanden. *Not all students passed the exam.*

negatives: kein

Kein negates a noun preceded by an indefinite article or no article at all. It has the same endings as **ein** (page 54) and **mein**:

Gibt es einen anderen Zug? *Is there another train?*
Nein, es gibt keinen anderen Zug. *No, there's no other train.*
Haben Sie Kinder? *Have you got any children?*
Wir haben keine Kinder. *We haven't got any children.*
Hast du Lust mit mir ins Kino zu gehen? *Do you feel like going to the cinema with me?*
Hast du keine Lust mit mir ins Kino zu gehen? *Don't you feel like going to the cinema with me?*
Ich will heute kein Frühstück. *I don't want any breakfast today.*
Er sollte unter keinen Umständen Alkohol trinken. *He shouldn't drink alcohol under any circumstances.*

In colloquial German the plural **keine** means *less than*:
Die Reparatur dauert keine zehn Minuten. *It will take less than ten minutes to repair.*

The negative adverbs **keinesfalls** *on no account* and **keineswegs** *by no means* are based on **kein**:
Schreiben Sie Passwörter keinesfalls auf. *On no account put passwords in writing.*
Das Buch war keineswegs so gut, wie du behauptet hast. *The book was by no means as good as you claimed.*

Gar and überhaupt *at all* can come before **nicht** or **kein**:
Es war gar nicht teuer. *It wasn't expensive at all.*
Er hatte überhaupt keine Symptome. *He had no symptoms at all.*

In response to a negative statement or question, you use **Doch**, not **ja**, when you disagree and want to say *yes* or *on the contrary*:
Das stimmt nicht. Doch, das stimmt. *That's not true. Yes it is!*
Gefällt dir diese Jacke nicht? Doch, sie gefällt mir sehr gut. *Don't you like this jacket? On the contrary, I like it very much.*

other negative words

niemand *nobody, not anybody*
nicht mehr *no longer, not any more*
nichts *nothing*
nie, niemals *never*
noch nicht *not yet*
noch nie *never … before*
nirgends, nirgendwo *nowhere*
weder … noch … *neither … nor …*
Unser Sohn wohnt nicht mehr bei uns. *Our son doesn't live with us any more.*
Ich habe nichts gesagt. *I didn't say anything.*
Das Frühstück ist noch nicht fertig. *Breakfast isn't ready yet.*
Ich war noch nie in Bayern. *I've never been to Bavaria before.*
Ich fühle mich nirgendwo zu Hause. *I don't feel at home anywhere.*
Sie trinkt weder Tee noch Kaffee. *She drinks neither tea nor coffee.*

Normal word order rules apply, so a negative word referring to time comes before manner and place:
Ich war nie mit meinen Kindern in diesem Museum. *I've never been in this museum with my children.*

- **Niemand** declines as follows:
  nominative: **niemand**
  accusative: **niemanden**
  dative: **niemandem**
  genitive: **niemandes**
  In spoken German, the accusative and dative endings can usually be omitted:
  Niemand weiß, wo er ist. *No one knows where he is.*
  Ich habe niemand(en) gesehen. *I didn't see anyone.*
  Teilen Sie Ihr Passwort niemandem mit. *Don't tell anyone your password.*
  Das ist niemandes Angelegenheit. *That's nobody's business.*

- As in English, sentences don't contain double negatives:
  Ich habe nie jemanden in diesem Büro gesehen. *I've never seen anyone in this office.*
  Ich habe noch nie etwas in diesem Geschäft gekauft. *I have never bought anything from this shop before.*

asking questions

- To ask a **closed question**, i.e. expecting the answer *yes* or *no*, German reverses the order of the subject and verb and doesn't add any extra words like *do/does*. The verb is now the first idea and the subject the second:

  Sind Sie Deutscher? *Are you German?*
  Wohnst du in München? *Do you live in Munich?*

  Word order in the rest of the question obeys the normal rules (time – manner – place, with past participles and infinitives at the end).

  Willst du am Samstag alleine zu Hause bleiben? *Do you want to stay at home alone on Saturday?*
  Hast du seinen neuen Film gesehen? *Have you seen his new film?*

  Nicht wahr or **oder** can be tagged at the very end of a statement – without inversion – to turn it into a closed question. These correspond to English question tags such as *isn't it*, *won't we*, *didn't he*, *aren't you*:
  Es war gut, nicht wahr? *It was good, wasn't it?*
  Du kannst ihn abholen, oder? *You can pick him up ... can't you?*

  In colloquial German **nicht wahr?** is often shortened to **nicht?**; **gell?** (from **gelten** *to be valid*) is heard frequently in southern Germany. These are used where *eh?* or *right?* might be used in English.

- **Open-ended questions** use question words such as **wann** *when* or **warum** *why*. These usually go at the beginning of the question (first idea), followed by the main verb (second idea), with the subject being the third idea. Normal word order rules apply in the rest of the sentence. There are no extras like *do/does*:

  Wann fängt das Konzert an? *When does the concert begin?*
  Warum bist du gestern nicht gekommen? *Why didn't you come yesterday?*

question words

German question words fall into two groups.

1 The following have no endings and don't change:

wann *when*	**wo** *where*
wohin *where to*	**woher** *where from*
wie *how*	**wie viel** *how much*
wie viele *how many*	**warum** *why*
was* *what*	

Wann fährt der nächste Zug? *When does the next train leave?*
Wie schreibt man das? *How do you spell* (lit. *write*) *that?*
Wie viele Leute werden da sein? *How many people will be there?*
Warum ist Sabine nicht hier? *Why is Sabine not here?*

- **Wo** *where*, **wohin** *where to*, **woher** *where from*
  Where is **wo**, when no movement is involved, **wohin** when movement
  <u>to</u> somewhere and away from the speaker is meant, and **woher** when
  movement <u>from</u> somewhere and towards the speaker is meant:
  Wo arbeiten Sie jetzt? *Where are you working now?*
  Wohin gehen Sie? *Where are you going (to)?*
  Woher sind alle diese Fliegen gekommen? *Where have all these flies
  come from?*

- **Was** *what*; with prepositions, **wo** is used instead of **was** and combines
  with the preposition: **womit, wofür, wozu**. An **r** is inserted to aid
  pronunciation if the preposition begins with a vowel: **woran, worüber**:
  Womit reinigt man diesen Stoff? *What do I clean this fabric with?* (Lit.
  With what do I clean this fabric?)
  Woran denkst du? *What are you thinking about?*

  ***Was** does have the genitive form **wessen** but this is not often used in
  spoken German. It appears mostly in writing with verbs that take the
  genitive: **Wessen bedarf er?** *What is he in need of?*

2 **Wer** *who, whom*, **welcher** *which* and **was für (ein)** *what sort of* have
  endings.

- **Wer** *who, whom* has case endings:

nominative: **wer**	accusative: **wen**
dative: **wem**	genitive: **wessen**

Wer weiß die Antwort? *Who knows the answer?*
Wer sind diese Leute? *Who are these people?*
Wen sollte ich einladen? *Who(m) should I invite?*
Mit wem haben Sie gesprochen? *Who did you talk to* (lit. *with*)?
Wessen Buch ist das? *Whose book is that?*

- **Welcher** *which, what* can be used as an adjective with a noun or as a pronoun. It has number, case and gender endings:

	masculine	feminine	neuter	plural
nominative	welcher	welche	welches	welche
accusative	welchen	welche	welches	welche
dative	welchem	welcher	welchem	welchen
genitive	welches	welcher	welches	welcher

Welches Hemd passt zu dieser Hose? *Which shirt goes with these trousers?*
Welches gefällt dir besser? *Which one* (i.e. shirt) *do you prefer?*
Welche Musik hörst du am liebsten? *What music do you most like listening to?*
Mit welchen Leuten sollte ich sprechen? *With which people should I speak?*

- **was für (ein)** *what sort of*
  Ein changes its endings depending on the gender and case of the noun that follows it. In the plural, **was für** is used on its own:
  Was für einen Computer brauchen Sie? *What sort of computer do you need?*
  Was für Kuchen gibt es? *What sort of cakes are there?*
  Mit was für Problemen kommen Patienten zu Ihnen? *With what sort of problems do patients come to you?*

Question words are also used to make exclamations.
Wer hätte das gedacht! *Who would have thought it!*
Was für ein schöner Tag! *What a lovely day!*

checkpoint 14

1 Write the negatives of these sentences.
   a Wir haben ein Auto.   b Das weiß ich.
   c Es war gut.   d Ich habe ihn gestern gesehen.
   e Er fährt nach Hamburg.   f Ich habe Hunger.

2 What do these mean? nichts, nie, wie viel, noch nicht

3 .... hat angerufen. Is the missing word niemand, niemanden, niemandes or niemandem?

4 Which three-letter word meaning *at all* is missing from this sentence? Sie will .... nichts essen.

5 Rearrange these words to form two sentences. Begin with the subject.
   a nicht ich sein hier morgen werde
   b Schottland war nie Ralf noch in

6 Which one of these question words changes to agree with a noun? wer, was, welcher, woher

7 What do you think worauf means in worauf sitzt du?

8 Rearrange these words to form two questions.
   a Zug Stuttgart wann der in an kommt
   b mir willst sprechen warum du mit

9 What would you tag on to Es war sehr interessant, ... if you want to know whether the other person agrees with you?

10 Complete these questions with a word from the box.
    a .... Leute gibt es hier?
    b .... machen wir heute Abend?
    c .... kommen Sie? – Aus Polen.
    d .... geht es deiner Mutter?
    e .... gehen Sie schon?
    f Für .... ist der Kaffee? – Für mich.

wie	was
wie viele	wen
warum	woher

Verbs: simple tenses

Simple tenses are one-word tenses, which don't use additional words such as *have*, *does*, *will*, *am*, *had*. German has two of these simple tenses: the present and the simple past/imperfect. The German present tense translates both the English *I work* and *I'm working*; the simple past translates *I worked*.

Both have a set of specific endings which show:
- when the action is taking place;
- who/what is doing it.

The present tense endings are the same for most verbs. However, in the simple past/imperfect the endings of weak and strong verbs follow slightly different patterns.

The endings are added to the stem of the verb. For regular weak verbs, the stem is what is left when you remove the **-n** or **-en** of the infinitive:

sagen *to say* → **sag**   **lächeln** *to smile* → **lächel**

However, strong verbs and irregular weak verbs undergo a stem change in the simple past/imperfect tense, and for many strong verbs the stem is different again in the **du** and **er/sie/es** form of the present tense:

essen *to eat* → **ess** and **iss** (present stem) → **aß** (simple past stem)

It's therefore best to learn strong and irregular weak verbs on an individual basis.

It's important to know that the simple past/imperfect tense is more common in written German, while in conversation and informal communications such as emails the perfect tense (pages 148–151) tends to be used instead. With modals, however, the simple past/imperfect is used much more frequently than the perfect in everyday German.

present tense

The present tense endings for most verbs are the same:
weak: **machen** *to make, do*; strong (no stem change): **gehen** *to go*

ich	mache	gehe
du	machst	gehst
er, sie, es	macht	geht
wir	machen	gehen
ihr	macht	geht
sie, Sie	machen	gehen

- If the stem ends in **-t** or **-d**, or in **-m** or **-n** preceded by a consonant other than l or r, an **e** is inserted between the stem and endings of the **du**, **er/sie/es** and **ihr** forms:
  arbeiten *to work*: ich arbeite, du arbeitest, er arbeitet, wir arbeiten, ihr arbeitet, sie/Sie arbeiten
  finden *to find*: ich finde, du findest, er findet, wir finden, ihr findet, sie/Sie finden
  atmen *to breathe*: ich atme, du atmest, er atmet, wir atmen, ihr atmet, sie/Sie atmen
  rechnen *to calculate*: ich rechne, du rechnest, er rechnet, wir rechnen, ihr rechnet, sie/Sie rechnen

- If the stem ends in **-s**, **-ß**, **-x** or **-z**, the **du** ending (**-st**) loses its **s**:
  reisen *to travel*: ich reise, du reist, er reist, wir reisen ...
  beißen *to bite*: ich beiße, du beißt, er beißt, wir beißen ...
  mixen *to mix*: ich mixe, du mixt, er mixt, wir mixen ...
  sitzen *to sit*: ich sitze, du sitzt, er sitzt, wir sitzen ...

- Verbs whose infinitives end in **-eln** lose the **e** of the stem in the **ich** form and the **e** of the ending in the **wir**, **sie** and **Sie** forms:
  lächeln *to smile*: ich läch(e)le, du lächelst, er lächelt, wir lächeln, ihr lächelt, sie/Sie lächeln

- Verbs whose infinitives end in **-ern** lose the **e** of the ending in the **wir**, **sie** and **Sie** forms. In spoken German, the **e** of the stem in the **ich** form can be omitted:
  wandern *to hike*: ich wand(e)re, du wanderst, er wandert, wir wandern, ihr wandert, sie/Sie wandern

- **Tun** *to do* loses the **e** of the ending in the plural forms:
  ich tue, du tust, er tut, wir tun, ihr tut, sie/Sie tun

- The stem of many strong verbs undergoes a vowel change, and occasionally a consonant change, in the **du** and **er/sie/es** forms. An **e** in the infinitive often changes to **i** or **ie**, while **a** often changes to **ä**:
  essen to *eat*: ich esse, du isst, er isst, wir essen, ihr esst, sie/Sie essen
  fahren to *go*: ich fahre, du fährst, er fährt, wir fahren, ihr fahrt, sie/Sie fahren
  fallen to *fall*: ich falle, du fällst, er fällt, wir fallen ...
  geben to *give*: ich gebe, du gibst, er gibt, wir geben ...
  laufen to *run*: ich laufe, du läufst, er läuft, wir laufen ...
  lesen to *read*: ich lese, du liest, er liest, wir lesen ...
  nehmen to *take*: ich nehme, du nimmst, er nimmt, wir nehmen ...
  sehen to *see*: ich sehe, du siehst, er sieht, wir sehen ...
  sprechen to *speak*: ich spreche, du sprichst, er spricht, wir sprechen ...
  When a prefix is added to these verbs, the stem change remains:
  ausgeben to *spend*: ich gebe ... aus, du gibst ... aus, er gibt ... aus
  versprechen to *promise*: ich verspreche, du versprichst, er verspricht ... aus

- If the stem of strong verbs ends in **-d** and the **er/sie/es** stem has an umlaut, it does not add an extra **e** to the ending. If the stem ends in **-t** and there's an umlaut, it does not add **e** or **t**:
  laden to *load*: ich lade, du lädst, er lädt, wir laden ...
  halten to *hold*: ich halte, du hältst, er hält, wir halten ...
  raten to *advise*: ich rate, du rätst, er rät, wir raten ...

- The prefix of separable verbs detaches from the main body of the verb and goes to the end of a main clause:
  ankommen to *arrive*: ich komme ... an, du kommst ... an
  zurückfahren to *go back*: ich fahre ... zurück, du fährst ... zurück
  If word order rules stipulate that the main verb is sent to the end of a subordinate clause (e.g. after a relative pronoun or subordinating conjunction), the two parts of the verb join up again:
  Wir wissen, dass er heute Abend ankommt. *We know (that) he's arriving tonight.*
  Ich kenne die Frau, die morgen zurückfährt. *I know the woman who's going back tomorrow.*

- The prefix of inseparable verbs does not detach from the main body of the verb:
  verstehen to *understand*: ich verstehe, du verstehst ...
  empfehlen to *recommend*: ich empfehle, du empfiehlst ...

common irregular verbs

Only a handful of verbs do not follow the endings pattern seen already. These are all the modal verbs and **haben**, **sein**, **werden** and **wissen**. **Sein** is highly irregular, but the others have irregularities only in the singular forms.

haben *to have*	sein *to be*	werden *to become*	wissen *to know*
ich habe	ich bin	ich werde	ich weiß
du hast	du bist	du wirst	du weißt
er hat	er ist	er wird	er weiß
wir haben	wir sind	wir werden	wir wissen
ihr habt	ihr seid	ihr werdet	ihr wisst
sie/Sie haben	sie/Sie sind	sie/Sie werden	sie/Sie wissen

können *can*	wollen *to want*	dürfen *may*
ich kann	ich will	ich darf
du kannst	du willst	du darfst
er kann	er will	er darf
wir können	wir wollen	wir dürfen
ihr könnt	ihr wollt	ihr dürft
sie/Sie können	sie/Sie wollen	sie/Sie dürfen

mögen *to like*	sollen *to be supposed*	müssen *must*
ich mag	ich soll	ich muss
du magst	du sollst	du musst
er mag	er soll	er muss
wir mögen	wir sollen	wir müssen
ihr mögt	ihr sollt	ihr müsst
sie/Sie mögen	sie/Sie sollen	sie/Sie müssen

when to use the present tense

- The present tense is used in German for the English present (*I do something*) and present continuous (*I'm doing something*). There is no present continuous tense in German:

  Ich arbeite in London. *I work in London.*
  Wir arbeiten heute in London. *We're working in London today.*
  Sie verkauft ihr Haus. *She's selling her house.*
  Immobilienmakler verkaufen Häuser. *Estate agents sell houses.*

- The present tense can be used to talk about the future if the context is clear:

  Ich arbeite morgen in London. *I'm working in London tomorrow.*
  Wir sehen uns bald wieder. *We'll see each other soon.*
  In einem Monat haben die Kinder Ferien. *The children (will) have holidays in a month.*

- In questions and negatives, German doesn't use extra words like *do, does, am, is, are*:

  Wo arbeiten Sie? *Where do you work?/Where are you working?*
  Arbeiten Sie morgen? *Are you working tomorrow?*
  Ich arbeite nicht. *I'm not working/I don't work.*

- You use the present tense with **seit** or **schon seit** *since/for* to talk about something which started in the past and is still going on, whereas English uses *have/has (done)* or *have/has been ...-ing*:

  Ich studiere (schon) seit drei Jahren Deutsch. *I've been studying German for three years.*
  Wir warten schon seit 30 Minuten auf den Zug. *We've been waiting 30 minutes for the train already.*
  Sie wohnen seit 2010 in Cardiff. *They've been living in Cardiff since 2010.*

  You also use the present tense after **Seit wann ...?** to form a question of the *How long have you been doing ...?* type:

  Seit wann studierst du Deutsch? *How long have you been studying German?*
  Seit wann wohnen Sie hier? *How long have you been living here?*

the simple past/imperfect

The simple past/imperfect endings differ depending on whether the verb is strong or weak.

Weak verbs add the following endings to the stem:

machen *to do, make*
ich mach**te**
du mach**test**
er, sie, es mach**te**
wir mach**ten**
ihr mach**tet**
sie/Sie mach**ten**

- If the stem ends in **-t** or **-d**, or in **-m** or **-n** preceded by a consonant other than **l** or **r**, an **e** is inserted between the stem and endings in all persons: **arbeiten** *to work*: **ich arbeitete, du arbeitetest, er arbeitete, wir arbeiteten, ihr arbeitetet, sie/Sie arbeiteten**

- Verbs ending **-ern** and **-eln** behave like other weak verbs: **lächeln** *to smile*: **ich lächelte, du lächeltest, er lächelte, wir lächelten, ihr lächeltet, sie/Sie lächelten**
  wandern *to hike*: **ich wanderte, du wandertest, er wanderte, wir wanderten, ihr wandertet, sie/Sie wanderten**

irregular weak verbs

The endings of the simple past/imperfect of irregular weak verbs such as **bringen**, **denken** *to think*, and **kennen** *to know* are the same as for regular weak verbs, but there's a vowel change in the stem (as with strong verbs). For this reason this group is often referred to as 'mixed verbs':

bringen *to bring*	denken *to think*	kennen *to know*
ich brachte	ich dachte	ich kannte
du brachtest	du dachtest	du kanntest
er brachte	er dachte	er kannte
wir brachten	wir dachten	wir kannten
ihr brachtet	ihr dachtet	ihr kanntet
sie/Sie brachten	sie/Sie dachten	sie/Sie kannten

strong verbs

The stems of most strong verbs look different from the infinitive stem in the simple past/imperfect. There's usually a vowel change, although there can be a consonant change too. There's sometimes a similarity between English and German strong verbs (**singen → sang, trinken → trank, schwimmen → schwamm**) but, on the whole, the simple past/imperfect of each verb has to be learnt individually.

The endings have some similarities to the weak endings, but the **ich** and **er/ sie/es** forms differ in that neither has an ending at all:

gehen *to go*	schreiben *to write*	sehen *to see*
ich ging	ich schrieb	ich sah
du gingst	du schriebst	du sahst
er ging	er schrieb	er sah
wir gingen	wir schrieben	wir sahen
ihr gingt	ihr schriebt	ihr saht
sie/Sie gingen	sie/Sie schrieben	sie/Sie sahen

- If the stem ends in **-s, -ß, -x** or **-z**, there are two possibilities for the **du** ending (**-st**): it loses its **s** or gains an **e** (the former is more common in modern German):
  lesen *to read*: **ich las, du last/lasest, er las, wir lasen, ihr last, sie/Sie lasen**
  sitzen *to sit*: **ich saß, du saßt/saßest, er saß, wir saßen, ihr saßt, sie/Sie saßen**

Some common simple past/imperfect stems are:

beginnen	→	begann	liegen *to lie, be lying* →		lag
bleiben *to stay*	→	blieb	rufen *to call*	→	rief
fahren *to go*	→	fuhr	stehen *to stand*	→	stand
fallen	→	fiel	trinken *to drink*	→	trank
fangen *to catch*	→	fing	tun *to do*	→	tat
finden	→	fand	verlieren *to lose*	→	verlor
fliegen *to fly*	→	flog	ziehen *to pull*	→	zog
heißen *to be called* →		hieß			
kommen *to come*	→	kam			

irregular verbs

The simple past/imperfect of **sein**, **haben**, **werden**, **wissen** and the modal verbs is irregular, although the endings show similarities with those seen so far:

sein *to be*	haben *to have*	werden *to become*
ich war	ich hatte	ich wurde
du warst	du hattest	du wurdest
er war	er hatte	er wurde
wir waren	wir hatten	wir wurden
ihr wart	ihr hattet	ihr wurdet
sie/Sie waren	sie/Sie hatten	sie/Sie wurden

wissen *to know*	müssen *to have to*	können *to be able to*
ich wusste	ich musste	ich konnte
du wusstest	du musstest	du konntest
er wusste	er musste	er konnte
wir wussten	wir mussten	wir konnten
ihr wusstet	ihr musstet	ihr konntet
sie/Sie wussten	sie/Sie mussten	sie/Sie konnten

dürfen *to be allowed to*	mögen *to like*	wollen *to want*
ich durfte	ich mochte	ich wollte
du durftest	du mochtest	du wolltest
er durfte	er mochte	er wollte
wir durften	wir mochten	wir wollten
ihr durftet	ihr mochtet	ihr wolltet
sie/Sie durften	sie/Sie mochten	sie/Sie wollten

sollen *to be supposed (to)* behaves like **wollen**.

separable and inseparable verbs

As in the present tense, separable prefixes detach from the main body of the verb provided that other word order rules don't apply. Inseparable prefixes do not detach from the main body of the verb.

Er kam gestern an. *He arrived yesterday.*
der Mann, der gestern ankam *the man who arrived yesterday*
Sie verloren alles. *They lost everything.*

when to use the simple past/imperfect

- The simple past/imperfect is used where in English we say *I did* to talk about an action or state in the past, one that is now finished:
  Ich ging ins Theater. *I went to the theatre.*
  Wir wohnten in Leipzig. *We lived in Leipzig.*

- It is more common in written German and in formal contexts. The perfect tense is used instead in conversation and in informal writing contexts like email.
  However, for modal verbs, the simple past/imperfect tense is used in preference to the perfect tense in spoken German:
  Ich konnte leider nicht gehen. *Unfortunately I couldn't go.*
  Sie wollte uns sehen. *She wanted to see us.*
  The simple past/imperfect of **haben** and **sein**, and of other very common verbs such as **bleiben, gehen, kommen** and **wissen**, is also often heard in conversation:
  Er war nicht da. *He wasn't there.* **Sie hatte keine Zeit.** *She had no time.*
  Es gab viel zu tun. *There was a lot to do.*
  Das wusste ich nicht. *I didn't know that.*

- The simple past/imperfect tense of **sein** can also translate the English *have/has been*:
  Ich war noch nie in Salzburg. *I've never been to Salzburg.*
  Waren Sie schon einmal in diesem Laden? *Have you ever been in this shop?*

- If you want to emphasise the continuation or repetition of an action in the past, as in the English *I was ...-ing* or *I used to ...,* you need to add a time expression to make the context clear:
  Er arbeitete. *He worked.* **Er arbeitete den ganzen Tag.** *He was working the whole day.*
  Sie blieben bei ihrer Großmutter. *They stayed with their grandmother.*
  Früher blieben sie bei ihrer Großmutter. *They used to stay with their grandmother.*

checkpoint 15

1   Write the present tense of these verbs:
    **sagen (du), studieren (wir), geben (er), erinnern (ich),
    bekommen (Sie), gefallen (es), sprechen (ihr), regnen (es),
    tun (ich)**

2   Translate these sentences into German:
    a   *We're arriving tomorrow.*
    b   *I've been living in Bremen for ten years.*

3   Which one of these verbs has a **du** form that ends in **-est** in the
    present tense?
    warten, halten, dürfen, ändern, tanzen

4   What is the infinitive of these simple past/imperfect forms?
    **verstand; rief … an; hatte; brachte; ging … zurück; wurde;
    gefiel; taten; fing … an; kannte**

5   Write the simple past/imperfect of these verbs:
    **geben (er); fragen (du); sitzen (ich); denken (wir); müssen (er);
    wissen (ihr); bleiben (Sie); fliegen (sie); sein (ihr); können (wir)**

6   **Erkennen** *to recognise* is an irregular weak verb and behaves like
    kennen. How do you say *I recognised* in the simple past?

7   Replace the ending of these infinitives with the person and tense
    in brackets.
finden (er present)	wollen (wir simple past/impf)
geben (du simple past/impf)	nehmen (er present)
reisen (du present)	schreiben (ihr simple past/impf)
halten (er present)	bleiben (ich simple past/impf)
sein (Sie present)	denken (ich simple past/impf)
werden (du simple past/impf)	wissen (Sie simple past/impf)
haben (ihr simple past/impf)	sprechen (du present)
anrufen (wir present)	tun (er present)

Verbs: compound tenses

Unlike **simple** tenses composed of one word, **compound** tenses consist of more than one element.

They have an auxiliary verb: *have, will* in English; **haben**, **sein**, **werden** in German. Some tenses team this with the infinitive of the main verb, others with the past participle; the future perfect teams it with both.

Regular English past participles end in *-ed*: *started*, *worked;* but many are irregular: *built, driven, found, sung*. Similarly, German has some that follow patterns and many others that have to be learnt individually.

In German the compound tenses are:

- **future**, which uses the present tense of **werden** plus the infinitive of the main verb: **ich werde ... machen** / *will make*; **ich werde ... gehen** / *will go*.

- **perfect**, which uses the present tense of **haben** or **sein** plus the past participle of the main verb: **ich habe ... gemacht** / *(have) made*; **ich bin ... gegangen** / *have gone./I went*.

- **pluperfect**, which uses the simple past/imperfect tense of **haben** or **sein** plus the past participle of the main verb: **ich hatte ... gemacht** / *had made*; **ich war ... gegangen** / *had gone*.

- **future perfect**, which uses the future of **haben** or **sein**, plus the past participle: **ich werde ... gemacht haben** / *will have made*; **ich werde ... gegangen sein** / *will have gone*.

The auxiliary verb goes in the usual verb position (second idea), while the past participle and/or infinitive go at the end of the clause, unless other word order rules apply.

the future tense

The future tense is made up of the present tense of **werden** plus the infinitive of the main verb. There are no exceptions.

	machen *to make, do*	**gehen** *to go*
ich	werde ... machen	werde ... gehen
du	wirst ... machen	wirst ... gehen
er, sie, es	wird ... machen	wird ... gehen
wir	werden ... machen	werden ... gehen
ihr	werdet ... machen	werdet ... gehen
sie	werden ... machen	werden ... gehen
Sie	werden ... machen	werden ... gehen

Werden goes in the usual verb slot, i.e. the second idea, and the infinitive goes at the end of the clause. If word order rules mean that **werden** is sent to the end, it comes after the infinitive:

Lena wird Deutsch an der Uni studieren. *Lena will/is going to study German at university.*

Ich weiß, dass Lena Deutsch an der Uni studieren wird. *I know that Lena will/is going to study German at university.*

Kennst du Lena, die Deutsch an der Uni studieren wird? *Do you know Lena, who's going to study German at university?*

when to use the future tense

- You use the future tense to express the English *I will/shall do something, I will/shall be doing something* or *I'm going to do something*:

  Wenn es regnet, werden wir zu Hause bleiben. *If it rains, we'll stay at home.*

  Ich habe eine neue Arbeitsstelle, aber ich weiß noch nicht, wo ich arbeiten werde. *I've got a new job, but I don't know yet where I'll be working.*

  Ich werde jeden Tag zehn neue Wörter lernen. *I'm going to learn ten new words every day.*

- As in English, you can use the future tense to make assumptions:

  Wo ist Christian? Er wird in seinem Büro sein. *Where is Christian? He'll be in his office.*

> It is very common in German to use the present tense to express the future. For more on this, see page 135.

the past participle

The past participle is used to form various tenses and moods, including the perfect, pluperfect, future and passive. It is a key form of German verbs, generally listed in verb lists after the infinitive and the **ich** form of the simple past/imperfect.

weak verbs

- To form the past participle of regular weak verbs you replace the **-en** or **-n** ending of the infinitive with **-t** and add **ge-** to the beginning of the word: **machen → gemacht; lächeln → gelächelt**.

- If the stem ends in **-t** or **-d**, or in **-m** or **-n** preceded by a consonant other than l or r, an **e** is inserted between the stem and final **-t**: **arbeiten → gearbeitet; rechnen → gerechnet**.

- Irregular weak verbs also add **ge-** and replace the **-en** of the infinitive with **-t**, but the past participle retains the stem change of the simple past/imperfect: **denken → gedacht; kennen → gekannt**.

- In separable verbs **ge-** goes between the separable prefix and the main body of the verb: **zumachen** *to shut* → **zugemacht; einkaufen** *to go shopping* → **eingekauft**.

- The following do not add **ge-**:

  Separable verbs which have a separable prefix followed by an inseparable one: **anerkennen** *to recognise* → **anerkannt; vorbereiten** *to prepare* → **vorbereitet**.

  Inseparable verbs: **besuchen** *to visit* → **besucht; gehören** *to belong* → **gehört**.

  Verbs ending **-ieren: studieren → studiert; reservieren → reserviert**. (**Frieren** *to freeze* and **verlieren** *to lose* are strong verbs so are not in this category.)

strong verbs

The past participle of strong verbs ends in **-en**.

As is the case for weak verbs:

- **ge-** is added to the beginning of verbs without prefixes;
- **ge-** is added between the prefix and the main body of separable verbs:
  anfangen *to begin* → **an<u>ge</u>fangen**;
- **ge-** is not added to inseparable verbs.

The stem is often different from the stem of the infinitive. Each verb needs to be learnt as you meet it, but there are some frequently occurring stem-change patterns:

- **i** often changes to **u** or **o**:

finden *to find*	→	**gefunden** *found*
gelingen *to succeed*	→	**gelungen** *succeeded*
misslingen *to fail*	→	**misslungen** *failed*
singen *to sing*	→	**gesungen** *sung*
trinken *to drink*	→	**getrunken** *drunk*
verschwinden *to disappear*	→	**verschwunden** *disappeared*
zwingen *to force*	→	**gezwungen** *forced*
beginnen *to begin*	→	**begonnen** *begun*
gewinnen *to win*	→	**gewonnen** *won*
schwimmen *to swim*	→	**geschwommen** *swum*

- **ei** often changes to **ie** or **i**:

bleiben *to stay*	→	**geblieben** *stayed*
leihen *to lend*	→	**geliehen** *lent*
scheiden *to separate*	→	**geschieden** *separated*
scheinen *to seem*	→	**geschienen** *seemed*
schreiben *to write*	→	**geschrieben** *written*
beißen *to bite*	→	**gebissen** *bitten*
greifen *to grasp*	→	**gegriffen** *grasped*
reiten *to ride (a horse)*	→	**geritten** *ridden*
schneiden *to cut*	→	**geschnitten** *cut*

- **ie** often changes to **o**:

bieten *to offer*	→	**geboten** *offered*
fliegen *to fly*	→	**geflogen** *flown*
genießen *to enjoy*	→	**genossen** *enjoyed*
schließen *to close*	→	**geschlossen** *closed*
verlieren *to lose*	→	**verloren** *lost*
ziehen *to pull*	→	**gezogen** *pulled*

- e often changes to **o**:

befehlen *to order*	→	befohlen *ordered*
brechen *to break*	→	gebrochen *broken*
empfehlen *to recommend*	→	empfohlen *recommended*
helfen *to help*	→	geholfen *helped*
nehmen *to take*	→	genommen *taken*
sprechen *to speak*	→	gesprochen *spoken*
stehlen *to steal*	→	gestohlen *stolen*
sterben *to die*	→	gestorben *died*
treffen *to meet*	→	getroffen *met*
werden *to become*	→	geworden *become*
werfen *to throw*	→	geworfen *thrown*

- Not all past participles of strong verbs have a different stem from the infinitive, including:

braten *to fry*	→	gebraten *roasted, fried*
einladen *to invite*	→	eingeladen *invited*
essen *to eat*	→	gegessen *eaten* (note the extra g)
fahren *to go*	→	gefahren *gone, been*
fangen *to catch*	→	gefangen *caught*
geben *to give*	→	gegeben *given*
geschehen *to happen*	→	geschehen *happened*
halten *to hold*	→	gehalten *held*
heißen *to call*	→	geheißen *called*
kommen *to come*	→	gekommen *come*
laden *to load*	→	geladen *loaded*
lassen *to let*	→	gelassen *let*
laufen *to run*	→	gelaufen *run*
lesen *to read*	→	gelesen *read*
rufen *to shout*	→	gerufen *shouted*
schlafen *to sleep*	→	geschlafen *slept*
schlagen *to hit*	→	geschlagen *hit*
sehen *to see*	→	gesehen *seen*
tragen *to carry*	→	getragen *carried*
vergessen *to forget*	→	vergessen *forgotten*
waschen *to wash*	→	gewaschen *washed*

the past participle: special cases

- The past participle of **sein** is completely irregular:
  sein *to be* → **gewesen** *been*

- The past participles of **haben** *to have* and **wissen** *to know* end in **-t**:
  haben → **gehabt**; **wissen** → **gewusst**

- **Tun** *to do* is the only strong verb to have a past participle that doesn't end in **-en**: **getan** *done*

- The past participles of several other common verbs are unpredictable:
  gehen *to go* → **gegangen** *gone*
  liegen *to lie (position)* → **gelegen** *lain*
  sitzen *to sit* → **gesessen** *sat*
  stehen *to stand* → **gestanden** *stood*

- Separable and inseparable verbs follow the same pattern as their equivalents without a prefix:
  anrufen *to phone* → **angerufen** *phoned*
  einladen *to invite* → **eingeladen** *invited*
  versprechen *to promise* → **versprochen** *promised*

- The past participles of the modal verbs end in **-t**.
  können *can* → **gekonnt** *could*
  müssen *must* → **gemusst** *had to*
  mögen *to like* → **gemocht** *liked*
  dürfen *be allowed to* → **gedurft** *allowed to*
  wollen *to want* → **gewollt** *wanted*
  sollen *to be supposed to* → **gesollt** *supposed to*

These are only used when the modal verb appears without another verb in the same clause: **Das habe ich nicht gewollt.** *I didn't want that.*
In practice, modal verbs rarely appear on their own, they're almost always followed by another verb, in which case the infinitive of the modal is used, not the past participle. It goes at the end of the clause, after the infinitive of the main verb, unless other word order rules apply:
Das hat er tun wollen. *He wanted to do it.*
Ich habe nicht gehen können. *I couldn't go.*

uses of the past participle

- The main use of the past participle is after **haben** and **sein** in compound verb forms: the perfect, pluperfect and future perfect tenses, the pluperfect subjunctive (page 113) and the passive:
  Ich habe ihn gestern angerufen. *I phoned him yesterday.*
  Er hatte das Auto schon verkauft. *He had already sold the car.*
  Der Zug wird abgefahren sein. *The train will have left.*
  Ich hätte es gemacht. *I would have done it.*

- It is also used to form the perfect infinitive:
  Das musst du gesehen haben. *You must have seen it.*
  Diese Wörter müssen gelernt werden. *These words must be learnt.*

- … and the passive:
  Das Fleisch wurde geschnitten. *The meat was cut.*
  Diese Gebäude müssen während des Krieges zerstört worden sein.
  These buildings must have been destroyed during the war.

- As in English, many past participles are used as adjectives. Before the noun they agree in number, case and gender with that noun:
  ein gekochtes Ei *a boiled egg*
  Wir möchten alle interessierten Studenten zur Veranstaltung einladen. *We'd like to invite all students who are interested (lit. interested students) to the event.*

- Some past participles (those that can also be used as adjectives – see Adjectival nouns, page 37) can be used as nouns, when they're written with a capital letter. They behave like adjectives: **der Angestellte/ein Angestellter** *employee* (from **anstellen** *to employ*):
  Ich habe mit dem Angestellten gesprochen. *I've spoken to the employee.*
  Die Polizei verhaftete den Dieb. *The police arrested the thief.*

the perfect tense i) with haben

The perfect tense of the vast majority of German verbs is made up of the present tense of **haben** *to have* plus the past participle of the main verb:

machen (weak, regular)

ich	habe	gemacht
du	hast	gemacht
er, sie, es	hat	gemacht
wir	haben	gemacht
ihr	habt	gemacht
sie	haben	gemacht
Sie	haben	gemacht

verstehen *to understand* (strong, inseparable)

ich	habe	verstanden
du	hast	verstanden
er, sie, es	hat	verstanden
wir	haben	verstanden
ihr	habt	verstanden
sie	haben	verstanden
Sie	haben	verstanden

- The past participle goes at the end of the clause unless other word order rules apply:
  Ich habe ihn gestern nicht gesehen. *I didn't see him yesterday.*
  Hat das Spiel schon angefangen? *Has the match begun yet?*
  Ich weiß nicht, ob das Spiel schon angefangen hat. *I don't know whether the match has begun yet.*

- All reflexive verbs form their perfect tense with **haben**:
  Ich habe mich schnell geduscht. *I quickly showered.*
  Wir haben uns gestern Abend entspannt. *We relaxed yesterday evening.*
  So habe ich es mir nicht vorgestellt. *That's not what I had in mind.*

ii) with sein

A smaller group of verbs forms the perfect tense with **sein** instead of **haben**. They can be weak, strong, separable or inseparable – it's the meaning of a verb that determines whether it takes **haben** or **sein**. As a rule of thumb, if a verb relates to movement or a change of state, it will form its perfect tense with **sein**; if not, it will take **haben**.

- Verbs directly concerned with movement or change of state:

gehen *to go*   **fallen** *to fall*   **klettern** *to climb*
fahren *to go*   **fliegen** *to fly*   **steigen** *to climb*
kommen *to come*   **reisen** *to travel*   **wandern** *to hike*
laufen *to run*   **einschlafen** *to fall asleep*   **sterben** *to die*
verschwinden *to disappear*

gehen

ich	bin	gegangen
du	bist	gegangen
er, sie, es	ist	gegangen
wir	sind	gegangen
ihr	seid	gegangen
sie	sind	gegangen
Sie	sind	gegangen

Other verbs that form their perfect tense with **sein** are:

- **werden**, **sein** and **bleiben**;

- verbs that mean *to succeed*: **gelingen**, **glücken**; and *to fail*: **misslingen**, **missglücken**;

- verbs that mean *to happen*: **geschehen**, **passieren**.

When a prefix is added to a verb, the meaning of the new verb must be considered before choosing **haben** or **sein**, regardless of which the base form of the verb takes:

schlafen *to sleep*: **ich habe geschlafen**
einschlafen *to fall asleep*: **ich bin eingeschlafen**
kommen *to come*: **ich bin gekommen**
bekommen *to get*: **ich habe bekommen**

verbs which can take haben or sein

In grammatical terms, verbs that take **sein** are intransitive, i.e. they don't take a direct object. Transitive verbs, which do take a direct object, take **haben**.

However, some verbs can be used transitively or intransitively, and so can take **sein** or **haben**, e.g:

Er ist nach Berlin gefahren. *He's gone to Berlin.*
Er hat sein neues Auto gefahren. *He drove his new car.*

Ich bin alleine in den Urlaub geflogen. *I flew off alone on holiday.*
Der Pilot hat uns nach Berlin geflogen. *The pilot flew us to Berlin.*

A few verbs of movement form their perfect tense with **sein** if they involve moving to a destination, but not if they merely describe doing the activity. The commonest such verbs are **schwimmen** *to swim*, **reiten** *to ride*, **segeln** *to sail*:
Sie ist von England nach Frankreich geschwommen. *She swam from England to France.*
Wir haben den ganzen Morgen im Mittelmeer geschwommen. *We spent the whole morning swimming in the Mediterranean Sea.*
Wir sind ans andere Ufer gesegelt. *We sailed to the other bank.*
Letztes Jahr habe ich auf dem Chiemsee gesegelt. *Last year I sailed on the Chiemsee.*

Verbs relating to movement are easy enough to recognise, but what about verbs relating to a change of state? These refer to a fundamental transformation of the bodily state (e.g. **einschlafen** *to fall asleep*, **aufwachen** *to wake up*) or of the essence of a thing (e.g. **verwelken** *to wilt*), and take **sein**:
Ich bin eingeschlafen/aufgewacht; Die Blumen sind schon verwelkt *The flowers have already wilted.* Changing a legal or official state or status doesn't count! **Unsere Freunde haben geheiratet/haben sich scheiden lassen** *Our friends have got married/divorced.*

when to use the perfect tense

- The perfect tense in German is used to convey the English *have +
past participle*: *I have worked, I have eaten*. In informal German, such
as conversation, letters and emails, the perfect tense is also used in
preference to the simple past/imperfect to refer to a completed action in
the past: *I worked, I went, I ate* etc.
  Ich habe zwei Karten gekauft. *I (have) bought two tickets.*
  Sie ist nach Dresden gefahren. *She has gone to Dresden./She went to
  Dresden.*
  Wir haben uns dort amüsiert. *We had a good time there.*
  Er ist um halb acht aufgestanden. *He got up at 7:30.*

- It is also used when the auxiliary verbs *did* or *didn't*, *have* or *haven't* are
used in English questions and negatives:
  Was haben Sie gestern gemacht? *What did you do yesterday?*
  Er ist noch nicht gekommen. *He hasn't arrived yet.*
  Wann hast du ihn kennengelernt? *When did you meet (i.e. get to know)
  him?*

- As in English, the perfect tense is used in subordinate time clauses which
refer to future time:
  Wenn ich das Buch gelesen habe, werde ich es dir leihen.
  When I have read the book, I'll lend it to you.
  Er darf mit euch gehen, sobald er die Hausaufgaben gemacht hat.
  He is allowed to go with you, as soon as he has finished his homework.

- It is used in negative sentences containing **seit** *for/since*, to mean *have/
has done* or *have/has been doing*, whereas the present tense is used in
positive sentences (page 135):
  Ich habe ihn seit vielen Jahren nicht gesehen.
  I haven't seen him for many years.
  Er hat seit fünf Monaten nicht gearbeitet.
  He hasn't worked for five months.

Beware of translating sentences such as *I've lived in this house for
ten years* and *They've known each other a long time* into German
using the perfect tense. In English, the perfect tense implies *I
still live in this house* and *They **still** know each other*, whereas in
German it means the action is in the past, possibly even a long
time in the past: **Ich habe zehn Jahre in diesem Haus gewohnt**
I lived in this house for ten years; **Sie haben einander gekannt**
They knew/used to know each other.

the pluperfect

You use the pluperfect when you say in English you *had done something*. In German, the only difference in the way the pluperfect and the perfect tenses are formed is that the pluperfect uses the simple past/imperfect of **haben** or **sein** instead of the present tense. The same verbs use **haben** or **sein**, the past participle is the same and the usual word order rules apply.

	machen	gehen
ich	hatte gemacht	war gegangen
du	hattest gemacht	warst gegangen
er, sie, es	hatte gemacht	war gegangen
wir	hatten gemacht	waren gegangen
ihr	hattet gemacht	wart gegangen
sie/Sie	hatten gemacht	waren gegangen

Alle hatten schon gegessen. *Everyone had already eaten.*
Er war drei Stunden gefahren, um sie abzuholen.
He had driven three hours to pick her up.
Sie war Englischlehrerin gewesen. *She had been an English teacher.*

- The pluperfect is often found in sentences containing **als** *when* or **nachdem** *after*:
  Als sie ankamen, hatte ich mich schon geduscht.
  When they arrived I had already showered.
  Nachdem der Film geendet hatte, gingen wir nach Hause.
  After the film had finished, we went home.
  In spoken German or informal writing, the perfect tense can be used instead of the simple past in the other half of the sentence:
  Nachdem der Film geendet hatte, sind wir nach Hause gegangen.
  After the film had finished, we went home.

- It's also used in negative sentences containing **seit** *for, since* to mean *had done/had been doing*.
  Ich hatte seit vielen Jahren überhaupt kein Deutsch gesprochen.
  I hadn't spoken any German at all for many years.

the future perfect

The future tense of **haben/sein** plus the past participle gives you the future perfect. The infinitive **haben** or **sein** is the last word in the clause, after the past participle, unless other word order rules send the conjugated verb to the end.

The same verbs use **haben** or **sein** as for the perfect and pluperfect tenses, the past participle is the same and the usual word order rules apply.

	machen
ich	werde gemacht haben
du	wirst gemacht haben
er, sie, es	wird gemacht haben
wir	werden gemacht haben
ihr	werdet gemacht haben
sie/Sie	werden gemacht haben

	gehen
ich	werde gegangen sein
du	wirst gegangen sein
er, sie, es	wird gegangen sein
wir	werden gegangen sein
ihr	werdet gegangen sein
sie/Sie	werden gegangen sein

You use the future perfect when in English you say *will have done something*:
Bis Montag wird sie von Wien zurückgekommen sein. *She will have come back from Vienna by Monday.*
Sie werden nichts gesehen haben. *They won't have seen anything.*

Like the future, the future perfect can be used to make assumptions. You'll often see the word **wohl** *probably* in such sentences:
Das wird er wohl gesagt haben. *I expect he said that.* (lit. *He will probably have said that.*)
Er wird wohl schon angekommen sein. *He'll probably have arrived by now.*

the passive

The passive is used when you want to highlight the action, rather than the person or thing *doing* the action.

- The passive in simple tenses, and the future, is formed with the appropriate tense of **werden** (see page 238) plus the past participle of the main verb.

  Das Auto wird repariert. *The car is being repaired.* (present)

  Neue Bücher werden gekauft werden. *New books will be bought.* (future)

  Das Fenster wurde gestern zerbrochen. *The window was smashed yesterday.* (simple past)

- The perfect and pluperfect are conjugated with **sein**. They lose the **ge-** of the past participle, which goes after the past participle of the main verb.

  Das Fenster ist gestern zerbrochen worden. *The window was smashed yesterday.* (perfect)

  Es war kalt, weil das Fenster vor einigen Tagen zerbrochen worden war. *It was cold because the window had been smashed a few days previously.* (pluperfect)

- The future perfect also uses **sein**. The infinitive (**sein**, never **haben**, because it goes with **werden**) goes at the end, unless other word order rules apply.

  Alles wird schon gegessen worden sein. *Everything will already have been eaten.*

  In the passive, the person who carries out the action is introduced by **von** + dative:

  Das Auto wird vom Mechaniker repariert. *The car is being repaired by the mechanic.*

  When the action is not carried out by a person, **durch** + accusative is used, although there's a growing tendency to use **von** for both people and things:

  Das Gebäude wurde durch ein Gewitter zerstört/von einem Gewitter zerstört. *The building was destroyed by a storm.*

  Mit + dative is used to indicate the instrument with which something is done:

  Der Brief wurde mit der Hand geschrieben. *The letter was written by hand.*

alternatives to the passive

The English passive can also be expressed by:

- the pronoun **man** *one, we, you, they* (page 83):
  Man sagt, dass … *It is said that …*
  Hier spricht man Englisch. *English is spoken here.*
  Man hat uns gesagt, dass … *We were told that …*

- a reflexive verb, in particular **sich lassen**, which has the sense of the English *can be*:
  Wie schreiben sich diese Namen? *How are these names spelt?*
  Diese Maschine lässt sich leicht reparieren. *This machine can be repaired easily.*

- The verbs **sein** *to be*, **bleiben** *to remain* and the impersonal expression **es gibt** *there is/are* can be followed by **zu** + infinitive, when they express possibility or necessity. The English translation sometimes includes a modal verb:
  Das Erdbeben war nicht vorauszusehen. *The earthquake could not have been foreseen.*
  Es bleibt noch zu klären. *It remains to be clarified.*
  Es gibt noch viel zu diskutieren. *There's still a lot to be discussed.*

the sein passive

In the present and simple past/imperfect tenses, German also uses a passive formed from **sein**. Used to refer to a state, as opposed to an action, it's not as common as the **werden** passive.
Das Fenster wurde gestern zerbrochen. *The window was smashed yesterday.* (action)
Das Fenster war zerbrochen. *The window was smashed.* (describing the state of the window, which had been smashed at an earlier point)

To say *was/were born*, German uses the **sein** passive of the verb **gebären** (past participle **geboren**) for people still living, but the **werden** passive for historical figures:
Ich bin 1978 geboren. *I was born in 1978.*
Goethe wurde 1749 geboren. *Goethe was born in 1749.*

checkpoint 16

1   What are the past participles of these verbs?

fragen	kennen	tun	zurückgehen
fahren	beginnen	warten	haben
besuchen	vergessen	anfangen	verkaufen
bringen	lernen	sagen	denken
lassen	fotografieren	kochen	verstehen
verlieren	werden	sterben	nehmen

2   Fill in the gaps to create the perfect tense:

ich .... getrunken   sie (sing) .... gearbeitet

wir .... gereist   ihr .... euch gewaschen

du .... gewandert   sie (pl) .... gefallen

wir .... bekommen   er .... angekommen

3   Choose the right form of the modal, and say what the sentences mean:

   a Ich habe Mathematik immer (gemocht/mögen)

   b Wir haben nicht gehen (gekonnt/können)

   c Wir werden nicht gehen (gekonnt/können)

4   Which of these verbs would you use to say when your son was born: er (ist/war/wurde) geboren?

5   Change these sentences from the present tense to the tense indicated:

   a Er kommt um neun Uhr an.   (future)

   b Sie tut das.   (future perfect)

   c Du läufst schnell.   (perfect)

   d Die Eier werden gekocht.   (perfect)

   e Ich gebe ihm das Buch.   (pluperfect)

   f Wir bleiben zu Hause.   (perfect)

   g Wir entspannen uns am Strand.   (future)

   h Sie fliegt nach Krakau.   (pluperfect)

   i Er ruft mich an.   (perfect)

   j Du musst diese Tabletten nehmen. (future)

Present participle, imperative, subjunctive, conditional

German verb endings and the prefix **ge-** not only provide information about whether things are happening in the past, present or future, they indicate other functions of the verb too.

These functions include:

- the **participles**: the past participle, which is used in compound tenses (pages 141–156), and the present participle, ending in **-(e)nd**, which is the equivalent of the -*ing* ending in English (although in German it's used much less and not always in the same way).

- the **imperative**, which is used to tell somebody what to do. In English there's only one version but there are three in German because of the three different words for you: **du**, **ihr**, **Sie**. There is also a **wir** imperative, used to say *let's*.

- the **subjunctive**, which is no longer used much in English but which is used more frequently in German. A verb in the subjunctive doesn't convey hard fact but usually expresses an attitude of doubt or uncertainty, or indicates that information has been obtained second-hand. It appears in **wenn** *if* sentences to indicate a hypothetical or impossible condition. There are two main sets of endings for the subjunctive, called **Konjunktiv I** and **Konjunktiv II**.

the present participle

The present participle ends in -ing in English and -(e)nd in German, formed by adding -d to the infinitive: **arbeitend** *working*, **lächelnd** *smiling*, **fahrend** *going*.

There are just two exceptions: **sein → seiend** *being*; **tun → tuend** *doing*.

The present participle of separable verbs does not separate: **ankommend** *arriving*, **vorbeigehend** *going past*.

- Many present participles have become standard German adjectives, which add endings when used before the noun they describe but not when used after **sein**:

  Das Dorf ist reizend. *The village is charming.*

  Ein reizendes Dorf. *A charming village.*

  Der Film war spannend. *The film was exciting.*

  Wir haben einen spannenden Film gesehen. *We saw an exciting film.*

  Meine Arbeit ist sehr anstrengend. *My work is very strenuous.*

  Ich habe sehr anstrengende Arbeit. *I have very strenuous work.*

  Other common examples include:

abwesend *absent*	**ansteckend** *contagious*
anstrengend *strenuous*	**anwesend** *present*
auffallend *conspicuous*	**bedeutend** *significant*
dringend *urgent*	**entscheidend** *decisive*
entzückend *delightful*	**gut aussehend** *good-looking*
reizend *charming*	**rührend** *touching*
spannend *exciting*	**überzeugend** *convincing*
umfassend *extensive*	**wütend** *angry*

- Present participles can also be used as adverbs, in which case they don't add endings. The actions expressed by the present participle and main verb must be going on at the same time and it must be the same person/people doing both actions:

  Das Kind ging lachend aus dem Zimmer. *The child laughed as he went out of the room.* (Lit. *The child went laughing out of the room.*)

  The present participle comes at the end of a clause:

  Ein Fußballlied singend, ging er die Straße entlang. *He walked along the road singing a football song.*

- Some present participles have become nouns, and are therefore written with a capital letter. They behave as adjectives:
  der/die Sterbende (ein Sterbender) *dying man/woman*
  der/die Vorsitzende *chairman/woman*
  50 000 Streikende *50,000 strikers*

... and when *not* to use it in German

The suffix *-ing* is extremely common in English, but it is usually not translated in German by the present participle. In English, words ending in *-ing*:

- are often part of a continuous tense: *The child is singing*; *She was playing*. In German, there are no continuous tenses – the present or the simple past/imperfect tenses are used instead: **das Kind singt**; **sie spielte**.

- come after verbs such as *like*, *enjoy*, *prefer*. German uses **gern** and **lieber**: **Ich tanze gern** *I like dancing*; **Ich schwimme lieber** *I prefer swimming*.

- come after verbs of perception: *I saw/heard him coming*. German uses the infinitive: **Ich sah/hörte ihn kommen**.

- come after prepositions: *before leaving*; *after eating*; *by watching*; *without speaking*; *instead of going*. German either uses a subordinating conjunction: **bevor (ich/sie) ... ausging**; **nachdem (er) ... gegessen hat**; **indem (ich) ... schaue** or an infinitive construction: **ohne ... zu sprechen**; **anstatt ... zu gehen**:
  Bevor sie ausging, telefonierte sie mit Stefan. *Before leaving, she phoned Stefan.*
  Kleine Kinder kommunizieren ohne zu sprechen. *Small children communicate without speaking.*
  Bevor sie ausging, telefonierte sie mit Stefan. *Before leaving, she phoned Stefan.*

- are often used as nouns: *Smoking is harmful to your health*. German uses a noun formed from an infinitive: **Das Rauchen schadet der Gesundheit.**

the imperative

The imperative, used to give instructions, has three main forms:

	sagen	kommen	essen	sich setzen
du	sag(e)!	komm(e)!	iss!	setz(e) dich!
ihr	sagt!	kommt!	esst!	setzt euch!
Sie	sagen Sie!	kommen Sie!	essen Sie!	setzen Sie sich!

- An exclamation mark is written after the imperative in German.

- The -e of the **du** form is optional except for:
  verbs whose stem ends in **-ig**: **entschuldige!** *excuse (me)*;
  weak verbs whose stem ends in **-t** or **-d**: **antworte!** *answer*, **rede!** *speak*;
  weak verbs whose stem ends in **-m** or **-n** preceded by a consonant other than **l** or **r**: **öffne!** *open*, **atme!** *breathe*;
  verbs whose infinitives end in **-eln** or **-ern**; **-eln** verbs lose the **e** of **-eln**, and **-ern** verbs have the option of omitting the **e** of **-ern**: **klingle!** *ring*, **flüst(e)re!** *whisper*.

- Strong verbs with a vowel change in the **du** and **er/sie/es** present tense forms have no final **-e** in the **du** form: **gib!** *give*, **sieh!** *see*. But strong verbs whose stem change only involves the addition of an umlaut behave like weak verbs: **fahr(e)!** *go* (**du fährst** is the present tense), **lauf(e)!** *run* (**du läufst**).

- Separable verbs separate: **Ruf mich morgen an!** *Call me tomorrow* (from **anrufen**).

- Reflexive pronouns come immediately after the verb: **Stell(e) dir mal vor!** *Just imagine.*

- **Nicht** comes in the place it would normally occupy: **Tu(e) das nicht!** *Don't do that*; **Seid nicht so dumm!** *Don't be so stupid!*

- The imperative forms of **sein** *to be* are **sei!**, **seid!** and **seien Sie!**

- There's a **wir** form of the imperative, which means *Let's …*: **Gehen wir!** *Let's go*. The **wir** imperative form of **sein** is **seien wir**: **Seien wir ehrlich/froh!** *Let's be honest/glad.*

- The imperative of the verb **lassen** *to let, allow* (**lass/ lasst/lassen Sie uns**) also means *Let's …*: **Lasst uns feiern!** *Let's celebrate.*

... and how to use it

You use the **du**, **ihr** and **Sie** imperatives to tell someone what to do and give advice, and the **wir** imperative to make suggestions:

du	**Denk(e) an deine Gesundheit!** *Think of your health.*
ihr	**Seid ruhig!** *Be quiet!*
Sie	**Gehen Sie links!** *Go left.*
wir	**Trinken wir auf die Freundschaft!/Lasst uns auf die Freundschaft trinken!** *Let's drink to friendship!*

Little words are often added to 'soften' an imperative and make it sound less brusque. They have no direct English translation:

Doch urges or encourages: **Komm doch mit!** <u>Do</u> come!

Ja reminds or warns: **Trink ja nicht zu viel!** *Don't drink too much, now!*

Mal tones down a command: **Komm mal her!** *Come here, will you!*

Nur intensifies the meaning: **Komm nur!** *Come on, now!*

Ruhig reassures: **Erzähl ruhig weiter!** *Do carry on.*

Schon shows impatience: **Nun komm schon!** *Hurry up, will you!*

alternatives to the imperative

- **Wir wollen ...** from **wollen** *to want*, can express *let's*: **wir wollen gehen**, *let's go* (the inverted **wollen wir gehen?** means *shall we go?*).

- The modal verb **sollen** *should, am to, is to* etc. is often used instead of the imperative: **du sollst jetzt lesen** *you should read now*.

- The infinitive is often used instead of the imperative in official contexts and when giving written instructions: **Aufstehen!** *Stand up!*; **Die Zwiebeln pellen und schneiden** *Peel and cut the onions.*

- Occasionally the past participle is used on its own as an imperative: **Stillgestanden!** *Stand to attention*! **Aufgepasst!** *Watch out!*

the subjunctive: formation

The subjunctive is a mood, which has tenses and a passive voice, just as the indicative mood does. There are two main sets of endings for the German subjunctive, called **Konjunktiv I** and **Konjunktiv II**.

Konjunktiv I (present subjunctive)

The **Konjunktiv I** form of all verbs except **sein** is formed the same way. Take the stem of the infinitive and add the following endings:

	mach(en) *to do, make*	ess(en) *to eat*	hab(en) *to have*	könn(en) *can*
ich	mache	esse	habe	könne
du	machest	essest	habest	könnest
er, sie, es	mache	esse	habe	könne
wir	machen	essen	haben	können
ihr	machet	esset	habet	könnet
sie/Sie	machen	essen	haben	können

The **Konjunktiv I** of **sein** is:

ich sei	wir seien
du sei(e)st	ihr seiet
er, sie, es sei	sie/Sie seien

- **Konjunktiv I** forms for all verbs except **sein** and the modal verbs are identical to the indicative except for the **du**, **ihr** and **er/sie/es** forms. Since the **du** and **ihr** forms are hardly ever used, you're only likely to come across the **er/sie/es** form. Verbs whose infinitives end in **-eln** or **-ern** have the option of dropping the **-e-** of the stem in the **ich** and **er/sie/es** forms: **ich läch(e)le, er läch(e)le, wir lächeln, Sie lächeln; ich wand(e)re, er wand(e)re, wir wandern, Sie wandern.**

The future subjunctive and the perfect subjunctive are formed from the **Konjunktiv I** of the verbs **werden**, **haben** and **sein**:

future subjunctive: **er werde ... machen**
perfect subjunctive: **er habe ... gemacht; er sei ... gegangen**

The present, future and perfect passive subjunctives are formed from the **Konjunktiv I** of **werden**:

present passive subjunctive: **es werde ... gemacht**
perfect passive subjunctive: **es sei ... gemacht worden**
future passive subjunctive: **es werde ... gemacht werden**

Konjunktiv II (past subjunctive)

The **Konjunktiv II** form of regular weak verbs is identical to the simple past/imperfect indicative. The endings are the same as those for **Konjunktiv I**. Strong verbs add these same endings to their simple past/imperfect stem:

	machen	gehen *to go*
ich	machte	ginge
du	machtest	gingest
er, sie, es	machte	ginge
wir	machten	gingen
ihr	machtet	ginget
sie/Sie	machten	gingen

Where possible (on **a**, **o** and **u**), an umlaut is added to the simple past/imperfect stem of irregular weak and strong verbs.

In spoken German, **Konjunktiv II**, like the simple past/imperfect indicative, is rarely used. However, it's common in newspaper reports and other formal written German contexts. Here are the **Konjunktiv II** forms of verbs which you are likely to meet when reading:

denken *to think*: ich dächte; du dächtest; er/sie/es dächte; wir dächten; ihr dächtet; sie/Sie dächten

essen *to eat*: ich äße; du äßest; er/sie/es äße; wir äßen; ihr äßet; sie/Sie äßen

fahren *to go*: ich führe; du führest; er/sie/es führe; wir führen; ihr führet; sie/Sie führen

finden *to find*: ich fände; du fändest; er/sie/es fände; wir fänden; ihr fändet; sie/Sie fänden

geben *to give*: ich gäbe; du gäbest; er/sie/es gäbe; wir gäben; ihr gäbet; sie/Sie gäben

halten *to hold*: ich hielte; du hieltest; er/sie/es hielte; wir hielten; ihr hieltet; sie/Sie hielten

kommen *to come*: ich käme; du kämest; er/sie/es käme; wir kämen; ihr kämet; sie/Sie kämen

lassen *to let*: ich ließe; du ließest; er/sie/es ließe; wir ließen; ihr ließet; sie/Sie ließen

tun *to do*: ich täte; du tätest; er/sie/es täte; wir täten; ihr tätet; sie/Sie täten

- Some strong verbs have an optional or obligatory change of vowel:

infinitive	simple past indicative	past subjunctive
helfen *to help*	half, halfst	hülfe, hülfest or hälfe, hälfest
stehen *to stand*	stand, standst	stünde, stündest or stände, ständest
sterben *to die*	starb, starbst	stürbe, stürbest
werfen *to throw*	warf, warfst	würfe, würfest

- The Konjunktiv II forms of sein, haben, werden and wissen, which **are** frequently encountered, are:

ich	wäre	hätte	würde	wüsste
du	wärest	hättest	würdest	wüsstest
er, sie, es	wäre	hätte	würde	wüsste
wir	wären	hätten	würden	wüssten
ihr	wäret	hättet	würdet	wüsstet
sie/Sie	wären	hätten	würden	wüssten

- The Konjunktiv II forms of the modal verbs are also common:

können *can*	müssen *must*	mögen *to like*	sollen *should*
ich könnte	müsste	möchte	sollte
du könntest	müsstest	möchtest	solltest
er könnte	müsste	möchte	sollte
wir könnten	müssten	möchten	sollten
ihr könntet	müsstet	möchtet	solltet
sie/Sie könnten	müssten	möchten	sollten

dürfen *might*: ich dürfte, du dürftest, er dürfte
wollen *to want*: ich wollte, du wolltest, er wollte

- The Konjunktiv II can alternatively be expressed using ich würde/ du würdest etc. + infinitive: ich machte = ich würde ... machen; ich ginge = ich würde ... gehen; ich dächte = ich würde ... denken *to think*. In practice, the würde form is usually used for weak verbs (including irregular weak verbs), as otherwise there would be no way of knowing whether the verb was in the indicative or subjunctive mood. However, the Konjunktiv II is used for modals and other common verbs:
ich möchte not ich würde ... mögen   ich hätte not ich würde ... haben
ich könnte not ich würde ... können   ich wäre not ich würde ... sein

- The pluperfect subjunctive is formed from the **Konjunktiv II** of the verbs **haben** or **sein** + past participle. All persons of the verb are different from the indicative, so all are used:

  pluperfect subjunctive: **ich hätte ... gemacht; du hättest ... gemacht; ich wäre ... gegangen; du wärest ... gegangen**

- The imperfect and pluperfect passive subjunctives are formed from the **Konjunktiv II** of **werden** (or **sein** for the **sein** passive):

  simple past/imperfect passive subjunctive: **es würde ... gemacht**
  sein passive form: **es wäre ... gemacht**
  pluperfect passive subjunctive: **es wäre ... gemacht worden**

when to use the subjunctive

In English, the subjunctive is confined to a few expressions like *If only it were true; They suggested that I be there.* In German, it's used much more widely – when you're reporting about something that you're not sure is true, when you're referring to hypothetical situations, and in order to be more polite or tentative. It is used in:

- **indirect speech** after verbs such as **sagen** *to say*, **behaupten** *to maintain*, **berichten** *to report* and after verbs of thinking and believing such as **denken**, **meinen** *to think*, **glauben** *to believe*:

  Er sagt/sagte, sie wolle kommen. *He says/said she wants/wanted to come.*
  Sie meint/meinte, er sei unglücklich. *She thinks/thought he is/was unhappy.*
  Sie sagt/sagte, sie werde kommen. *She says/said she will/would come.*
  Er sagt/sagte, sie habe es nicht gemacht. *He says/said she hasn't done it/ didn't do it/hadn't done it.*

  Konjunktiv I is used if the form is distinguishable from the indicative. If not, **Konjunktiv II** is used:

  Sie sagt/sagte, die Kinder hätten nicht geschlafen. *She says/said the children haven't slept/didn't sleep/hadn't slept.*

  Er glaubt/glaubte, sie kämen erst später. *He believes/believed they're coming/will be coming/would be coming later.*

  The comma is obligatory in these sentences. The conjunction **dass** *that* can introduce the clause after **er sagt(e)**, **meint(e)** etc., which means the verb goes to the end. If **dass** is used, the indicative is frequently used instead of the subjunctive: **Er sagte, dass sie es nicht gemacht hat/habe.**

- **indirect questions** (**Konjunktiv I** or **II** as above)
  Question words used in indirect questions and **ob** *if, whether* send the verb to the end of the clause:
  Sie fragte ihn, ob er Zeit habe. *She asked him if he had time.*
  Er fragte sie, wann sie kommen könne. *He asked her when she could come.*
  Sie fragte uns, was die Frau wolle, die eben gekommen sei. *She asked us what the woman who had just come wanted.*
  Ich habe sie gefragt, warum sie das wissen wolle. *I asked her why she wanted to know that.*

- **indirect commands** with **sollen** (**Konjunktiv I** or **II** as above)
  Sie sagte ihm, er solle sofort kommen. *She told him to come immediately.*
  Er sagte mir, ich solle ihn in Ruhe lassen. *He told me to leave him alone.*

In informal German, **Konjunktiv II** or the indicative is frequently used instead of **Konjunktiv I** in indirect speech, questions and commands:
Sie sagt/sagte, sie wird/würde kommen. *She says/said she will/would come.*
Sie sagte ihm, er soll/sollte sofort kommen. *She told him to come immediately.*
Sie hat mir gesagt, ich soll/solle unten warten. *She told me to wait downstairs.*

---

other uses of the subjunctive

- to make a request sound more polite (**Konjunktiv II**):
  Ich hätte gern einen Apfelsaft. *I'd like an apple juice.*
  Ich möchte den Käsekuchen bitte. *I'd like the cheesecake, please.*
  Könnten Sie mir bitte sagen, wie ich zum Alexanderplatz komme?
  Could you please tell me how I get to Alexanderplatz?
  Würden Sie mir bitte sagen, wie spät es ist? *Would you tell me the time, please?*

- to express a wish (**Konjunktiv II**):
  Ich wünschte, ich könnte fliegen. *I wish I could fly.*
  Ich wünschte, sie wäre hier. *I wish she was here.*
  Wir wünschten, wir hätten hier den ganzen Urlaub verbracht.
  We wish we'd spent the whole holiday here.

- to express *if only* (**Konjunktiv II**):
  Hätte er nur fleißiger gearbeitet. *If only he'd worked harder.*
  Wenn sie nur hier wären. *If only they were here.*
  Hätten wir nur mehr Zeit gehabt. *If only we'd had more time.*

- after **als ob** *as if* (**Konjunktiv I** or **II**):
  Sie sieht aus, als ob sie krank sei/wäre. *She looks as if she's ill.*
  Er tat, als ob er schliefe. *He pretended to be asleep.* (Lit. *He did as if he were asleep.*)
  Er benimmt sich, als ob nichts geschehen wäre. *He's acting as if nothing has happened.*

- in a few set phrases (**Konjunktiv I**):
  Es lebe der König! *Long live the king!*
  Gott sei Dank! *Thank God.*
  Wehe dir! *Woe betide you.*

the conditional

The conditional in German is neither a tense nor a mood. It is a type of sentence that usually includes the word **wenn** *if*; if **wenn** isn't there, it is implied.

Some conditional sentences express 'possible' conditions, while others express 'impossible' conditions.

possible conditions

Possible (or 'open') conditions express the idea that if one thing happens (and this is entirely possible) then something else will happen.

They use the present and future tenses of the indicative (see pages 112–113), the present in the **wenn** clause and the future in the main clause: **Wenn es regnet, werden wir zu Hause bleiben** *If it rains, we'll stay at home*. In this sentence, the indicative shows that the speaker believes that rain is possible.

impossible conditions

Impossible (or 'unreal') conditions, those that the speaker thinks are unlikely or impossible, use the subjunctive in German. Such sentences can express conditions in the future or in the past: if one thing were to happen (and this is unlikely) then something else would happen/if one thing had happened (but it didn't) then something else would have happened.

- If the sentence expresses a condition in the future, the Konjunktiv II or **würde** form is used in both clauses: **Wenn ich Zeit hätte, würde ich mitkommen./Wenn ich Zeit hätte, käme ich mit.** *If I had time I would come with you.* (The second option is more formal.) In this sentence, the subjunctive shows that the speaker does not believe that they have time.

  The **würde** form is usually used for weak verbs, since **Konjunktiv II** is identical to the simple past indicative, and also for strong verbs whose past subjunctive is considered archaic (this is the case for **gewönne**, the past subjunctive of **gewinnen**: **würde gewinnen** is used instead). **Konjunktiv II** is used for **haben**, **sein**, the modals and other common verbs.

- If the sentence expresses a condition in the past, the pluperfect subjunctive is used in both clauses: **Wenn ich Zeit gehabt hätte, dann wäre ich mitgekommen**. *If I'd had time, I would have come.* (The implication is that I didn't have time, so I didn't come.)
  Ich hätte ihm gesimst, wenn ich seine Handynummer gewusst hätte. *I would have texted him if I'd known his mobile number.* (The implication is that I didn't know his mobile number, so I didn't text him.)

- A conditional sentence can start with either the **wenn** clause or the main clause. If it starts with the **wenn** clause, the main clause can be introduced by **so** or **dann**, but this is optional:
  Ich würde ihm simsen, wenn ich seine Handynummer wüsste. *I would text him if I knew his mobile number.*
  Wenn Sie kommen könnten, (so/dann) würden wir uns freuen. *If you could come we'd be delighted.*
  Wenn er Zeit hätte, ginge er spazieren. *If he had time he'd go for a walk.*

- **Wenn** can be omitted, in which case the **wenn** clause begins with the verb:
  Hätte er Zeit, ginge er spazieren. *If he had time he'd go for a walk/Had he time he'd go for a walk.*

- **Falls** *in case, if* is sometimes used instead of **wenn**, especially when there's ambiguity in meaning (since **wenn** can mean *when* or *whenever*, as well as *if*). In practice, ambiguity is most likely in present indicative sentences:
  Wenn sie anruft, sag ihr ... *When she rings, tell her* ...
  Falls sie anruft, sag ihr ... *If she rings, tell her* ...

Be careful of the word *would* when translating it into German. In English it can be conditional (*We would buy it if* ...), but it can also relate to the past (*We would go to the beach every summer when we were children*).

checkpoint 17

1 Write the **du**, **ihr** and **Sie** imperative forms of the verbs below. Check the present tense stems of the strong verbs on pages 132–133.
   nehmen, warten, schreiben, sich beeilen, waschen, verändern, anfangen, studieren, sich anziehen

2 What is another way of saying **Lasst uns zurückgehen!**, using the wir form of **zurückgehen**?

3 Replace the underlined clauses with the present participle, changing the word order as necessary:
   a Der Junge, <u>der weinte</u>, lief über die Brücke.
   b Ein Baum ist auf ein Auto, <u>das vorbeifuhr</u>, gefallen.

4 Which of these verb forms are subjunctive only and which could be indicative or subjunctive?
   ich habe; er sei; er wollte; sie ginge; wir hätten; ich müsse; wir kommen; es wäre; wir wüssten; sie werden

5 How would you say?
   a *I'd like a glass of wine.* (two possibilities)
   b *I wish I had more money.*
   c *He pretended to be working.*
   d *Could you tell me how I get to the station?*

6 Match the two halves of these sentences:

a Wenn er fleißiger gelernt hätte,	1 wäre er fitter.
b Wenn er jeden Tag trainieren würde,	2 wären wir an den Strand gefahren.
c Wenn heute schönes Wetter gewesen wäre,	3 wenn das Wetter besser gewesen wäre.
d Wenn du kommen könntest,	4 hätte er die Prüfung bestanden.
e Sie wäre länger geblieben,	5 wäre das wunderschön.

Key verbs

In German, as in most languages, some verbs are used more frequently than others. These include verbs like **gehen** *to go*, **sagen** *to say*, **essen** *to eat* and **denken** *to think*, which relate to basic human activity. Others are:

- **dürfen** *to be allowed to*, **können** *to be able to*, **mögen** *to like*, **müssen** *to have to*, **sollen** *to be (supposed) to* and **wollen** *to want to*. These are known as modal verbs and are used with the infinitive of a second verb. **Lassen** *to let*, though not a modal, has similarities.

- **sein** *to be* and **haben** *to have*, which are used with a past participle to form past tenses (pages 148–150). **Haben** also features in several expressions that don't use the word *have* in English.

- **werden** *to become*, used with an infinitive to form the future tense and the conditional, and with a past participle to form the passive.

- **machen** *to do/make* and **gehen** *to go*, which can be used in situations that are not translated as *do*, *make* or *go* in English.

German has a number of different ways of expressing the English verb *to like*: it uses the verb **gefallen** *to be pleasing*, the modal verb **mögen** *to like* or the adverb **gern**. It also has the verb **schmecken**, used when talking about liking food.

All the above, except **sagen**, **machen** and **schmecken**, are either strong or irregular; they're written out in full in the Verb tables (pages 191–242).

Some common German verbs don't have a direct equivalent in English. Both **wissen** and **kennen** are translated as *to know*, but they're not at all interchangeable. **Wissen** means to know information and facts, whereas you use **kennen** when you're talking about knowing or being acquainted with a person, place, thing or concept.

modal verbs

There are six modal verbs in German: **dürfen** *to be allowed to*, **können** *to be able to*, **mögen** *to like*, **müssen** *to have to*, **sollen** *to be (supposed) to, should* and **wollen** *to want to*. The modal verbs don't usually impart much information on their own, so are followed by another verb in the infinitive, or sometimes by a noun. The verbs are all irregular (see pages 134 and 138), but behave in a similar way.

- Modal verbs are followed by a straight infinitive, not an infinitive prefaced by **zu** as is the case for most verbs. This infinitive goes to the end of the clause, unless the modal itself is sent to the end of a subordinate clause:
  Ich will/möchte nach Österreich fahren. *I want/I'd like to go to Austria.*
  Ich musste lange warten. *I had to wait a long time.*
  Darf ich mal hereinkommen? *May I come in?*
  Was soll man tun, wenn man nicht einschlafen kann? *What should you do if you can't get to sleep?*

- **Mögen** and **wollen** are the only modal verbs that can have a noun or pronoun object:
  Das wollte ich nicht. *I didn't want that.*
  Ich möchte ein Glas Wein. *I'd like a glass of wine.*

- In the future tense the modal infinitive is placed at the very end of the sentence:
  Ich werde nicht kommen können. *I won't be able to come.*
  Wir werden früh weggehen müssen. *We'll have to get away early.*

- In the perfect tense, the modal verbs use **haben**. Although they do have a past participle beginning **ge-** and ending **-t** (**gedurft, gekonnt, gemocht, gemusst, gesollt, gewollt**), these are only used if there's no other verb in the clause. Otherwise the infinitive is used instead. Since modal verbs usually **are** accompanied by another verb, the infinitive is far more common in compound tenses than the past participle:
  Das habe ich nicht gewollt. *I didn't want it.*
  Sie hat nicht kommen wollen. *She didn't want to come.*
  Er hätte das Haus nicht verlassen sollen. *He shouldn't have left the house.*

- The simple past/imperfect of modals is used much more frequently than the perfect in everyday German:
  Ich wollte mit ihnen gehen. *I wanted to go with them.* (in preference to **Ich habe mit ihnen gehen wollen.**)
  Wir mussten warten. *We had to wait.* (in preference to **Wir haben warten müssen.**)
  Ich konnte seine Nummer nicht finden. *I couldn't find his number.* (in preference to **Ich habe seine Nummer nicht finden können.**)

- The **Konjunktiv II** of modal verbs is used to convey politeness:
  Könnten Sie mir sagen, …? *Could you tell me …?*
  Möchten Sie sich zu uns setzen? *Would you like to sit with us?*
  Dürfte ich fragen? *Might I possibly ask?*

- Verbs of motion (e.g. **gehen** *to go*, **kommen** *to come*) and **tun** *to do*, can be omitted after a modal verb:
  Ich will nach München. *I want to go to Munich.*
  Darf ich zur Toilette? *May I go to the toilet?*
  Ich kann nicht mehr. *I can't eat/go on any more.*

- If there are two infinitives in a subordinate clause, the auxiliary verb **werden** or **haben** comes before the two infinitives, not at the end, as is normal in subordinate clauses:
  Obwohl wir früh werden weggehen müssen, … *Although we will have to get away early, …*
  Er ist nicht gekommen, weil er die Kinder hatte abholen müssen. *He didn't come because he had to pick up the children.*
  Ich wusste, dass er es nicht hätte wissen können. *I knew he couldn't have known.*

dürfen

- **Dürfen** is the equivalent of *may, can* or *be allowed to* and has to do with asking for and getting permission. In the negative it means *must not, not be allowed to*:
  Darf ich rauchen? *May I smoke?*
  Ihre Kinder durften alles machen. *Their children were allowed to do everything.*
  Du darfst nicht hereinkommen. *You must not enter./You're not allowed to come in.*

- It's used in polite formulaic expressions:
  Was darf es sein? *What would you like?/Can I help you?* (in a shop)
  Darf/(Dürfte) ich Sie bitten, das Fenster zuzumachen?
  Would you/(Would you be so kind as to) close the window?

- In the **Konjunktiv II** form it expresses likelihood:
  Das dürfte der Grund sein. *That, most likely, is the reason.*
  Morgen dürfte es Regen geben. *It looks as if it might rain tomorrow.*

können

- **Können** is the equivalent of the English *can, be able to*:
  Ich kann meine Schlüssel nicht finden. *I can't find my keys.*
  Kannst du es beweisen? *Can you prove it?*
  Er konnte nicht kommen, weil er krank war. *He couldn't come because he was ill.*

- It can also express possibility, its sense overlapping with, although not as strong as, **dürfen**:
  Das kann sein. *That may be the case.*
  Er kann jeden Augenblick kommen. *He could come at any moment.*

- It can be used with languages, without a following infinitive, to mean *can speak* or *know*:
  Du kannst gut Deutsch. *You can speak/know German very well.*

- It appears in idioms meaning *cannot help (doing)*:
  Ich kann nichts dafür. *I can't help it.*
  Ich konnte mir nicht helfen, ich musste lachen. *I couldn't help laughing.*

mögen

- **Mögen** *to like* can be followed by a noun, a pronoun or an infinitive. It's very common in the **Konjunktiv II** to mean the polite *would like*:
  Ich mag die deutsche Sprache. *I like the German language.*
  Er mag mich nicht. *He doesn't like me.*
  Was möchten Sie – Tee oder Kaffee? *What would you like – tea or coffee?*
  Wir möchten länger bleiben. *We'd like to stay longer.*

- It can indicate possibility or translate *may* or *might*:
  (Das) mag sein. *That may be so./Maybe.*
  Er mochte zwischen dreißig und vierzig Jahren alt sein. *He might have been/was perhaps between thirty and forty.*

sollen

- **Sollen** *to be (supposed) to, should* expresses a sense of obligation:
  Was soll ich tun? *What should I do?/What am I to do?*
  Wir sollen hier bleiben. *We are supposed to stay here.*
  Was sollte er tun? *What was he to do?*
  Du sollst nicht stehlen/töten. *Thou shalt not steal/kill.*

- **Sollte** (**Konjunktiv II**) translates *should* or *ought*, expressing duty:
  Er sollte seine Eltern öfter besuchen. *He ought to visit his parents more often.*
  Du solltest dich schämen. *You should be ashamed of yourself.*

- **Sollte** (**Konjunktiv II**) is often used in **wenn** *if* clauses:
  Wenn du ihn sehen solltest, sag ihm bitte, dass … *If you (should) see him, please tell him that …*

- It is used in indirect commands. The use of **sollen** on its own is enough to give the force of a command:
  (Sag ihm,) er soll sofort kommen. *Tell him to come at once.*

- **Sollen** in the present tense also translates *it is said that*:
  Das Hotel soll sehr gut sein. *It's said that the hotel is very good./The hotel is supposed to be very good.*

müssen

- **Müssen** translates the English *must* or *have to*. The negative translates the English *don't have to* or *needn't* (**not** *must not,* for which **dürfen** is used):
  Ich muss jetzt gehen. *I must go now.*
  Sie muss hier gewesen sein. *She must have been here.*
  Bei jedem Workout muss man diese Übungen nicht machen. *You don't have to do these exercises every workout.*

- It translates *can't help (doing)*:
  Ich musste lachen. *I couldn't help laughing.*

- It's used in some common expressions:
  Muss das sein? *Is that really necessary?*
  Wenn es (unbedingt) sein muss. *If it's (absolutely) necessary.*

wollen

- **Wollen** *to want to* can be followed by a noun or by a verb in the infinitive:
  Willst du Wein oder Bier? *Do you want wine or beer?*
  Ich will den neuen Film mit Brad Pitt sehen. *I want to see the new Brad Pitt film.*
  Sie wollte länger bleiben. *She wanted to stay for longer.*

- Sometimes it can be translated by the English *will* or *won't*, but only if it means *(don't) want to, refuse to*; the English *will* is not the future here:
  Er will nicht studieren. *He won't study* (i.e. *He refuses to study*).
  Willst du mitkommen? *Will you come with us?*

- **Wollen wir?** *shall we?* is used when making a suggestion:
  Wollen wir ins Kino gehen? *Shall we go to the cinema?*

- **Wollen** followed by **eben** in the past tense means *was just about to (do)*:
  Ich wollte dich eben anrufen. *I was just about to call you.*
  Die Sonne wollte eben untergehen. *The sun was just about to set.*

lassen

- Although not a modal verb, **lassen** *to let, leave* has a lot in common with them: it is followed by a straight infinitive, not **zu** + infinitive; it uses its infinitive instead of its past participle if there's already another infinitive in the clause; and the auxiliary verb goes before two infinitives in a subordinate clause, not at the end:

  Er ließ mich wissen, dass ... *He let me know that ...*
  Er hat sein Handy auf dem Tisch liegen lassen.
  He's left his mobile phone (lying) on the table.
  Ich habe meinen Koffer nicht aus den Augen gelassen.
  I didn't let the suitcase out of my sight.

- It means *make* (someone else) *do something*:

  Er lässt mich immer lange warten. *He always makes me wait a long time.*
  Es war unhöflich, dass er dich so lange hat warten lassen.
  It was rude of him to make you wait so long.
  Der Lehrer hat ihn nachsitzen lassen.
  The teacher made him stay behind for detention.

- It means *get/have something done*:

  Wo kann ich meinen Computer reparieren lassen?
  Where can I get my computer fixed?
  Ich habe mir die Haare schneiden lassen. *I've had my hair cut.*

- **Lass/lasst/lassen Sie uns!** *let's* is an alternative to the **wir** imperative (see page 160):

  Lass uns jetzt zurückgehen! *Let's go back now.* (talking to one person you call **du**)
  Lasst uns ein Picknick machen! *Let's have a picnic.*
  Lassen Sie uns darüber reden! *Let's talk about it.*

- It can be used reflexively, **sich lassen**, when it's translated by the English passive or *can be*:

  Das Fenster lässt sich leicht öffnen.
  The window opens easily/is easy to open.
  Das lässt sich erklären. *It can be explained.*

sein

Sein *to be* is a very common irregular verb in both German and English.

- As well as its basic meaning, **sein** is used with a past participle to form compound tenses:
  Sie sind spät angekommen. *They arrived late.*
  Sie ist letztes Jahr gestorben. *She died last year.*
  Nachdem er weggegangen war, … *After he had left, …*
  Wenn ich länger geblieben wäre, … *If I'd stayed longer, …*

- It is used with a past participle to form the **sein** passive describing a state:
  Das Geschäft war geschlossen. *The shop was closed.*
  Ich bin in Polen geboren. *I was born in Poland.*
  Er ist schon einmal verheiratet gewesen. *He has already been married once.*

- Adjectives appearing on their own are in the dictionary form after **sein** – they do not add endings. Nouns and noun phrases that go with the verb *to be* are in the nominative case:
  Das Wetter ist schön. *The weather is lovely.*
  Es war ein schöner Tag. *It was a lovely day.*
  Der Rhein ist der längste Fluss in Deutschland. *The Rhine is the longest river in Germany.*

- **Sein** can be followed by **zu** + another infinitive to express necessity or possibility, instead of a passive construction with **müssen** or **können**:
  Solche Medikamente sind unbedingt zu vermeiden. *Such drugs must definitely be avoided.* (= **Solche Medikamente müssen unbedingt vermieden werden.**)
  Der Lehrgang ist in einem Jahr gut zu schaffen. *It's possible to get through the course in a year.* (= **Der Lehrgang kann in einem Jahr geschafft werden.**)

Hamlet's famous soliloquy beginning *To be or not to be, that is the question* is **Sein oder Nichtsein, das ist hier die Frage** in German.

haben

- **Haben** translates the English *to have, have got*:
  Ich habe kein Geld. *I haven't got any money.*
  Er hat Zahnschmerzen. *He's got toothache.*
  Sie hat eine Erkältung/einen Schnupfen. *She's got a cold.*
  Du hast ein Talent für Sprachen. *You've got a talent for languages.*
  Sie haben die Möglichkeit, tolle Preise zu gewinnen. *You've got the possibility of winning great prizes.*

- It is used with the past participle to form compound past tenses:
  Haben Sie verstanden? *Did you understand?/Have you understood?*
  Er hatte schon gegessen. *He had already eaten.*
  Die Kinder haben sich die Zähne geputzt. *The children (have) cleaned their teeth.*
  Ich hätte ihm gesagt, ... *I would have told him ...*

- It features in expressions that don't use *have* in English, particularly those describing how you feel:
  Hunger haben *to be hungry*
  Durst haben *to be thirsty*
  Angst haben *to be afraid*
  Lust haben *to feel like, fancy*
  Geduld haben *to be patient*
  Heimweh haben *to be homesick*
  Glück haben *to be lucky*
  Pech haben *to be unlucky*
  jemanden/etwas satt haben *to be fed up with someone/something*
  Hast du Hunger? *Are you hungry?*
  Ich habe ihn satt. *I'm fed up with him.*
  Wir hatten Glück, dass das Wetter so gut war. *We were lucky that the weather was so good.*
  Pech gehabt! *Hard luck!/Tough!*
  The expressions containing nouns are made negative with **kein**:
  Ich habe keine Lust zur Arbeit zu gehen. *I don't feel like going to work.*
  Hab keine Angst! *Don't be afraid.*

werden

When **werden** stands alone without an accompanying verb, it means *to become, get*:

Es wird dunkel. *It's getting dark.*
Das Wetter wurde schlechter. *The weather got worse.*
Sie ist eben dreißig geworden. *She's just turned thirty.*
Er wurde Lehrer. *He became a teacher.*

Werden is most frequently used as an auxiliary verb, in conjunction with other verbs:

● The present tense of **werden** + infinitive forms the future and future perfect tenses:
   Es wird bald regnen. *It's going to rain soon.*
   Bis Montag werden wir die Arbeit beendet haben. *We'll have finished the work by Monday.*

● The **Konjunktiv II** form of **werden** (**würde**) + infinitive translates the English *would (do)*:
   Ich würde sagen, ... *I'd say ...*
   Wir würden uns freuen, wenn er käme. *We'd be pleased if he came.*

● The **würde** + infinitive form of a verb is the equivalent of the **Konjunktiv II** form of that verb. It is often seen in **wenn** *if* clauses (see page 168):
   Wir würden uns freuen, wenn er kommen würde is equivalent to **Wir freuten uns, wenn er käme** *We'd be pleased if he came.*

● **Werden** in the appropriate tense + past participle forms the passive:
   Das Haus wird renoviert. *The house is being renovated.*
   Zu viele dumme Fehler wurden gemacht. *Too many stupid mistakes were made.*

● The past participle of **werden**, when it stands alone, is **geworden**, but this loses the **ge-** in passive compound tenses where there's already another past participle in the clause:
   Er ist Lehrer geworden. *He became a teacher.*
   Das Paket ist vor zwei Tagen geschickt worden. *The parcel was sent two days ago.*

machen

- Machen *to do, make* is not used as often as the English *do* as it is not an auxiliary verb. It is followed by a direct object in the accusative case:
  Was machst du? *What are you doing?*
  Er machte dieses Spielzeug aus Holz. *He made this toy out of wood.*

- It means *make*, in the sense of *cause to be*, with adjectives:
  Das macht mich wütend/froh. *That makes me angry/happy.*
  Das macht mich verrückt. *That drives me crazy.*

- Machen is used in some idioms and expressions which don't use *do* or *make* in English:
  Spaß machen *to be fun*: **Hat es euch Spaß gemacht?** *Did you enjoy it?*
  Was macht das? *How much is it?/What does it come to?*
  (Das/Es) macht nichts. *It doesn't matter.*
  Mach's gut! *Take care!*

gehen

- The basic meaning of **gehen** is *to go* or *walk*:
  Gehen Sie links! *Go/Turn left.*
  Ich muss zum Zahnarzt gehen. *I must go to the dentist's.*

- It means *to work* when talking about machines and devices:
  Meine Uhr geht nicht mehr. *My watch has stopped.*
  Die Maschine geht nicht. *The machine isn't working.*

- It can indicate possibility:
  Freitag geht auch nicht. *Friday's not possible either.*
  Das geht nicht. *That can't be done./That's impossible.*

- **Es geht** is used impersonally when asking about someone's health or well-being:
  Wie geht es Ihnen? *How are you?* **Es geht.** *Okay./So-so.*
  Es geht ihm schlecht. *He's not well./He's doing badly.*

- **es geht um** (+ accusative) means *it's about/to do with*:
  Worum geht es in diesem Film? *What's this film about?*
  Es geht um Geld. *It's to do with money.*

likes and dislikes

In English, the verb *to like* takes a direct object: *My mother likes tulips*; *I liked the picture*; *You'll like him*; *Do you like it?* German uses other, different ways to express what you like and don't like.

gefallen

Gefallen + the dative means *to be pleasing (to)*, so that to translate the above examples, what you literally say is:

Tulips are pleasing to my mother. **Tulpen gefallen meiner Mutter.**
The picture was pleasing to me. **Das Bild hat mir gefallen/Das Bild gefiel mir.**
He will be pleasing to you. **Er wird dir gefallen.**
Is it pleasing to you? **Gefällt es dir?**

You can begin with the dative, or the person being pleased. It's very common to start sentences with a dative pronoun:

Meiner Mutter gefallen Tulpen.
Mir hat das Bild gefallen/Mir gefiel das Bild.

The impersonal **es gefällt mir/ihm** etc. (lit. *it is pleasing to me/him* etc.) can be followed by **zu** + an infinitive or **dass**:

Es gefällt ihm nicht allein zu sein. *He doesn't like being alone.*
Es gefällt mir, dass du gekommen bist. *I'm pleased you've come.*

gern

Gern(e) is used with a verb to say you like *doing* something:

Wir wandern gern in den Bergen. *We like hiking in the mountains.*
Als Kind ging ich nicht gern zur Schule.
When I was a child (lit. *as a child*) *I didn't like going to school.*

mögen

The modal verb **mögen** also means *to like* but it's used less often than **gern**. It's followed by a direct object:

Ich mag Schnee. *I like snow.*
Sie hat mich nie gemocht. *She's never liked me.*

schmecken

Schmecken *to taste (good)* can be used to say you like food.
Hat es Ihnen geschmeckt? *Did you like it (the meal)?*
(Lit. *Did it taste good to you?*)
Mir schmeckt deutsches Bier. *I like German beer.*

impersonal verbs

Impersonal verbs exist only in the **es** *it* form. They include:

- weather words
  Es regnet/schneit. *It's raining/snowing.*
  Es hat geblitzt und gedonnert. *There was thunder and lightning.*

- some personal verbs used impersonally when there's no subject:
  Es klopfte an die Tür. *There was a knock at the door.*
  Es klingelt. *Someone's ringing the doorbell.*
  Es zieht. *There's a draught.*
  Es brennt. *Something's burning.*

- **es gibt**, from **geben** *to give*, meaning *there is/are*:
  Es gab viele Möglichkeiten. *There were a lot of possibilities.*
  Gibt es noch etwas? *Is there anything else?*

- **es geht**, when asking about health:
  Wie geht es Ihnen? *How are you?*
  Wie geht's? *How are things?*

- certain verbs when used impersonally:
  Es handelt sich um (+ acc.) ... *It's about ...*
  Es hängt von (+ dat.) **ab .../Es kommt auf** (+ acc.) **an ...** *It depends on ...*

In German, people don't say *I am cold/hot* etc. to talk about senses and feelings, but use the impersonal **es ist** + the indirect object pronoun (**mir**, **dir** etc.) + adjective (**kalt/heiß** etc.). The **es** is dropped unless it's the first word in the clause:
Es war mir kalt/Mir war kalt. *I was cold.*
Es ist ihm übel/Ihm ist übel. *He's feeling sick.*

Some impersonal expressions are followed by a comma + **dass** clause:
Es ärgert mich, dass ... *It annoys me that ...*
They frequently begin with the object pronoun:
Mich ärgert, dass ... *It annoys me that ...*
The examples below can also be reworded beginning **es**, as above:
Mich enttäuscht, dass ... *I'm disappointed that ...*
Mich erstaunt/wundert, dass ... *I'm surprised that ...*
Mich freut, dass ... *I'm pleased that ...*
Mich interessiert, dass ... *It interests me that ...*

checkpoint 18

1   Match the two halves of the sentence.

a Mir gefallen	1 er nicht.
b Es gefällt mir	2 die Suppe?
c Schmeckt dir	3 München?
d Gefällt Ihnen	4 in der Sonne zu sitzen.
e Mir gefällt	5 diese Blumen

2   Fill each gap with one of the words from the box.

a Ich .... meinen Laptop reparieren.
b Mein Mann .... in Wien geboren.
c Solche Fehler müssen vermieden ....
d .... du Lust, ins Kino zu gehen?
e Ich .... mitkommen, wenn ich Zeit hätte.
f Wie .... es Ihnen? Gut, danke.
g .... ihr Durst?
h Um zwei Uhr .... es einen Zug.
i Es .... uns, dass ihr gekommen seid.

> werden
> habt
> hast
> lasse
> freut
> geht
> gibt
> würde
> ist

3   Fill in each blank with a modal verb:

a Ich .... jetzt gehen. *I'd like to go now.*
b Ihr .... warten. *You ought to wait.*
c .... du anfangen? *Do you want to start?*
d Wir .... nicht kommen. *We couldn't come.*
e Sie .... morgen arbeiten. *She has to work tomorrow.*
f .... man hier parken? *Is one allowed to park here?*
g Sie .... mit uns spielen. *They wanted to play with us.*
h .... du Arabisch? *Can you speak Arabic?*
i .... Sie mir bitte helfen? *Could you help me please?*
j Wir .... lachen. *We couldn't help laughing.*

4   Are the following questions likely to come from a shop
    assistant or a customer?

a Was macht das?
b Was darf es sein?

Verbs + prepositions

In both English and German, there are verb + preposition combinations, known as prepositional verbs. English examples include *to look **at***, *to send **for***, *to join **in***, *to rely **on***, *to deal **with***.

German examples include **denken an** *to think about*, **bestehen auf** *to insist on,* **sich freuen über** *to be glad about*, **sich sorgen um** *to worry about* and **warnen vor** *to warn against/about*.

As these show, the preposition used in many German prepositional verbs is different from the one used in the English equivalent. For instance, English uses *for* in *to ask for* and *to wait for*, whereas the German equivalents are **bitten um** and **warten auf**.

A few German prepositional verbs don't include a preposition in English: **antworten auf** *to answer* (a question), **aufhören mit** *to stop* (doing something), **sich erinnern an** *to remember,* **hören auf** *to obey*

... and vice versa: *to apply for* **beantragen**, *to pay for* **bezahlen**.

Verb + preposition combinations have specific meanings when used together. In English, *to look at, to look after, to look into, to look for* and *to look over* have quite different meanings. The same is true for German: **bestehen auf** *to insist on*, **bestehen aus** *to consist of*; **sich freuen auf** *to look forward to*, **sich freuen über** *to be pleased about*. Prepositional verbs therefore need to be thought of as combinations rather than as separate words and should be learnt as units.

prepositional verbs

- The preposition used as part of many German prepositional verbs is different from the one used in the English equivalent:
  Wir warten auf den Bus. *We're waiting for the bus.*
  Alles hängt vom Wetter ab. *Everything depends on the weather.*
  Ich freue mich über deinen Besuch. *I'm delighted about your visit.*
  Erinnerst du dich an unsere erste Begegnung? *Do you remember our first meeting?*

- The relevant preposition must accompany the verb, even where there's no noun or pronoun. In these circumstances the prefix **da-** (**dar-** before a vowel) is added to **an**, **auf**, **von**, etc: **daran**, **darauf**, **davon**. These are called **prepositional adverbs**.
  Es kommt darauf an/Es hängt davon ab. *It depends.*
  Ich gehe davon aus, dass ... *I assume that ...*

  Prepositional adverbs are needed when the object of the preposition is a neuter pronoun, or something abstract or unspecified:
  Ich erinnere mich daran. *I remember (it/that).*
  However, a personal pronoun is used when a person is involved:
  Ich erinnere mich an ihn. *I remember him.*

  Prepositional adverbs are also used when a prepositional verb is followed by a clause or an infinitive phrase (often translated in English by the *-ing* verb ending):
  Ich verlasse mich darauf, dass ihr kommt. *I rely on you coming.*
  Er hat sich daran gewöhnt hier zu wohnen. *He's got used to living here.*
  Es hängt davon ab, ob du kommen kannst oder nicht. *It depends on whether you can come or not.*

- In questions, the preposition combines with **wo-** (**wor-** + vowel):
  Woran arbeitest du gerade? *What are you working on at the moment?*
  Womit soll ich anfangen? *How should I start?*
  Wofür interessierst du dich? *What are you interested in?*

- **an + accusative**
  denken an *to think of*
  erinnern an *to remind of*
  sich erinnern an *to remember*
  sich gewöhnen an *to get used to*
  glauben an *to believe in*
  Bitte denkt an mich! *Please think of me.*

- **an + dative**
  erkennen an *to recognise by*
  fehlen an *to be lacking in*
  leiden an *to suffer from*
  sterben an *to die of*
  teilnehmen an *to take part in*
  zweifeln an *to doubt*
  Es fehlt an politischer Führung. *There's a lack of political leadership.*
  Hast du am Spiel teilgenommen? *Did you take part in the game?*

- **auf + accusative**
  achten auf *to pay attention to*
  ankommen auf *to depend on*
  aufpassen auf *to look after*
  sich beziehen auf *to refer to*
  sich freuen auf *to look forward to*
  trinken auf *to drink to, toast*
  sich vorbereiten auf *to prepare for*
  sich verlassen auf *to rely on*
  warten auf *to wait for*
  Es kommt auf das Wetter an. *It depends on the weather.*
  Wir bereiten uns auf unseren Urlaub vor. *We're preparing for our holiday.*

- **auf + dative**
  beruhen auf *to be based on*
  bestehen auf *to insist on*
  Die Politik beruht auf Illusionen. *The policy is based on illusions.*
  Er bestand auf seinen Rechten. *He insisted on his rights.*

An and **auf** prepositional verbs can take either the accusative or dative. There are no rules to help you decide which case to use so it's best to learn these verbs individually. However, **an** prepositional verbs are far more likely to be followed by the dative and **auf** prepositional verbs by the accusative.

- aus + dative
  bestehen aus *to consist of*
  entstehen aus *to originate in, arise from*
  resultieren aus *to result from*
  schließen aus *to conclude from*
  Das Leben besteht aus einem Geben und Nehmen. *Life consists of give and take.*

- bei + dative
  halten bei *to hold by*
  helfen bei *to help with*
  Er hielt seinen Sohn bei der Hand. *He held his son by the hand.*
  Sie half uns bei der Arbeit. *She helped us with our work.*

- für + accusative
  sich interessieren für *to be interested in*
  halten für *to consider to be*
  Er interessiert sich für alle Sportarten. *He's interested in all sports.*
  Ich halte ihn für einen Dummkopf. *I consider him to be an idiot.*

- in + accusative
  einsteigen in *to get on (vehicle)*
  sich verlieben in *to fall in love with*
  einbrechen in *to break into, burgle*
  einfallen in *to invade*
  Er hat sich in ein deutsches Mädchen verliebt. *He's fallen in love with a German girl.*

- mit + dative
  telefonieren mit *to telephone*
  winken mit *to wave*
  Ich habe gerade mit Max telefoniert. *I've just phoned Max.*
  Sie winkte mit der Hand. *She waved her hand.*

- nach + dative
  fragen nach *to enquire about*
  riechen nach *to smell of*
  schicken nach *to send for*
  schmecken nach *to taste of*
  Mein Mantel riecht nach Zigarettenrauch. *My coat smells of cigarette smoke.*
  Sie schickte nach dem Arzt. *She sent for the doctor.*

- über + accusative

  sich ärgern über *to be annoyed with*
  sich beklagen über *to complain about*
  sich freuen über *to be glad about*
  sprechen über *to speak about*
  Emma ärgert sich über ihren Computer. *Emma is annoyed with her computer.*
  Sie beklagte sich über die Medien. *She complained about the media.*

- um + accusative

  sich bewerben um *to apply for*; **bitten um** *to ask for*
  sich handeln um *to be a question/matter of*
  Ich bewerbe mich um eine Lehrstelle. *I'm applying for an apprenticeship.*
  Es handelt sich um eine ernste Erkrankung. *This is a serious illness.*

- von + dative

  abhängen von *to depend on*; **leben von** *to live on*
  überzeugen von *to convince of*; **halten von** *to think of*
  Wovon lebt er? *What does he live on?*
  Jan hat mich von meinem Erfolg überzeugt. *Jan convinced me of my success.*

- vor + dative

  Angst haben vor *to be afraid of*
  sich in Acht nehmen vor *to be careful, mind*
  retten vor *to save from*; **schützen vor** *to protect from*
  Nimm dich in Acht davor! *Be careful!*
  Der Hund rettete die Familie vor dem Feuer. *The dog saved the family from the fire.*

- zu + dative

  gratulieren zu *to congratulate on*; **passen zu** *to go with, match*
  Ich gratuliere zu deinem Geburtstag! *I congratulate (you) on your birthday!*
  Die Krawatte passt zum Anzug. *The tie goes with the suit.*

Some verbs can be followed by more than one preposition:
sich bedanken bei (+ dat.) **für** (+ acc.) *to thank someone for …*
übereinstimmen mit (+ dat.) **in** (+ dat.) *to agree with someone about …*
Leni hat sich bei mir für die schönen Blumen bedankt. *Leni thanked me for the lovely flowers.*
Darin stimmen wir völlig mit Ihnen überein. *We completely agree with you (about it).*

checkpoint 19

1   Put the correct preposition in the gap:

> an (x 2)   mit   auf (x 2)   von   um   für   nach   über

a   **Er ärgert sich** .... **dich.** *He's annoyed with you.*

b   **Ich habe mich schon** .... **dieses Klima gewöhnt.** *I've already got used to this climate.*

c   **Wir halten ihn** .... **ein Genie.** *We consider him to be a genius.*

d   **Ich erkannte sie** .... **der Stimme.** *I recognised her by her voice.*

e   **Ich bewerbe mich** .... **eine neue Arbeitsstelle.** *I'm applying for a new job.*

f   **Es riecht hier** .... **Fisch.** *It smells of fish here.*

g   **Ich verlasse mich** .... **dich.** *I'm relying on you.*

h   **Hast du** .... **ihm telefoniert?** *Have you phoned him?*

i   **Wir konnten ihn nicht** .... **der Wahrheit überzeugen.** *We couldn't convince him of the truth.*

j   **Es kommt** .... **das Wetter an.** *It depends on the weather.*

2   How would you say these in German?

a   *Are you (du) waiting for me?*

b   *I'm interested in sport.*

c   *It depends.*

d   *Does she remember me?*

e   *He relies on his parents.*

f   *I'm afraid of it.*

g   *What are you thinking of?*

h   *They are preparing for their exam.*

i   *You (ihr) must pay attention to the teacher.*

j   *She paid for everything.*

3   Does **Wir freuen uns auf den Kurs** mean *We're pleased about the course* or *We're looking forward to the course*?

Verb tables

The following pages present 50 key verbs, which are listed on page 242 for easy reference. They include:

- **fragen** *to ask*, which provides the pattern for most weak verbs;
- **arbeiten** *to work*, which provides the pattern for weak verbs whose stems end in **-t** or **-d**; **lächeln** *to smile* and **wandern** *to go hiking,* which provide the pattern for weak verbs ending in **-eln** and **-ern**; and **studieren** *to study*, which provides the pattern for weak verbs ending in **-ieren**;
- the commonest strong verbs, including **fahren** *to drive, to go*, **gehen** *to go* and **kommen** *to come*;
- irregular weak verbs, such as **denken** *to think* and **kennen** *to know, to be acquainted with*;
- verbs which are also used to form tenses – **haben** *to have,* **sein** *to be* and **werden** *to become*;
- the modal verbs **dürfen** *to be allowed to*, **können** *to be able to*, **mögen** *to like*, **müssen** *to have to, must*, **sollen** *to be supposed to, should* and **wollen** *to want to*;
- the irregular verb **wissen** *to know* (a fact);
- the reflexive verb **sich entscheiden** *to decide*.

All 50 verbs are written out in all persons in the present, future, conditional, simple past/imperfect and perfect tenses, and **Konjunktiv I** and **Konjunktiv II**.

The perfect tense shows you whether the verb takes **haben** or **sein** and this will allow you to form the future perfect and pluperfect.

A few verbs have alternative forms in some tenses/moods. The most commonly used version is listed first.

Verbs which behave similarly are given below each table. The symbol **|** (e.g. **an|kommen** *to arrive*) indicates a separable verb and (*) indicates that the verb takes **sein**).

1 arbeiten *to work*

	present	future	conditional
ich	arbeite	werde ... arbeiten	würde ... arbeiten
du	arbeitest	wirst ... arbeiten	würdest ... arbeiten
er/sie/es	arbeitet	wird ... arbeiten	würde ... arbeiten
wir	arbeiten	werden ... arbeiten	würden ... arbeiten
ihr	arbeitet	werdet ... arbeiten	würdet ... arbeiten
sie/Sie	arbeiten	werden ... arbeiten	würden ... arbeiten

	simple past/imperfect	perfect
ich	arbeitete	habe ... gearbeitet
du	arbeitetest	hast ... gearbeitet
er/sie/es	arbeitete	hat ... gearbeitet
wir	arbeiteten	haben ... gearbeitet
ihr	arbeitetet	habt ... gearbeitet
sie/Sie	arbeiteten	haben ... gearbeitet

	Konjunktiv I	Konjunktiv II
ich	arbeite	arbeitete
du	arbeitest	arbeitetest
er/sie/es	arbeite	arbeitete
wir	arbeiten	arbeiteten
ihr	arbeitet	arbeitetet
sie/Sie	arbeiten	arbeiteten

present participle **arbeitend**

past participle **gearbeitet**

imperative **arbeit(e)! arbeitet! arbeiten Sie! arbeiten wir!**

2   bleiben *to stay*

	present	future	conditional
ich	bleibe	werde ... bleiben	würde ... bleiben
du	bleibst	wirst ... bleiben	würdest ... bleiben
er/sie/es	bleibt	wird ... bleiben	würde ... bleiben
wir	bleiben	werden ... bleiben	würden ... bleiben
ihr	bleibt	werdet ... bleiben	würdet ... bleiben
sie/Sie	bleiben	werden ... bleiben	würden ... bleiben

	simple past/imperfect	perfect
ich	blieb	bin ... geblieben
du	bliebst	bist ... geblieben
er/sie/es	blieb	ist ... geblieben
wir	blieben	sind ... geblieben
ihr	bliebt	seid ... geblieben
sie/Sie	blieben	sind ... geblieben

	Konjunktiv I	Konjunktiv II
ich	bleibe	bliebe
du	bleibest	bliebest
er/sie/es	bleibe	bliebe
wir	bleiben	blieben
ihr	bleibet	bliebet
sie/Sie	bleiben	blieben

present participle **bleibend**

past participle **geblieben**

imperative **bleib(e)! bleibt! bleiben Sie! bleiben wir!**

Verbs that follow the same pattern as **bleiben** include **weg|bleiben** (*) *to stay away/out*.

3 brechen *to break*

	present	future	conditional
ich	breche	werde ... brechen	würde ... brechen
du	brichst	wirst ... brechen	würdest ... brechen
er/sie/es	bricht	wird ... brechen	würde ... brechen
wir	brechen	werden ... brechen	würden ... brechen
ihr	brecht	werdet ... brechen	würdet ... brechen
sie/Sie	brechen	werden ... brechen	würden ... brechen

	simple past/imperfect	perfect
ich	brach	habe ... gebrochen
du	brachst	hast ... gebrochen
er/sie/es	brach	hat ... gebrochen
wir	brachen	haben ... gebrochen
ihr	bracht	habt ... gebrochen
sie/Sie	brachen	haben ... gebrochen

	Konjunktiv I	Konjunktiv II
ich	breche	bräche
du	brechest	brächest
er/sie/es	breche	bräche
wir	brechen	brächen
ihr	brechet	brächet
sie/Sie	brechen	brächen

present participle **brechend**

past participle **gebrochen**

imperative **brich! brecht! brechen Sie! brechen wir!**

Verbs that follow the same pattern as **brechen** include **ein|brechen** *to break in*, **unterbrechen** *to interrupt*, **zerbrechen** *to smash*.

4   denken *to think*

	present	future	conditional
ich	denke	werde ... denken	würde ... denken
du	denkst	wirst ... denken	würdest ... denken
er/sie/es	denkt	wird ... denken	würde ... denken
wir	denken	werden ... denken	würden ... denken
ihr	denkt	werdet ... denken	würdet ... denken
sie/Sie	denken	werden ... denken	würden ... denken

	simple past/imperfect	perfect
ich	dachte	habe ... gedacht
du	dachtest	hast ... gedacht
er/sie/es	dachte	hat ... gedacht
wir	dachten	haben ... gedacht
ihr	dachtet	habt ... gedacht
sie/Sie	dachten	haben ... gedacht

	Konjunktiv I	Konjunktiv II
ich	denke	dächte
du	denkest	dächtest
er/sie/es	denke	dächte
wir	denken	dächten
ihr	denket	dächtet
sie/Sie	denken	dächten

present participle **denkend**

past participle **gedacht**

imperative **denk(e)! denkt! denken Sie! denken wir!**

Verbs that follow the same pattern as **denken** include **bedenken** *to consider* and **nach|denken** *to think about something.*

5 dürfen *to be allowed to, may*

	present	future	conditional
ich	darf	werde ... dürfen	würde ... dürfen
du	darfst	wirst ... dürfen	würdest ... dürfen
er/sie/es	darf	wird ... dürfen	würde ... dürfen
wir	dürfen	werden ... dürfen	würden ... dürfen
ihr	dürft	werdet ... dürfen	würdet ... dürfen
sie/Sie	dürfen	werden ... dürfen	würden ... dürfen

	simple past/imperfect	perfect
ich	durfte	habe ... gedurft/dürfen
du	durftest	hast ... gedurft/dürfen
er/sie/es	durfte	hat ... gedurft/dürfen
wir	durften	haben ... gedurft/dürfen
ihr	durftet	habt ... gedurft/dürfen
sie/Sie	durften	haben ... gedurft/dürfen

	Konjunktiv I	Konjunktiv II
ich	dürfe	dürfte
du	dürfest	dürftest
er/sie/es	dürfe	dürfte
wir	dürfen	dürften
ihr	dürfet	dürftet
sie/Sie	dürfen	dürften

present participle **dürfend**

past participle **gedurft** (**dürfen** after another verb)

no imperative

Verbs that follow the same pattern as **dürfen** include **bedürfen** (+ genitive) *to require.*

6 sich entscheiden *to decide*

	present	future	conditional
ich	entscheide mich	werde ... mich entscheiden	würde ... mich entscheiden
du	entscheidest dich	wirst ... dich entscheiden	würdest ... dich entscheiden
er/sie/es	entscheidet sich	wird ... sich entscheiden	würde ... sich entscheiden
wir	entscheiden uns	werden ... uns entscheiden	würden ... uns entscheiden
ihr	entscheidet euch	werdet ... euch entscheiden	würdet ... euch entscheiden
sie/Sie	entscheiden sich	werden ... sich entscheiden	würden ... sich entscheiden

	simple past/imperfect	perfect
ich	entschied mich	habe ... mich entschieden
du	entschied(e)st dich	hast ... dich entschieden
er/sie/es	entschied sich	hat ... sich entschieden
wir	entschieden uns	haben ... uns entschieden
ihr	entschiedet euch	habt ... euch entschieden
sie/Sie	entschieden sich	haben ... sich entschieden

	Konjunktiv I	Konjunktiv II
ich	entscheide mich	entschiede mich
du	entscheidest dich	entschiedest dich
er/sie/es	entscheide sich	entschiede sich
wir	entscheiden uns	entschieden uns
ihr	entscheidet euch	entschiedet euch
sie/Sie	entscheiden sich	entschieden sich

present participle (sich) entscheidend

past participle (sich) entschieden

imperative entscheid(e) dich! entscheidet euch! entscheiden Sie sich! entscheiden wir uns!

7 essen *to eat*

	present	future	conditional
ich	esse	werde ... essen	würde ... essen
du	isst	wirst ... essen	würdest ... essen
er/sie/es	isst	wird ... essen	würde ... essen
wir	essen	werden ... essen	würden ... essen
ihr	esst	werdet ... essen	würdet ... essen
sie/Sie	essen	werden ... essen	würden ... essen

	simple past/imperfect	perfect
ich	aß	habe ... gegessen
du	aßest	hast ... gegessen
er/sie/es	aß	hat ... gegessen
wir	aßen	haben ... gegessen
ihr	aßt	habt ... gegessen
sie/Sie	aßen	haben ... gegessen

	Konjunktiv I	Konjunktiv II
ich	esse	äße
du	essest	äßest
er/sie/es	esse	äße
wir	essen	äßen
ihr	esset	äßet
sie/Sie	essen	äßen

present participle **essend**

past participle **gegessen**

imperative **iss! esst! essen Sie! essen wir!**

Verbs that follow the same pattern as **essen** include **mit|essen** *to join someone in eating*, **auf|essen** *to eat (everything) up.*

8 **fahren** *to go* (in a vehicle)

	present	future	conditional
ich	fahre	werde ... fahren	würde ... fahren
du	fährst	wirst ... fahren	würdest ... fahren
er/sie/es	fährt	wird ... fahren	würde ... fahren
wir	fahren	werden ... fahren	würden ... fahren
ihr	fahrt	werdet ... fahren	würdet ... fahren
sie/Sie	fahren	werden ... fahren	würden ... fahren

	simple past/imperfect	perfect
ich	fuhr	bin ... gefahren
du	fuhrst	bist ... gefahren
er/sie/es	fuhr	ist ... gefahren
wir	fuhren	sind ... gefahren
ihr	fuhrt	seid ... gefahren
sie/Sie	fuhren	sind ... gefahren

	Konjunktiv I	Konjunktiv II
ich	fahre	führe
du	fahrest	führest
er/sie/es	fahre	führe
wir	fahren	führen
ihr	fahret	führet
sie/Sie	fahren	führen

present participle **fahrend**

past participle **gefahren**

imperative **fahr(e)! fahrt(!) fahren Sie! fahren wir!**

Verbs that follow the same pattern as **fahren** include **erfahren** *to find out*, **fort|fahren (*)** *to continue.*

9   fallen *to fall*

	present	future	conditional
ich	falle	werde ... fallen	würde ... fallen
du	fällst	wirst ... fallen	würdest ... fallen
er/sie/es	fällt	wird ... fallen	würde ... fallen
wir	fallen	werden ... fallen	würden ... fallen
ihr	fallt	werdet ... fallen	würdet ... fallen
sie/Sie	fallen	werden ... fallen	würden ... fallen

	simple past/imperfect	perfect
ich	fiel	bin ... gefallen
du	fielst	bist ... gefallen
er/sie/es	fiel	ist ... gefallen
wir	fielen	sind ... gefallen
ihr	fielt	seid ... gefallen
sie/Sie	fielen	sind ... gefallen

	Konjunktiv I	Konjunktiv II
ich	falle	fiele
du	fallest	fielest
er/sie/es	falle	fiele
wir	fallen	fielen
ihr	fallet	fielet
sie/Sie	fallen	fielen

present participle **fallend**

past participle **gefallen**

imperative **fall(e)! fallt! fallen Sie! fallen wir!**

Verbs that follow the same pattern as **fallen** include **auf|fallen (*)** *to stand out*, **ein|fallen (*)** *to occur to*, **gefallen** *to please*.

10 finden *to find*

	present	future	conditional
ich	finde	werde ... finden	würde ... finden
du	findest	wirst ... finden	würdest ... finden
er/sie/es	findet	wird ... finden	würde ... finden
wir	finden	werden ... finden	würden ... finden
ihr	findet	werdet ... finden	würdet ... finden
sie/Sie	finden	werden ... finden	würden ... finden

	simple past/imperfect	perfect
ich	fand	habe ... gefunden
du	fandest	hast ... gefunden
er/sie/es	fand	hat ... gefunden
wir	fanden	haben ... gefunden
ihr	fandet	habt ... gefunden
sie/Sie	fanden	haben ... gefunden

	Konjunktiv I	Konjunktiv II
ich	finde	fände
du	findest	fändest
er/sie/es	finde	fände
wir	finden	fänden
ihr	findet	fändet
sie/Sie	finden	fänden

present participle **findend**

past participle **gefunden**

imperative **find(e)! findet! finden Sie! finden wir!**

Verbs that follow the same pattern as **finden** include **erfinden** *to invent*, **statt|finden** *to take place*.

11 fliegen *to fly*

	present	future	conditional
ich	fliege	werde ... fliegen	würde ... fliegen
du	fliegst	wirst ... fliegen	würdest ... fliegen
er/sie/es	fliegt	wird ... fliegen	würde ... fliegen
wir	fliegen	werden ... fliegen	würden ... fliegen
ihr	fliegt	werdet ... fliegen	würdet ... fliegen
sie/Sie	fliegen	werden ... fliegen	würden ... fliegen

	simple past/imperfect	perfect
ich	flog	bin ... geflogen
du	flogst	bist ... geflogen
er/sie/es	flog	ist ... geflogen
wir	flogen	sind ... geflogen
ihr	flogt	seid ... geflogen
sie/Sie	flogen	sind ... geflogen

	Konjunktiv I	Konjunktiv II
ich	fliege	flöge
du	fliegest	flögest
er/sie/es	fliege	flöge
wir	fliegen	flögen
ihr	flieget	flöget
sie/Sie	fliegen	flögen

present participle **fliegend**

past participle **geflogen**

imperative **flieg(e)! fliegt! fliegen Sie! fliegen wir!**

Verbs that follow the same pattern as **fliegen** include **ab|fliegen** *to depart by plane*, **fort|fliegen** *to fly away*, **weg|fliegen** *to fly away, off*.

12   fragen *to ask*

	present	future	conditional
ich	frage	werde ... fragen	würde ... fragen
du	fragst	wirst ... fragen	würdest ... fragen
er/sie/es	fragt	wird ... fragen	würde ... fragen
wir	fragen	werden ... fragen	würden ... fragen
ihr	fragt	werdet ... fragen	würdet ... fragen
sie/Sie	fragen	werden ... fragen	würden ... fragen

	simple past/imperfect	perfect
ich	fragte	habe ... gefragt
du	fragtest	hast ... gefragt
er/sie/es	fragte	hat ... gefragt
wir	fragten	haben ... gefragt
ihr	fragtet	habt ... gefragt
sie/Sie	fragten	haben ... gefragt

	Konjunktiv I	Konjunktiv II
ich	frage	fragte
du	fragest	fragtest
er/sie/es	frage	fragte
wir	fragen	fragten
ihr	fraget	fragtet
sie/Sie	fragen	fragten

present participle **fragend**

past participle **gefragt**

imperative **frag(e)! fragt! fragen Sie! fragen wir!**

Verbs that follow the same pattern as **fragen** include **hinterfragen** *to ask again, to get to the bottom of something.*

13 geben *to give*

	present	future	conditional
ich	gebe	werde ... geben	würde ... geben
du	gibst	wirst ... geben	würdest ... geben
er/sie/es	gibt	wird ... geben	würde ... geben
wir	geben	werden ... geben	würden ... geben
ihr	gebt	werdet ... geben	würdet ... geben
sie/Sie	geben	werden ... geben	würden ... geben

	simple past/imperfect	perfect
ich	gab	habe ... gegeben
du	gabst	hast ... gegeben
er/sie/es	gab	hat ... gegeben
wir	gaben	haben ... gegeben
ihr	gabt	habt ... gegeben
sie/Sie	gaben	haben ... gegeben

	Konjunktiv I	Konjunktiv II
ich	gebe	gäbe
du	gebest	gäbest
er/sie/es	gebe	gäbe
wir	geben	gäben
ihr	gebet	gäbet
sie/Sie	geben	gäben

present participle **gebend**

past participle **gegeben**

imperative **gib! gebt! geben Sie! geben wir!**

Verbs that follow the same pattern as geben include **auf|geben** *to give up*, **aus|geben** *to spend*, **umgeben** *to surround*, **zu|geben** *to admit*, **zurück|geben** *to give back*.

14 gehen *to go* (on foot)

	present	future	conditional
ich	gehe	werde ... gehen	würde ... gehen
du	gehst	wirst ... gehen	würdest ... gehen
er/sie/es	geht	wird ... gehen	würde ... gehen
wir	gehen	werden ... gehen	würden ... gehen
ihr	geht	werdet ... gehen	würdet ... gehen
sie/Sie	gehen	werden ... gehen	würden ... gehen

	simple past/imperfect	perfect
ich	ging	bin ... gegangen
du	gingst	bist ... gegangen
er/sie/es	ging	ist ... gegangen
wir	gingen	sind ... gegangen
ihr	gingt	seid ... gegangen
sie/Sie	gingen	sind ... gegangen

	Konjunktiv I	Konjunktiv II
ich	gehe	ginge
du	gehest	gingest
er/sie/es	gehe	ginge
wir	gehen	gingen
ihr	gehet	ginget
sie/Sie	gehen	gingen

present participle **gehend**

past participle **gegangen**

imperative **geh(e)! geht! gehen Sie! gehen wir!**

Verbs that follow the same pattern as **gehen** include **aus|gehen** (*) *to go out*, **weg|gehen** (*) *to go away*, **zurück|gehen** (*) *to go back*.

15 haben *to have*

	present	future	conditional
ich	habe	werde ... haben	würde ... haben
du	hast	wirst ... haben	würdest ... haben
er/sie/es	hat	wird ... haben	würde ... haben
wir	haben	werden ... haben	würden ... haben
ihr	habt	werdet ... haben	würdet ... haben
sie/Sie	haben	werden ... haben	würden ... haben

	simple past/imperfect	perfect
ich	hatte	habe ... gehabt
du	hattest	hast ... gehabt
er/sie/es	hatte	hat ... gehabt
wir	hatten	haben ... gehabt
ihr	hattet	habt ... gehabt
sie/Sie	hatten	haben ... gehabt

	Konjunktiv I	Konjunktiv II
ich	habe	hätte
du	habest	hättest
er/sie/es	habe	hätte
wir	haben	hätten
ihr	habet	hättet
sie/Sie	haben	hätten

present participle **habend**

past participle **gehabt**

imperative **hab(e)! habt! haben Sie! haben wir!**

Verbs that follow the same pattern as **haben** include **vor|haben** *to plan*.

16 halten *to hold, to stop*

	present	future	conditional
ich	halte	werde ... halten	würde ... halten
du	hältst	wirst ... halten	würdest ... halten
er/sie/es	hält	wird ... halten	würde ... halten
wir	halten	werden ... halten	würden ... halten
ihr	haltet	werdet ... halten	würdet ... halten
sie/Sie	halten	werden ... halten	würden ... halten

	simple past/imperfect	perfect
ich	hielt	habe ... gehalten
du	hielt(e)st	hast ... gehalten
er/sie/es	hielt	hat ... gehalten
wir	hielten	haben ... gehalten
ihr	hieltet	habt ... gehalten
sie/Sie	hielten	haben ... gehalten

	Konjunktiv I	Konjunktiv II
ich	halte	hielte
du	haltest	hieltest
er/sie/es	halte	hielte
wir	halten	hielten
ihr	haltet	hieltet
sie/Sie	halten	hielten

present participle **haltend**

past participle **gehalten**

imperative **halt(e)! haltet! halten Sie! halten wir!**

Verbs that follow the same pattern as **halten** include **erhalten** *to receive*, **unterhalten** to *entertain, maintain*, **sich unterhalten** *to converse.*

17 helfen *to help*

	present	future	conditional
ich	helfe	werde ... helfen	würde ... helfen
du	hilfst	wirst ... helfen	würdest ... helfen
er/sie/es	hilft	wird ... helfen	würde ... helfen
wir	helfen	werden ... helfen	würden ... helfen
ihr	helft	werdet ... helfen	würdet ... helfen
sie/Sie	helfen	werden ... helfen	würden ... helfen

	simple past/imperfect	perfect
ich	half	habe ... geholfen
du	halfst	hast ... geholfen
er/sie/es	half	hat ... geholfen
wir	halfen	haben ... geholfen
ihr	halft	habt ... geholfen
sie/Sie	halfen	haben ... geholfen

	Konjunktiv I	Konjunktiv II
ich	helfe	hülfe (or hälfe)
du	helfest	hülfest (or hälfest)
er/sie/es	helfe	hülfe (or hälfe)
wir	helfen	hülfen (or hälfen)
ihr	helfet	hülfet (or hälfet)
sie/Sie	helfen	hülfen (or hälfen)

present participle **helfend**

past participle **geholfen**

imperative **hilf! helft! helfen Sie! helfen wir!**

Verbs that follow the same pattern as **helfen** include **mit|helfen** *to join in helping, to give someone a hand.*

18 kennen *to know, to be acquainted with*

	present	future	conditional
ich	kenne	werde ... kennen	würde ... kennen
du	kennst	wirst ... kennen	würdest ... kennen
er/sie/es	kennt	wird ... kennen	würde ... kennen
wir	kennen	werden ... kennen	würden ... kennen
ihr	kennt	werdet ... kennen	würdet ... kennen
sie/Sie	kennen	werden ... kennen	würden ... kennen

	simple past/imperfect	perfect
ich	kannte	habe ... gekannt
du	kanntest	hast ... gekannt
er/sie/es	kannte	hat ... gekannt
wir	kannten	haben ... gekannt
ihr	kanntet	habt ... gekannt
sie/Sie	kannten	haben ... gekannt

	Konjunktiv I	Konjunktiv II
ich	kenne	kannte
du	kennest	kanntest
er/sie/es	kenne	kannte
wir	kennen	kannten
ihr	kennet	kanntet
sie/Sie	kennen	kannten

present participle **kennend**

past participle **gekannt**

imperative **kenn(e)! kennt! kennen Sie! kennen wir!**

Verbs that follow the same pattern as **kennen** include **an|erkennen** *to recognise* and **erkennen** *to recognise*.

19 kommen *to come*

	present	future	conditional
ich	komme	werde ... kommen	würde ... kommen
du	kommst	wirst ... kommen	würdest ... kommen
er/sie/es	kommt	wird ... kommen	würde ... kommen
wir	kommen	werden ... kommen	würden ... kommen
ihr	kommt	werdet ... kommen	würdet ... kommen
sie/Sie	kommen	werden ... kommen	würden ... kommen

	simple past/imperfect	perfect
ich	kam	bin ... gekommen
du	kamst	bist ... gekommen
er/sie/es	kam	ist ... gekommen
wir	kamen	sind ... gekommen
ihr	kamt	seid ... gekommen
sie/Sie	kamen	sind ... gekommen

	Konjunktiv I	Konjunktiv II
ich	komme	käme
du	kommest	kämest
er/sie/es	komme	käme
wir	kommen	kämen
ihr	kommet	kämet
sie/Sie	kommen	kämen

present participle **kommend**

past participle **gekommen**

imperative **komm(e)! kommt! kommen Sie! kommen wir!**

Verbs that follow the same pattern as **kommen** include **an|kommen (*)** *to arrive*, **bekommen** *to get*, **entkommen (*)** *to escape*, **herein|kommen (*)** *to come in*, **mit|kommen (*)** *to come with* (me/us etc.).

20 können *to be able to, can*

	present	future	conditional
ich	kann	werde ... können	würde ... können
du	kannst	wirst ... können	würdest ... können
er/sie/es	kann	wird ... können	würde ... können
wir	können	werden ... können	würden ... können
ihr	könnt	werdet ... können	würdet ... können
sie/Sie	können	werden ... können	würden ... können

	simple past/imperfect	perfect
ich	konnte	habe ... gekonnt/können
du	konntest	hast ... gekonnt/können
er/sie/es	konnte	hat ... gekonnt/können
wir	konnten	haben ... gekonnt/können
ihr	konntet	habt ... gekonnt/können
sie/Sie	konnten	haben ... gekonnt/können

	Konjunktiv I	Konjunktiv II
ich	könne	könnte
du	könnest	könntest
er/sie/es	könne	könnte
wir	können	könnten
ihr	könnet	könntet
sie/Sie	können	könnten

present participle **könnend**

past participle **gekonnt** (**können** after another verb)

no imperative

21   lächeln *to smile*

	present	future	conditional
ich	läch(e)le	werde ... lächeln	würde ... lächeln
du	lächelst	wirst ... lächeln	würdest ... lächeln
er/sie/es	lächelt	wird ... lächeln	würde ... lächeln
wir	lächeln	werden ... lächeln	würden ... lächeln
ihr	lächelt	werdet ... lächeln	würdet ... lächeln
sie/Sie	lächeln	werden ... lächeln	würden ... lächeln

	simple past/imperfect	perfect
ich	lächelte	habe ... gelächelt
du	lächeltest	hast ... gelächelt
er/sie/es	lächelte	hat ... gelächelt
wir	lächelten	haben ... gelächelt
ihr	lächeltet	habt ... gelächelt
sie/Sie	lächelten	haben ... gelächelt

	Konjunktiv I	Konjunktiv II
ich	lächle	lächelte
du	lächelst	lächeltest
er/sie/es	lächle	lächelte
wir	lächeln	lächelten
ihr	lächelt	lächeltet
sie/Sie	lächeln	lächelten

present participle **lächelnd**

past participle **gelächelt**

imperative **lächle! lächelt! lächeln Sie! lächeln wir!**

Verbs that follow the same pattern as **lächeln** include **an|lächeln**, **zu|lächeln** *to smile at*.

22 lassen *to let*

	present	future	conditional
ich	lassen	werde ... lassen	würde ... lassen
du	lässt	wirst ... lassen	würdest ... lassen
er/sie/es	lässt	wird ... lassen	würde ... lassen
wir	lassen	werden ... lassen	würden ... lassen
ihr	lasst	werdet ... lassen	würdet ... lassen
sie/Sie	lassen	werden ... lassen	würden ... lassen

	simple past/imperfect	perfect
ich	ließ	habe ... gelassen/lassen
du	ließest	hast ... gelassen/lassen
er/sie/es	ließ	hat ... gelassen/lassen
wir	ließen	haben ... gelassen/lassen
ihr	ließt	habt ... gelassen/lassen
sie/Sie	ließen	haben ... gelassen/lassen

	Konjunktiv I	Konjunktiv II
ich	lasse	ließe
du	lassest	ließest
er/sie/es	lasse	ließe
wir	lassen	ließen
ihr	lasset	ließet
sie/Sie	lassen	ließen

present participle **lassend**

past participle **gelassen** (**lassen** after another verb)

imperative **lass(e)! lasst! lassen Sie! lassen wir!**

Verbs that follow the same pattern as **lassen** include **aus|lassen** *to omit*, **verlassen** *to leave*.

23 laufen *to run*

	present	future	conditional
ich	laufe	werde ... laufen	würde ... laufen
du	läufst	wirst ... laufen	würdest ... laufen
er/sie/es	läuft	wird ... laufen	würde ... laufen
wir	laufen	werden ... laufen	würden ... laufen
ihr	lauft	werdet ... laufen	würdet ... laufen
sie/Sie	laufen	werden ... laufen	würden ... laufen

	simple past/imperfect	perfect
ich	lief	bin ... gelaufen
du	liefst	bist ... gelaufen
er/sie/es	lief	ist ... gelaufen
wir	liefen	sind ... gelaufen
ihr	lieft	seid ... gelaufen
sie/Sie	liefen	sind ... gelaufen

	Konjunktiv I	Konjunktiv II
ich	laufe	liefe
du	laufest	liefest
er/sie/es	laufe	liefe
wir	laufen	liefen
ihr	laufet	liefet
sie/Sie	laufen	liefen

present participle **laufend**

past participle **gelaufen**

imperative **lauf(e)! lauft! laufen Sie! laufen wir!**

Verbs that follow the same pattern as **laufen** include **auf|laufen** *to accumulate*.

24 lesen *to read*

	present	future	conditional
ich	lese	werde ... lesen	würde ... lesen
du	liest	wirst ... lesen	würdest ... lesen
er/sie/es	liest	wird ... lesen	würde ... lesen
wir	lesen	werden ... lesen	würden ... lesen
ihr	lest	werdet ... lesen	würdet ... lesen
sie/Sie	lesen	werden ... lesen	würden ... lesen

	simple past/imperfect	perfect
ich	las	habe ... gelesen
du	las(es)t	hast ... gelesen
er/sie/es	las	hat ... gelesen
wir	lasen	haben ... gelesen
ihr	last	habt ... gelesen
sie/Sie	lasen	haben ... gelesen

	Konjunktiv I	Konjunktiv II
ich	lese	läse
du	lesest	läsest
er/sie/es	lese	läse
wir	lesen	läsen
ihr	leset	läset
sie/Sie	lesen	läsen

present participle **lesend**

past participle **gelesen**

imperative **lies! lest! lesen Sie! lesen wir!**

Verbs that follow the same pattern as **lesen** include **vor|lesen** *to read aloud*.

25 liegen *to be lying*

	present	future	conditional
ich	liege	werde ... liegen	würde ... liegen
du	liegst	wirst ... liegen	würdest ... liegen
er/sie/es	liegt	wird ... liegen	würde ... liegen
wir	liegen	werden ... liegen	würden ... liegen
ihr	liegt	werdet ... liegen	würdet ... liegen
sie/Sie	liegen	werden ... liegen	würden ... liegen

	simple past/imperfect	perfect
ich	lag	habe (bin*) ... gelegen
du	lagst	hast (bist) ... gelegen
er/sie/es	lag	hat (ist) ... gelegen
wir	lagen	haben (sind) ... gelegen
ihr	lagt	habt (seid) ... gelegen
sie/Sie	lagen	haben (sind) ... gelegen

	Konjunktiv I	Konjunktiv II
ich	liege	läge
du	liegest	lägest
er/sie/es	liege	läge
wir	liegen	lägen
ihr	lieget	läget
sie/Sie	liege	lägen

present participle **liegend**

past participle **gelegen**

imperative **lieg(e)! liegt! liegen Sie! liegen wir!**

Verbs that follow the same pattern as **liegen** include **sich nieder|legen** *to lie down*.

* Used with **sein** in southern Germany, Austria and Switzerland.

26 mögen *to like, may*

	present	future	conditional
ich	mag	werde ... mögen	würde ... mögen
du	magst	wirst ... mögen	würdest ... mögen
er/sie/es	mag	wird ... mögen	würde ... mögen
wir	mögen	werden ... mögen	würden ... mögen
ihr	mögt	werdet ... mögen	würdet ... mögen
sie/Sie	mögen	werden ... mögen	würden ... mögen

	simple past/imperfect	perfect
ich	mochte	habe ... gemocht/mögen
du	mochtest	hast ... gemocht/mögen
er/sie/es	mochte	hat ... gemocht/mögen
wir	mochten	haben ... gemocht/mögen
ihr	mochtet	habt ... gemocht/mögen
sie/Sie	mochten	haben ... gemocht/mögen

	Konjunktiv I	Konjunktiv II
ich	möge	möchte
du	mögest	möchtest
er/sie/es	möge	möchte
wir	mögen	möchten
ihr	möget	möchtet
sie/Sie	mögen	möchten

present participle **mögend**

past participle **gemocht** (**mögen** after another verb)

no imperative

27 müssen *to have to, must*

	present	future	conditional
ich	muss	werde ... müssen	würde ... müssen
du	musst	wirst ... müssen	würdest ... müssen
er/sie/es	muss	wird ... müssen	würde ... müssen
wir	müssen	werden ... müssen	würden ... müssen
ihr	müsst	werdet ... müssen	würdet ... müssen
sie/Sie	müssen	werden ... müssen	würden ... müssen

	simple past/imperfect	perfect
ich	musste	habe ... gemusst/müssen
du	musstest	hast ... gemusst/müssen
er/sie/es	musste	hat ... gemusst/müssen
wir	mussten	haben ... gemusst/müssen
ihr	musstet	habt ... gemusst/müssen
sie/Sie	mussten	haben ... gemusst/müssen

	Konjunktiv I	Konjunktiv II
ich	müsse	müsste
du	müssest	müsstest
er/sie/es	müsse	müsste
wir	müssen	müssten
ihr	müsset	müsstet
sie/Sie	müssen	müssten

present particple **müssend**

past participle **gemusst** (**müssen** after another verb)

no imperative

28 nehmen *to take*

	present	future	conditional
ich	nehme	werde ... nehmen	würde ... nehmen
du	nimmst	wirst ... nehmen	würdest ... nehmen
er/sie/es	nimmt	wird ... nehmen	würde ... nehmen
wir	nehmen	werden ... nehmen	würden ... nehmen
ihr	nehmt	werdet ... nehmen	würdet ... nehmen
sie/Sie	nehmen	werden ... nehmen	würden ... nehmen

	simple past/imperfect	perfect
ich	nahm	habe ... genommen
du	nahmst	hast ... genommen
er/sie/es	nahm	hat ... genommen
wir	nahmen	haben ... genommen
ihr	nahmt	habt ... genommen
sie/Sie	nahmen	haben ... genommen

	Konjunktiv I	Konjunktiv II
ich	nehme	nähme
du	nehmest	nähmest
er/sie/es	nehme	nähme
wir	nehmen	nähmen
ihr	nehmet	nähmet
sie/Sie	nehmen	nähmen

present participle **nehmend**

past participle **genommen**

imperative **nimm! nehmt! nehmen Sie! nehmen wir!**

Verbs that follow the same pattern as **nehmen** include **ab|nehmen** *to lose weight*, **an|nehmen** *to accept*, **auf|nehmen** *to take (photos)*, *to record*, **teil|nehmen** *to take part*, **unternehmen** *to undertake*, **sich vor|nehmen** *to plan*, **weg|nehmen** *to take away*, **zu|nehmen** *to put on weight*.

29 rufen *to call*

	present	future	conditional
ich	rufe	werde ... rufen	würde ... rufen
du	rufst	wirst ... rufen	würdest ... rufen
er/sie/es	ruft	wird ... rufen	würde ... rufen
wir	rufen	werden ... rufen	würden ... rufen
ihr	ruft	werdet ... rufen	würdet ... rufen
sie/Sie	rufen	werden ... rufen	würden ... rufen

	simple past/imperfect	perfect
ich	rief	habe ... gerufen
du	riefst	hast ... gerufen
er/sie/es	rief	hat ... gerufen
wir	riefen	haben ... gerufen
ihr	rieft	habt ... gerufen
sie/Sie	riefen	haben ... gerufen

	Konjunktiv I	Konjunktiv II
ich	rufe	riefe
du	rufest	riefest
er/sie/es	rufe	riefe
wir	rufen	riefen
ihr	rufet	riefet
sie/Sie	rufen	riefen

present participle **rufend**

past participle **gerufen**

imperative **ruf(e)! ruft! rufen Sie! rufen wir!**

Verbs that follow the same pattern as **rufen** include **an|rufen** *to telephone*, **widerrufen** *to retract*.

30 schlafen *to sleep*

	present	future	conditional
ich	schlafe	werde ... schlafen	würde ... schlafen
du	schläfst	wirst ... schlafen	würdest ... schlafen
er/sie/es	schläft	wird ... schlafen	würde ... schlafen
wir	schlafen	werden ... schlafen	würden ... schlafen
ihr	schlaft	werdet ... schlafen	würdet ... schlafen
sie/Sie	schlafen	werden ... schlafen	würden ... schlafen

	simple past/imperfect	perfect
ich	schlief	habe ... geschlafen
du	schliefst	hast ... geschlafen
er/sie/es	schlief	hat ... geschlafen
wir	schliefen	haben ... geschlafen
ihr	schlieft	habt ... geschlafen
sie/Sie	schliefen	haben ... geschlafen

	Konjunktiv I	Konjunktiv II
ich	schlafe	schliefe
du	schlafest	schliefest
er/sie/es	schlafe	schliefe
wir	schlafen	schliefen
ihr	schlafet	schliefet
sie/Sie	schlafen	schliefen

present participle **schlafend**

past participle **geschlafen**

imperative **schlaf(e)! schlaft! schlafen Sie! schlafen wir!**

Verbs that follow the same pattern as **schlafen** include **ein|schlafen** (*) *to fall asleep*, **verschlafen** *to oversleep*.

31 schließen *to close*

	present	future	conditional
ich	schließe	werde ... schließen	würde ... schließen
du	schließt	wirst ... schließen	würdest ... schließen
er/sie/es	schließt	wird ... schließen	würde ... schließen
wir	schließen	werden ... schließen	würden ... schließen
ihr	schließt	werdet ... schließen	würdet ... schließen
sie/Sie	schließen	werden ... schließen	würden ... schließen

	simple past/imperfect	perfect
ich	schloss	habe ... geschlossen
du	schlossest	hast ... geschlossen
er/sie/es	schloss	hat ... geschlossen
wir	schlossen	haben ... geschlossen
ihr	schlosst	habt ... geschlossen
sie/Sie	schlossen	haben ... geschlossen

	Konjunktiv I	Konjunktiv II
ich	schließe	schlösse
du	schließest	schlössest
er/sie/es	schließe	schlösse
wir	schließen	schlössen
ihr	schließet	schlösset
sie/Sie	schließen	schlössen

present participle **schließend**

past participle **geschlossen**

imperative **schließ(e)! schließt! schließen Sie! schließen wir!**

Verbs that follow the same pattern as **schließen** include **aus|schließen** *to exclude* and **ein|schließen** *to include.*

32   schreiben *to write*

	present	future	conditional
ich	schreibe	werde ... schreiben	würde ... schreiben
du	schreibst	wirst ... schreiben	würdest ... schreiben
er/sie/es	schreibt	wird ... schreiben	würde ... schreiben
wir	schreiben	werden ... schreiben	würden ... schreiben
ihr	schreibt	werdet ... schreiben	würdet ... schreiben
sie/Sie	schreiben	werden ... schreiben	würden ... schreiben

	simple past/imperfect	perfect
ich	schrieb	habe ... geschrieben
du	schriebst	hast ... geschrieben
er/sie/es	schrieb	hat ... geschrieben
wir	schrieben	haben ... geschrieben
ihr	schriebt	habt ... geschrieben
sie/Sie	schrieben	haben ... geschrieben

	Konjunktiv I	Konjunktiv II
ich	schreibe	schriebe
du	schreibest	schriebest
er/sie/es	schreibe	schriebe
wir	schreiben	schrieben
ihr	schreibet	schriebet
sie/Sie	schreiben	schrieben

present participle **schreibend**

past participle **geschrieben**

imperative **schreib(e)! schreibt! schreiben Sie! schreiben wir!**

Verbs that follow the same pattern as **schreiben** include **auf|schreiben** *to write down*, **beschreiben** *to describe*, **unterschreiben** *to sign*.

33 sehen *to see*

	present	future	conditional
ich	sehe	werde ... sehen	würde ... sehen
du	siehst	wirst ... sehen	würdest ... sehen
er/sie/es	sieht	wird ... sehen	würde ... sehen
wir	sehen	werden ... sehen	würden ... sehen
ihr	seht	werdet ... sehen	würdet ... sehen
sie/Sie	sehen	werden ... sehen	würden ... sehen

	simple past/imperfect	perfect
ich	sah	habe ... gesehen
du	sahst	hast ... gesehen
er/sie/es	sah	hat ... gesehen
wir	sahen	haben ... gesehen
ihr	saht	habt ... gesehen
sie/Sie	sahen	haben ... gesehen

	Konjunktiv I	Konjunktiv II
ich	sehe	sähe
du	sehest	sähest
er/sie/es	sehe	sähe
wir	sehen	sähen
ihr	sehet	sähet
sie/Sie	sehen	sähen

present participle **sehend**

past participle **gesehen**

imperative **sieh! seht! sehen Sie! sehen wir!**

Verbs that follow the same pattern as **sehen** include **aus|sehen** *to look*, **zu|sehen** *to watch*.

34 sein *to be*

	present	future	conditional
ich	bin	werde ... sein	würde ... sein
du	bist	wirst ... sein	würdest ... sein
er/sie/es	ist	wird ... sein	würde ... sein
wir	sind	werden ... sein	würden ... sein
ihr	seid	werdet ... sein	würdet ... sein
sie/Sie	sind	werden ... sein	würden ... sein

	simple past/imperfect	perfect
ich	war	bin ... gewesen
du	warst	bist ... gewesen
er/sie/es	war	ist ... gewesen
wir	waren	sind ... gewesen
ihr	wart	seid ... gewesen
sie/Sie	waren	sind ... gewesen

	Konjunktiv I	Konjunktiv II
ich	sei	wäre
du	sei(e)st	wärest
er/sie/es	sei	wäre
wir	seien	wären
ihr	seiet	wäret
sie/Sie	seien	wären

present participle **seiend**

past participle **gewesen**

imperative **sei! seid! seien Sie! seien wir!**

35 sitzen *to be sitting*

	present	future	conditional
ich	sitze	werde ... sitzen	würde ... sitzen
du	sitzt	wirst ... sitzen	würdest ... sitzen
er/sie/es	sitzt	wird ... sitzen	würde ... sitzen
wir	sitzen	werden ... sitzen	würden ... sitzen
ihr	sitzt	werdet ... sitzen	würdet ... sitzen
sie/Sie	sitzen	werden ... sitzen	würden ... sitzen

	simple past/imperfect	perfect
ich	saß	habe (bin*) ... gesessen
du	saß(es)t	hast (bist) ... gesessen
er/sie/es	saß	hat (ist) ... gesessen
wir	saßen	haben (sind) ... gesessen
ihr	saßt	habt (seid) ... gesessen
sie/Sie	saßen	haben (sind) ... gesessen

	Konjunktiv I	Konjunktiv II
ich	sitze	säße
du	sitzest	säßest
er/sie/es	sitze	säße
wir	sitzen	säßen
ihr	sitzet	säßet
sie/Sie	sitzen	säßen

present participle **sitzend**

past participle **gesessen**

imperative **sitz(e)! sitzt! sitzen Sie! sitzen wir!**

* Used with **sein** in southern Germany, Austria and Switzerland.

36 sollen *to be supposed to, should*

	present	future	conditional
ich	soll	werde … sollen	würde … sollen
du	sollst	wirst … sollen	würdest … sollen
er/sie/es	soll	wird … sollen	würde … sollen
wir	sollen	werden … sollen	würden … sollen
ihr	sollt	werdet … sollen	würdet … sollen
sie/Sie	sollen	werden … sollen	würden … sollen

	simple past/imperfect	perfect
ich	sollte	habe … gesollt/sollen
du	solltest	hast … gesollt/sollen
er/sie/es	sollte	hat … gesollt/sollen
wir	sollten	haben … gesollt/sollen
ihr	solltet	habt … gesollt/sollen
sie/Sie	sollten	haben … gesollt/sollen

	Konjunktiv I	Konjunktiv II
ich	solle	sollte
du	sollest	solltest
er/sie/es	solle	sollte
wir	sollen	sollten
ihr	sollet	solltet
sie/Sie	sollen	sollten

present participle **sollend**

past participle **gesollt** (**sollen** after another verb)

no imperative

37 sprechen *to speak*

	present	future	conditional
ich	spreche	werde ... sprechen	würde ... sprechen
du	sprichst	wirst ... sprechen	würdest ... sprechen
er/sie/es	spricht	wird ... sprechen	würde ... sprechen
wir	sprechen	werden ... sprechen	würden ... sprechen
ihr	sprecht	werdet ... sprechen	würdet ... sprechen
sie/Sie	sprechen	werden ... sprechen	würden ... sprechen

	simple past/imperfect	perfect
ich	sprach	habe ... gesprochen
du	sprachst	hast ... gesprochen
er/sie/es	sprach	hat ... gesprochen
wir	sprachen	haben ... gesprochen
ihr	spracht	habt ... gesprochen
sie/Sie	sprachen	haben ... gesprochen

	Konjunktiv I	Konjunktiv II
ich	spreche	spräche
du	sprechest	sprächest
er/sie/es	spreche	spräche
wir	sprechen	sprächen
ihr	sprechet	sprächet
sie/Sie	sprechen	sprächen

present participle **sprechend**

past participle **gesprochen**

imperative **sprich! sprecht! sprechen Sie! sprechen wir!**

Verbs that follow the same pattern as **sprechen** include **aus|sprechen** *to pronounce*, **versprechen** *to promise*, **widersprechen** *to contradict*.

38 stehen *to stand*

	present	future	conditional
ich	stehe	werde ... stehen	würde ... stehen
du	stehst	wirst ... stehen	würdest ... stehen
er/sie/es	steht	wird ... stehen	würde ... stehen
wir	stehen	werden ... stehen	würden ... stehen
ihr	steht	werdet ... stehen	würdet ... stehen
sie/Sie	stehen	werden ... stehen	würden ... stehen

	simple past/imperfect	perfect
ich	stand	habe (bin*) ... gestanden
du	stand(e)st	hast (bist) ... gestanden
er/sie/es	stand	hat (ist) ... gestanden
wir	standen	haben (sind) ... gestanden
ihr	standet	habt (seid) ... gestanden
sie/Sie	standen	haben (sind) ... gestanden

	Konjunktiv I	Konjunktiv II
ich	stehe	stünde (or stände)
du	stehest	stündest (or ständest)
er/sie/es	stehe	stünde (or stände)
wir	stehen	stünden (or ständen)
ihr	stehet	stündet (or ständet)
sie/Sie	stehen	stünden (or ständen)

present participle **stehend**

past participle **gestanden**

imperative **steh(e)! steht! stehen Sie! stehen wir!**

Verbs that follow the same pattern as **stehen** include **auf|stehen (*)** *to get up*, **missverstehen** *to misunderstand*, **verstehen** *to understand*, **widerstehen** *to resist*.

* Used with **sein** in southern Germany, Austria and Switzerland.

39 sterben *to die*

	present	future	conditional
ich	sterbe	werde ... sterben	würde ... sterben
du	stirbst	wirst ... sterben	würdest ... sterben
er/sie/es	stirbt	wird ... sterben	würde ... sterben
wir	sterben	werden ... sterben	würden ... sterben
ihr	sterbt	werdet ... sterben	würdet ... sterben
sie/Sie	sterben	werden ... sterben	würden ... sterben

	simple past/imperfect	perfect
ich	starb	bin ... gestorben
du	starbst	bist ... gestorben
er/sie/es	starb	ist ... gestorben
wir	starben	sind ... gestorben
ihr	starbt	seid ... gestorben
sie/Sie	starben	sind ... gestorben

	Konjunktiv I	Konjunktiv II
ich	sterbe	stürbe (or stärbe)
du	sterbest	stürbest (or stärbest)
er/sie/es	sterbe	stürbe (or stärbe)
wir	sterben	stürben (or stärben)
ihr	sterbet	stürbet (or stärbet)
sie/Sie	sterben	stürben (or stärben)

present participle **sterbend**

past participle **gestorben**

imperative **stirb! sterbt! sterben Sie! sterben wir!**

Verbs that follow the same pattern as **sterben** include **aus|sterben (*)** *to die out*.

40 studieren *to study*

	present	future	conditional
ich	studiere	werde ... studieren	würde ... studieren
du	studierst	wirst ... studieren	würdest ... studieren
er/sie/es	studiert	wird ... studieren	würde ... studieren
wir	studieren	werden ... studieren	würden ... studieren
ihr	studiert	werdet ... studieren	würdet ... studieren
sie/Sie	studieren	werden ... studieren	würden ... studieren

	simple past/imperfect	perfect
ich	studierte	habe ... studiert
du	studiertest	hast ... studiert
er/sie/es	studierte	hat ... studiert
wir	studierten	haben ... studiert
ihr	studiertet	habt ... studiert
sie/Sie	studierten	haben ... studiert

	Konjunktiv I	Konjunktiv II
ich	studiere	studierte
du	studierest	studiertest
er/sie/es	studiere	studierte
wir	studieren	studierten
ihr	studieret	studiertet
sie/Sie	studieren	studierten

present participle **studierend**

past participle **studiert**

imperative **studier(e)! studiert! studieren Sie! studieren wir!**

41 tragen to carry, to wear

	present	future	conditional
ich	trage	werde ... tragen	würde ... tragen
du	trägst	wirst ... tragen	würdest ... tragen
er/sie/es	trägt	wird ... tragen	würde ... tragen
wir	tragen	werden ... tragen	würden ... tragen
ihr	tragt	werdet ... tragen	würdet ... tragen
sie/Sie	tragen	werden ... tragen	würden ... tragen

	simple past/imperfect	perfect
ich	trug	habe ... getragen
du	trugst	hast ... getragen
er/sie/es	trug	hat ... getragen
wir	trugen	haben ... getragen
ihr	trugt	habt ... getragen
sie/Sie	trugen	haben ... getragen

	Konjunktiv I	Konjunktiv II
ich	trage	trüge
du	tragest	trügest
er/sie/es	trage	trüge
wir	tragen	trügen
ihr	traget	trüget
sie/Sie	tragen	trügen

present participle **tragend**

past participle **getragen**

imperative **trag(e)! tragt! tragen Sie! tragen wir!**

Verbs that follow the same pattern as **tragen** include **vertragen** to tolerate, to endure and **vor|tragen** to perform, to declaim.

42 trinken *to drink*

	present	future	conditional
ich	trinke	werde ... trinken	würde ... trinken
du	trinkst	wirst ... trinken	würdest ... trinken
er/sie/es	trinkt	wird ... trinken	würde ... trinken
wir	trinken	werden ... trinken	würden ... trinken
ihr	trinkt	werdet ... trinken	würdet ... trinken
sie/Sie	trinken	werden ... trinken	würden ... trinken

	simple past/imperfect	perfect
ich	trank	habe ... getrunken
du	trankst	hast ... getrunken
er/sie/es	trank	hat ... getrunken
wir	tranken	haben ... getrunken
ihr	trankt	habt ... getrunken
sie/Sie	tranken	haben ... getrunken

	Konjunktiv I	Konjunktiv II
ich	trinke	tränke
du	trinkest	tränkest
er/sie/es	trinke	tränke
wir	trinken	tränken
ihr	trinket	tränket
sie/Sie	trinken	tränken

present participle **trinkend**

past participle **getrunken**

imperative **trink(e)! trinkt! trinken Sie! trinken wir!**

Verbs that follow the same pattern as **trinken** include **ertrinken** (*) *to drown.*

43 tun *to do*

	present	future	conditional
ich	tue	werde ... tun	würde ... tun
du	tust	wirst ... tun	würdest ... tun
er/sie/es	tut	wird ... tun	würde ... tun
wir	tun	werden ... tun	würden ... tun
ihr	tut	werdet ... tun	würdet ... tun
sie/Sie	tun	werden ... tun	würden ... tun

	simple past/imperfect	perfect
ich	tat	habe ... getan
du	tat(e)st	hast ... getan
er/sie/es	tat	hat ... getan
wir	taten	haben ... getan
ihr	tatet	habt ... getan
sie/Sie	taten	haben ... getan

	Konjunktiv I	Konjunktiv II
ich	tue	täte
du	tuest	tätest
er/sie/es	tue	täte
wir	tuen	täten
ihr	tuet	tätet
sie/Sie	tun	täte

present participle **tuend**

past participle **getan**

imperative **tu(e)! tut! tun Sie! tun wir!**

Verbs that follow the same pattern as **tun** include **leid|tun** *to be sorry*, **weh|tun** *to hurt*.

44 vergessen *to forget*

	present	future	conditional
ich	vergesse	werde ... vergessen	würde ... vergessen
du	vergisst	wirst ... vergessen	würdest ... vergessen
er/sie/es	vergisst	wird ... vergessen	würde ... vergessen
wir	vergessen	werden ... vergessen	würden ... vergessen
ihr	vergesst	werdet ... vergessen	würdet ... vergessen
sie/Sie	vergessen	werden ... vergessen	würden ... vergessen

	simple past/imperfect	perfect
ich	vergaß	habe ... vergessen
du	vergaß(es)t	hast ... vergessen
er/sie/es	vergaß	hat ... vergessen
wir	vergaßen	haben ... vergessen
ihr	vergaßt	habt ... vergessen
sie/Sie	vergaßen	haben ... vergessen

	Konjunktiv I	Konjunktiv II
ich	vergesse	vergäße
du	vergessest	vergäßest
er/sie/es	vergesse	vergäße
wir	vergessen	vergäßen
ihr	vergesset	vergäßet
sie/Sie	vergessen	vergäßen

present participle **vergessend**

past participle **vergessen**

imperative **vergiss! vergesst! vergessen Sie! vergessen wir!**

45 verlieren *to lose*

	present	future	conditional
ich	verliere	werde ... verlieren	würde ... verlieren
du	verlierst	wirst ... verlieren	würdest ... verlieren
er/sie/es	verliert	wird ... verlieren	würde ... verlieren
wir	verlieren	werden ... verlieren	würden ... verlieren
ihr	verliert	werdet ... verlieren	würdet ... verlieren
sie/Sie	verlieren	werden ... verlieren	würden ... verlieren

	simple past/imperfect	perfect
ich	verlor	habe ... verloren
du	verlorst	hast ... verloren
er/sie/es	verlor	hat ... verloren
wir	verloren	haben ... verloren
ihr	verlort	habt ... verloren
sie/Sie	verloren	haben ... verloren

	Konjunktiv I	Konjunktiv II
ich	verliere	verlöre
du	verlierest	verlörest
er/sie/es	verliere	verlöre
wir	verlieren	verlören
ihr	verlieret	verlöret
sie/Sie	verlieren	verlören

present participle **verlierend**

past participle **verloren**

imperative **verlier(e)! verliert! verlieren Sie! verlieren wir!**

46 wandern *to go hiking*

	present	future	conditional
ich	wand(e)re	werde ... wandern	würde ... wandern
du	wanderst	wirst ... wandern	würdest ... wandern
er/sie/es	wandert	wird ... wandern	würde ... wandern
wir	wandern	werden ... wandern	würden ... wandern
ihr	wandert	werdet ... wandern	würdet ... wandern
sie/Sie	wandern	werden ... wandern	würden ... wandern

	simple past/imperfect	perfect
ich	wanderte	bin ... gewandert
du	wandertest	bist ... gewandert
er/sie/es	wanderte	ist ... gewandert
wir	wanderten	sind ... gewandert
ihr	wandertet	seid ... gewandert
sie/Sie	wanderten	sind ... gewandert

	Konjunktiv I	Konjunktiv II
ich	wand(e)re	wanderte
du	wand(e)rest	wandertest
er/sie/es	wand(e)re	wanderte
wir	wandern	wanderten
ihr	wandert	wandertet
sie/Sie	wandern	wanderten

present participle **wandernd**

past participle **gewandert**

imperative **wand(e)re! wandert! wandern Sie! wandern wir!**

Verbs that follow the same pattern as **wandern** include **aus|wandern (*)** *to emigrate* and **ein|wandern (*)** *to immigrate*.

47 werden *to become*

	present	future	conditional
ich	werde	werde ... werden	as Konjunktiv II
du	wirst	wirst ... werden	
er/sie/es	wird	wird ... werden	
wir	werden	werden ... werden	
ihr	werdet	werdet ... werden	
sie/Sie	werden	werden ... werden	

	simple past/imperfect	perfect
ich	wurde	bin ... geworden
du	wurdest	bist ... geworden
er/sie/es	wurde	ist ... geworden
wir	wurden	sind ... geworden
ihr	wurdet	seid ... geworden
sie/Sie	wurden	sind ... geworden

	Konjunktiv I	Konjunktiv II
ich	werde	würde
du	werdest	würdest
er/sie/es	werde	würde
wir	werden	würden
ihr	werdet	würdet
sie/Sie	werden	würden

present participle **werdend**

past participle **geworden**

imperative **werde! werdet! werden Sie! werden wir!**

Verbs that follow the same pattern as **werden** include **los|werden (*)** *to get rid of.*

48 wissen *to know*

	present	future	conditional
ich	weiß	werde ... wissen	würde ... wissen
du	weißt	wirst ... wissen	würdest ... wissen
er/sie/es	weiß	wird ... wissen	würde ... wissen
wir	wissen	werden ... wissen	würden ... wissen
ihr	wisst	werdet ... wissen	würdet ... wissen
sie/Sie	wissen	werden ... wissen	würden ... wissen

	simple past/imperfect	perfect
ich	wusste	habe ... gewusst
du	wusstest	hast ... gewusst
er/sie/es	wusste	hat ... gewusst
wir	wussten	haben ... gewusst
ihr	wusstet	habt ... gewusst
sie/Sie	wussten	haben ... gewusst

	Konjunktiv I	Konjunktiv II
ich	wisse	wüsste
du	wissest	wüsstest
er/sie/es	wisse	wüsste
wir	wissen	wüssten
ihr	wisset	wüsstet
sie/Sie	wissen	wüssten

present participle wissend

past participle gewusst

imperative wisse! wisst! wissen Sie! wissen wir!

49 wollen *to want to*

	present	future	conditional
ich	will	werde ... wollen	würde ... wollen
du	willst	wirst ... wollen	würdest ... wollen
er/sie/es	will	wird ... wollen	würde ... wollen
wir	wollen	werden ... wollen	würden ... wollen
ihr	wollt	werdet ... wollen	würdet ... wollen
sie/Sie	wollen	werden ... wollen	würden ... wollen

	simple past/imperfect	perfect
ich	wollte	habe ... gewollt/wollen
du	wolltest	hast ... gewollt/wollen
er/sie/es	wollte	hat ... gewollt/wollen
wir	wollten	haben ... gewollt/wollen
ihr	wolltet	habt ... gewollt/wollen
sie/Sie	wollten	haben ... gewollt/wollen

	Konjunktiv I	Konjunktiv II
ich	wolle	wollte
du	wollest	wolltest
er/sie/es	wolle	wollte
wir	wollen	wollten
ihr	wollet	wolltet
sie/Sie	wollen	wollten

present participle **wollend**

past participle **gewollt** (**wollen** after another verb)

no imperative

50 ziehen to pull, to draw, to move

	present	future	conditional
ich	ziehe	werde ... ziehen	würde ... ziehen
du	ziehst	wirst ... ziehen	würdest ... ziehen
er/sie/es	zieht	wird ... ziehen	würde ... ziehen
wir	ziehen	werden ... ziehen	würden ... ziehen
ihr	zieht	werdet ... ziehen	würdet ... ziehen
sie/Sie	ziehen	werden ... ziehen	würden ... ziehen

	simple past/imperfect	perfect
ich	zog	habe (bin*) ... gezogen
du	zogst	hast (bist) ... gezogen
er/sie/es	zog	hat (ist)... gezogen
wir	zogen	haben (sind) ... gezogen
ihr	zogt	habt (seid) ... gezogen
sie/Sie	zogen	haben (sind) ... gezogen

	Konjunktiv I	Konjunktiv II
ich	ziehe	zöge
du	ziehest	zögest
er/sie/es	ziehe	zöge
wir	ziehen	zögen
ihr	ziehet	zöget
sie/Sie	ziehen	zögen

present participle **ziehend**

past participle **gezogen**

imperative **zieh(e)! zieht! ziehen Sie! ziehen wir!**

Verbs that follow the same pattern as **ziehen** include **an|ziehen** *to put on*, **aus|ziehen** *to pull out, to take off*, **um|ziehen** (*) *to move (house)*, **sich um|ziehen** *to get changed*.

* With **haben**, **ziehen** means *to pull*, *to draw* and with **sein** it means *to move*.

Verb index

Pages 192–241

Irregular verbs are also highlighted on the following pages:

Grammar terms

The **accusative case** is used to indicate the **direct object** of a verb.

Adjectives are words that describe or add information to nouns and pronouns: *small car; It was superb; German wine; first class; my name; which hotel?; those people.*

Adverbs are words that say how, when or where something happens or is (*quickly*, *early*, *here*); they add an extra dimension to adjectives and other adverbs (*very*, *too*) or to a whole sentence (*luckily*).

Agreement Unlike English, adjectives and articles in German change according to the noun/pronoun they relate to, needing to agree, i.e. match, in terms of gender (masculine/feminine/neuter), number (singular/plural) and case (nominative/ accusative/dative/genitive).

Articles are *the* (definite article) and *a/an* (indefinite article).

Auxiliary verbs are verbs that support the main verb: *We have eaten, Will she go?* In English, but not German, *do/does* is used as an auxiliary verb in questions like *Do you understand?*

Cardinal numbers are *one*, *two*, *three*, *four*, etc.

Case shows the role that a noun, pronoun or adjective plays in a clause. Case is typically shown by means of different endings.

A **clause** is a meaningful sequence of words that includes a verb. See **Main clause** and **Subordinate clause**.

Comparatives are used when making comparisons. English has two ways of comparing with adjectives: adding *-er* as in *bigger*, *cheaper* and using the word *more* as in *more expensive*. German normally adds **-er**.

Compound tenses are two-word tenses e.g. the perfect *I have waited*, the pluperfect *I had waited*, the future *I will wait*.

The **conditional** is a verb form used to talk about possible or imaginary situations: *I would go if …; I would have gone if …*

Conjunctions are linking words like *and*, *but*, *while*, *because*.

Consonants and vowels make up the alphabet. The vowels are **a**, **e**, **i**, **o**, **u**; the rest: **b**, **c**, **d**, **f**, etc. are the consonants.

Continuous tenses are used to say *I am/was doing* something. German has no continuous tenses.

The **dative case** is used to indicate the **indirect object** of a verb.

The **definite article** is the word *the*, which has several German equivalents.

Demonstrative words are used to point things out. *This*, *these*, *that*, *those* are demonstrative adjectives; *this one*, *that one*, *these (ones)*, *those (ones)* are demonstrative pronouns.

A **direct object** is directly at the receiving end of a verb. In the sentence *We saw John*, *we* is the subject, *saw* is the verb and *John* is the direct object. Compare with **indirect object**.

Direct object pronouns are *me, us, you, him, her, it, them*.

Feminine See **Gender**.

The **future** tense of a verb translates the English *will*: *We will be there; I'll go later; She'll be at work*.

The **future perfect** translates *will have*: *She will have gone to work*.

Formal is used to describe **Sie**, the word for *you* when talking to someone, or people, you don't know well.

Gender Every German noun is masculine, feminine or neuter. Articles and adjectives have masculine, feminine and neuter forms to **agree** with the gender of the noun they relate to.

The **genitive case** is used to indicate possession (like *'s* in English).

Imperative is the verb form used to give instructions or commands: ***Wait** for me; **Don't do** that; **Turn** the top clockwise*.

The **imperfect** tense of a verb is used to describe a completed action, actions, or a state, in the past. In German it is also called the **simple past**: *She **was** furious; We **watched** the match; We **went** to the cinema*. It is more common in written German than spoken German.

An **impersonal verb** is a verb that is used in the *it* form: *It's raining*.

The **indefinite article** is *a/an* in English, which has several German equivalents.

The **indicative mood** is used for factual statements: *He **goes** to school*.

An **indirect object** is sometimes separated from its verb by *to* or, if *to* is not said explicitly, it is implied. In the sentences *We talked to John* and *We told John,* we is the subject, *talked/told* is the verb and *John* is the indirect object. Compare with **Direct object**.

Indirect object pronouns, *to me, to him etc.*, are expressed using the dative case in German: **mir**, **ihm** etc.

Indirect speech communicates what someone else said, without using exactly the same words.

Infinitive German verbs are listed in a dictionary in the infinitive form, ending in **-en**, **-ern**, **-eln** or **-n**. The English equivalent uses *to*: **essen** *to eat*, **sein** *to be*, **lächeln** *to smile*.

Informal is used to describe **du** and **ihr**, the words for *you* when talking to someone (or people) you call by their first name.

Inseparable verbs are verbs whose prefix never detaches from the main body of the verb. See also **Separable verbs**.

Interrogative words are used in questions, e.g. *who*, *what*, *when*, *where*, *how*, *why*, *how much/many*.

Intransitive verbs need only a subject to make sense: *go*, *laugh*; unlike transitive verbs which need a subject and a direct object.

Invariable words don't change to agree with/match anything else.

Irregular nouns, verbs or adjectives don't behave in a predictable way like regular ones and have to be learnt separately.

Konjunktiv is the German word for the subjunctive mood. There are two sets of endings **Konjunktiv I** (sometimes called present subjunctive) and **Konjunktiv II** (sometimes called past subjunctive).

A **main clause** may not be a full sentence, but it does not need any extra information to make sense: *Although the sun is shining,* ***it's cold***.

Masculine See **Gender**.

Modal verbs are verbs like *want*, *be able to*, *must*, which are usually followed by other verbs: *I* ***want*** *to stay here; I* ***can*** *swim.*

The **mood** of a verb defines how it's used. See **Indicative mood** and **Subjunctive**.

Negatives are words like *not, never, nothing, not … anybody*.

Neuter See **Gender**.

The **nominative case** is used to indicate the **subject** of a clause.

Nouns are the words for living beings, things, places and concepts: *son, doctor, dog, table, house, Scotland, time, freedom*. See also **Proper nouns**.

Number refers to the difference between singular (one) and plural (more than one).

Numbers See **Cardinal numbers** and **Ordinal numbers**.

The **object** of a sentence is at the receiving end of the verb. It can be direct: *They have **two children***; or indirect: *Anna talks **to the children***.

Object pronoun. See **Direct/Indirect object pronouns**.

Ordinal numbers are *first, second, third, fourth*, etc.

Parts of speech are the grammatical building blocks of a sentence: *adjective, article, noun, pronoun, verb*, etc.

The **passive** describes something done <u>to</u> the **subject** rather than <u>by</u> it: *The meat is cooked in the oven; The room was booked by my friend*.

The **past participle** of a verb is used with *have* when talking about the past: *I have **finished**, he has **eaten**, they had **gone***. Some past participles can also be used as adjectives: *the **finished** product*.

The **perfect** tense of a verb is used in spoken German to talk about the past; it is equivalent to the English *I worked* and *I have worked*.

The **person** of a verb indicates who or what is doing something:

1st person = the speaker: *I* (singular), *we* (plural)

2nd person = the person(s) being addressed: *you*

3rd person = who/what is being talked about: *he/she/it/they*

Personal pronouns are words like *I, you, we, she, her, them*.

The **pluperfect tense** translates *had* done something: *She had worked hard all day*.

Plural means more than one.

Possessive relates to ownership: the **possessive adjectives** are *my, our, your, his/her/its, their*; the **possessive pronouns** are *mine, ours, yours, his/ hers, theirs*.

A **prefix** is a group of letters attached to the beginning of a word that modifies its meaning. *Mis-, dis-* and *un-* are English prefixes. German verbal prefixes may become detached from the main body of the verb.

A **prepositional** phrase is made up of a preposition plus noun, pronoun or word ending in *-ing*. It consists of a minimum of two words (*from London*;

with them) but can also include adjectives, articles and other modifying words (*with my two friends*; *after a long discussion*).

Prepositions are words like *by, in, on, with, for, through, next to*. They relate a noun/pronoun to another part of the sentence by place, time, purpose, etc: *It's **on** the back seat*; *We're here **until** Friday*; *I've got a letter **for** Tom*.

The **present** tense of a verb is used to talk about things being done now: *I work, I'm working*.

Present participles end in *-ing* in English, although all English words that end in *-ing* are not necessarily present participles. In German they end in **-end** and are almost always used as adjectives.

Pronouns replace nouns to avoid the need to repeat them. They can be personal: *we, she, us*; demonstrative: *this one, those*; possessive: *mine, theirs*.

Proper nouns are the names of specific people, places or organisations. They're written with a capital letter: *Sally, Cambridge, European Union*.

Reflexive pronouns are **mich/mir**, **dich/dir**, **sich**, **uns**, **euch**, used as an integral part of reflexive verbs in German.

The infinitive of **reflexive verbs** includes **sich**. There's no consistent English equivalent, although some reflexive verbs include *get* or *oneself* in the translation: **sich waschen** *to get washed*, **sich amüsieren** *to enjoy oneself*.

Regular nouns, adjectives, verbs etc. behave in a predictable way, conforming to the pattern for that particular part of speech.

Relative pronouns are words like *which, who, that*, used to join together parts of a sentence without repeating the noun.

Separable verbs are verbs which have a prefix that detaches from the main body of the verb in some tenses and verb forms. See also **Inseparable verbs**.

The **simple past tense** is e.g. *I worked, we ate, they spoke*. The simple past tense in German is also known as the imperfect. It is used mostly in writing.

Simple tenses are one-word tenses like *I play, I played*.

Singular means one.

The **stem** of a German verb is what's left when you remove the **-en**, **-eln** or **-ern** ending of the infinitive. You can then add other endings to this stem.

Strong verbs change their vowel in one or more tenses: **singen – sang – habe gesungen**. Their past participles end in **-n**. See **Weak verbs**.

The **subject** of a sentence is whoever or whatever is carrying out the verb: *They* have two children; *Anna* reads the paper; *This house* cost a lot of money; *Peace* is possible.

Subject pronouns are *I, we, you, he, she, it, they*.

Subjunctive is a form of a verb that's more widely used in German than English. It equates to the English *may* or *were*: **May** all your dreams come true; *If I* **were** rich, but it's also used in reported speech and indirect questions, and to form conditional sentences.

A **subordinate clause** is a clause that does not make sense on its own, but needs another, main, clause to form a full sentence: **Although the sun is shining**, it's cold.

Superlative is the *most/least* ... when comparing several things. In English you can add *-est* to many adjectives: *biggest, cheapest*, or you can use *most*: *most expensive*. German normally adds **-st** plus the appropriate adjective ending.

A **syllable** is a unit that contains a vowel and consists of a single sound: *can* has one syllable, *can-ter* has two, while *Can-ter-bu-ry* has four.

The **tense** of a verb indicates when something is done:

in the past	perfect tense: *I (have) worked*
	imperfect/simple past tense: *I worked*
now	present tense: *I work, I'm working*
in the future	future tense: *I will work*

Transitive verbs need both a subject and a direct object: *use, give*; unlike intransitive verbs which need only a subject.

An **umlaut** is represented by two dots over the vowels **a**, **o** and **u** (ä, ö, ü), and changes the sound slightly.

Verbs are words like *to go, to sleep, to eat, to like, to have, to be, to think* that refer to doing and being.

Vowels and consonants make up the alphabet. Vowels are the sounds made by the letters **a**, **e**, **i**, **o**, **u**; the rest: **b**, **c**, **d**, **f**, etc. are the consonants.

Weak verbs are usually regular and have a **t** in the imperfect/simple past tense and in their past participle: **fragen – fragte – gefragt** *to ask*. See **Strong verbs**.

Answers

Getting started Page 9

1 *a* Sofia N; glossy ADJ; magazine N; organises V; interviews N; hires V; professional ADJ; models N; photographers N; travels V; world N; boyfriend N; well-known ADJ; actor N

   b my ADJ; father N; comes V; Bonn N; lives V; Düsseldorf N; works V; central ADJ; office N; large ADJ; company N

   c prepared V; fantastic ADJ; meal N; ate V; grilled ADJ; fish N; fresh ADJ; asparagus N; new ADJ; potatoes N; drank V; superb ADJ; German ADJ; white ADJ; wine N; dessert N; incredible ADJ.

2 *a* very ADV; reasonable ADJ; rather ADV; dilapidated ADJ; really ADV; small ADJ; overgrown ADJ

   b superbly ADV; terribly ADV; uneven ADJ; deliberately ADV; unfair ADJ

Checkpoint 1 Page 22

1 The first ü is pronounced long because it's followed by h; the second ü is pronounced short because it's followed by two consonants (ck).

2 Sand; sie; Fantasie

3 a – Anton; c – Cäsar; n – Nordpol; o – Otto

4 veh veh veh

5 on the first syllable

6 Pol<u>it</u>ik (last syllable); Mu<u>sik</u> (last syllable); pro<u>bie</u>ren (second to last syllable); ge<u>macht</u> (second syllable); Fleisch<u>erei</u> (last syllable)

7 Ich (because it's at the beginning of the sentence); Tasse; Tee; Milch; Zucker

8 Herr Peters, kommen Sie aus England? Nein, ich komme aus Schottland.

9 ä; ö; ü; ß

10 Schifffahrt

11 ei

12 Ich denke, dass London interessant ist. (A comma is needed before a subordinate clause in German.)

13 Bischof – bishop (f → p); scharf – sharp (sch → sh and f → p); gut – good (u → oo and t → d); Ding – thing (d → th)

Checkpoint 2 Page 30

1 null

2 einhundertzweiundsechzig (162); einhundertsechsundzwanzig is 126

3 8 acht; 18 achtzehn; 28 achtundzwanzig; 88 achtundachtzig

4 2.374.000/2 374 000

5 *a* It is five (o'clock); *b* at seven in the evening/at seven pm; *c* after midnight; *d* yesterday evening at seven (o'clock); *e* at half past six; *f* a week ago; *g* It's quarter past one; *h* next week; *i* at one (o'clock) on the dot; *j* between four and six (o'clock)

6 *a* Es ist elf Uhr; *b* um Mitternacht; *c* um halb acht; *d* Es ist Viertel vor drei; *e* Es ist zwanzig nach vier; *f* morgen um zehn Uhr; *g* gestern um fünf; *h* am Sonntag um sechzehn Uhr; *i* jeden Tag um sieben Uhr; *j* genau um vier Uhr

7 *a* im; *b* am; *c* um

8 März

9 der fünfundzwanzigste Dezember; der einunddreißigste Dezember

10 the day after tomorrow

11 21.42

12 neunzig

13 the 18th century (1760)

14 Frühling (Herbst means autumn)

15 fünfundsiebzig Prozent

Checkpoint 3 Page 42

1 Arzt m; Ärztin f; Montag m; Tasche f; Schwimmen nt; Thema nt; Astrologie f; Kultur f; September m; Kino nt; Universität f; Kind nt

2 Berufe; Theater; Freunde; Mütter; Füße; Cafés; Fragen; Museen; Sonnen; Städte; Zeitungen; Äpfel; Kinder; Länder; Bankerinnen; Filme; Geschenke; Handys; Häuser; Partys

3 neuter

4 Der See means the lake; die See means the sea.

5 Name – although it ends in e, it's masculine

6 several female students

7 die Person

8 *a* -ant, -ig, -ismus, -ling, -or; *b* -e, -ei, -heit, -keit, -ie, -ik, -ion, -schaft, -tät, -ung, -ur; *c* -chen, -lein, -ing, -ma, -ment, -o, -um

9 the last noun

10 die Internetfirma; der Zeitungsartikel

11 Kennst du Herrn Kahn?/Kennen Sie Herrn Kahn?

12 Bruder and Onkel

13 Übersetzerin

Checkpoint 4 Page 50

1 *a* she – subject, the car – direct object; *b* my friend – subject, my

son – indirect object, a present – direct object

2 der for masculine nouns; die for feminine nouns; das for neuter nouns; die for all plural forms; only the masculine form changes (from der to den)

3 eine Schwester; einen Bruder

4 dem – einem (masculine singular); der – einer (feminine singular); dem – einem (neuter singular)

5 *a* Er (subject), ein Sportmagazin (direct object); *b* Sie (subject), ein Eis (direct object), den Kindern (indirect object); *c* ich (subject), eine Freundin (direct object); *d* Er (subject), eine Flasche Wein (direct object), dem Nachbarn (indirect object)

6 n

7 any three of: antworten, begegnen, danken, drohen, folgen, gehören, gratulieren, helfen, schaden, trauen, zuhören

8 dem Mann; der Frau; dem Kind

9 Mit, which takes the dative. The other three are followed by the accusative.

10 Mir

11 des Computers; der Frau

12 Das ist Peters Auto. There is no apostrophe. (Alternatively: Das ist das Auto von Peter.)

Checkpoint 5 Page 56

1 der Mann; die Frau; der Kaffee; das Kind; die Türkei; das Baby; die Freiheit; der Bruder; der Junge; das Brötchen; die Zeitung; die Universität

2 *a* die; *b* eine; *c* der; *d* ein; *e* der; *f* die

3 *a* ein; *b* eine; *c* einen, ein; *d* eine; *e* einen; *f* eine, einen

4 einem, einer, einem

5 Er wohnt in der Schillerstraße.

6 *a* Sind Sie Berliner?; *b* Sind Sie Student?; *c* Spielen Sie Klavier?; *d* Fahren Sie mit dem Auto?

Checkpoint 6 Page 64

1 e and en

2 *a* e; *b* e; *c* en

3 *a* modisch; *b* gut; *c* neu; *d* teuer; *e* gesund; *f* süß; *g* stark; *h* dunkel

4 *a* er; *b* e; *c* en; *d* en; *e* en

5 deutsches, deutschen

6 He is very unlikeable.

7 Das ist ein teures Auto. (or Dies ist ein teures Auto.)

8 Hamburger Hauptbahnhof, Hamburger Flughafen

9 *a* en; *b* e; *c* en; *d* en

10 *a* Sie kauft die blaue Jacke und den weißen Rock. *b* Er trägt eine weiße Jacke mit einem blauen T-Shirt and weißen Schuhen.

Checkpoint 7 Page 72

1 *a* Er kocht schlecht. *b* Sie tanzt sehr gut. *c* Sie sprechen schnell.

2 *a* spät; *b* unten; *c* rechts; *d* genau; *e* oft; *f* nie; *g* nachher; *h* weit; *i* hier; *j* zuletzt

3 *a* Ich bin wirklich müde. *b* Er geht nie einkaufen. *c* Sie spielen gern Badminton. *d* Das ist viel zu teuer.

4 billiger; am wärmsten; höher, am höchsten; interessanter, am interessantesten; runder, am rundesten; kommerzieller, am kommerziellsten; gern, am liebsten; besser, am besten

5 *a* London ist größer als Berlin. *b* Ich trinke lieber Kaffee als Tee. *c* Barcelona ist so interessant wie Paris. *d* Die Pizza schmeckt so gut wie in Italien. *e* Rebecca ist älter

als Leon. Aber Valentin ist am ältesten.

6 *a* e; *b* en; *c* es; *d* en; *e* e

Checkpoint 8 Page 80

1 *a* Ich möchte dieses Buch hier. *b* Wer ist diese Frau dort? *c* Diese Autos kommen aus Japan.

2 Das ist meine Schwester/Dies ist meine Schwester.

3 *a* dieses; *b* die; *c* jenes; *d* jene

4 *a* Jede Jacke kostet fünfzig Euro. *b* Einige Leute sind nett. *c* Sie sind alle zu Hause. *d* Niemand ist hier. *e* Alles ist zu teuer.

5 Because it's unstressed, i.e. it has no real emphasis in the sentence.

6 jemand

7 *a* ihr; *b* seine; *c* ihren; *d* ihrem; *e* unsere

8 Man glaubt, dass …

9 *a* meins; *b* ihre; *c* seins; *d* unsere; *e* deinem

Checkpoint 9 Page 88

1 *a* du; *b* Sie; *c* ihr; *d* Sie; *e* du; *f* ihr

2 *a* Louise – Sie; *b* Die Kinder – Sie; *c* Die Pizza – Sie; *d* Das Auto – Es; *e* Die Blumen – Sie

3 selber or selbst: Das habe ich selber gemacht./Das habe ich selbst gemacht.

4 Man darf hier nicht parken./ Hier darf man nicht parken.

5 *a* do; *b* io; *c* do; *d* io; *e* do, io

6 du: dich and dir; Sie: Sie and Ihnen; er: ihn and ihm; sie: sie and ihr

7 *a* ihn; *b* sie; *c* sie dir; *d* es ihm; *e* sie ihr

8 *a* Ich bin es. *b* Hier spricht man Deutsch. *c* Angela spielt mit ihm. *d* Nico schickt ihnen eine E-Mail. *e* Können Sie mir helfen, bitte?/

Können Sie mir bitte helfen?
f Ich liebe dich.

Checkpoint 10 **Page 94**

1   *a* Sie kommt morgen um neun
    Uhr. *b* Mein Bruder hat mir
    Blumen gekauft. *c* Wir sind
    am Montag mit dem Zug nach
    Hamburg gefahren.
2   *a* Er geht ins Kino, aber ich bleibe
    zu Hause. *b* Er geht ins Kino,
    obwohl ich zu Hause bleibe.
    c Er geht ins Kino, deswegen
    bleibe ich zu Hause.
3   sonst

Checkpoint 11 **Page 98**

1   *a* andererseits; *b* Was meinst du?
    c Zum Schluss ...; *d* Ich bin der
    Meinung, dass ... *e* Das stimmt.
    Also is left over; it means well or
    so.
2   *a* der; *b* den; *c* denen; *d* die;
    e deren; *f* dem
3   wo
4   ich weiß
5   Das stimmt.
6   nun; also
7   that's just the way it is/things are

Checkpoint 12 **Page 110**

1   *a* accusative; *b* genitive;
    c accusative; *d* dative;
    e accusative; *f* dative.
2   Nach because it takes the dative.
    All the others are followed by the
    accusative.
3   Er lebt seit fünf Jahren in London.
4   *a* em; *b* er; *c* en; *d* em
5   *a* ins, im; *b* an die, an der
6   *a* zur; *b* aufs; *c* zum; *d* ans; *e* beim
7   *a* Sie geht nach Hause. *b* Sie ist
    zu Hause. *c* Sie sind im Urlaub.

d Sie kommt trotz des schlechten
Wetters.

Checkpoint 13 **Page 122**

1   arrival; deep
2   dream
3   -eln; -ern
4   tense
5   I; they
6   -en, the same as 3rd person plural
7   -t
8   *a* inseparable; *b* inseparable;
    c separable
9   inseparable
10 zu
11 organisieren
12 to come again; to misunderstand

Checkpoint 14 **Page 130**

1   *a* Wir haben kein Auto. *b* Das
    weiß ich nicht. *c* Es war nicht
    gut. *d* Ich habe ihn gestern nicht
    gesehen. *e* Er fährt nicht nach
    Hamburg. *f* Ich habe keinen
    Hunger.
2   nothing; never; how much; not
    yet
3   niemand
4   gar
5   *a* Ich werde morgen nicht hier
    sein. *b* Ralf war noch nie in
    Schottland.
6   welcher, wer and das
7   on what
8   *a* Wann kommt der Zug in
    Stuttgart an? *b* Warum willst du
    mit mir sprechen?
9   nicht wahr or oder
10 *a* wie viele; *b* was; *c* woher; *d* wie;
    e warum; *f* wen

Checkpoint 15 **Page 140**

1   du sagst; wir studieren; er gibt;
    ich erinn(e)re; Sie bekommen;
    es gefällt; ihr sprecht; es regnet;
    ich tue

2 a Wir kommen morgen an.
b Ich wohne seit zehn Jahren in Bremen.

3 warten

4 verstehen; anrufen; haben; bringen; zurückgehen; werden; gefallen; tun; anfangen; kennen

5 er gab; du fragtest; ich saß; wir dachten; er musste; ihr wusstet; Sie blieben; sie flogen; ihr wart; wir konnten

6 ich erkannte

7 er findet; wir wollten; du gabst; er nimmt; du reist; ihr schriebt; er hält; ich blieb; Sie sind; ich dachte; du wurdest; Sie wussten; ihr hattet; du sprichst; wir rufen an; er tut

Checkpoint 16 **Page 156**

1 gefragt; gekannt; getan; zurückgegangen; gefahren; begonnen; gewartet; gehabt; besucht; vergessen; angefangen; verkauft; gebracht; gelernt; gesagt; gedacht; gelassen; fotografiert; gekocht; verstanden; verloren; geworden; gestorben; genommen

2 habe; hat; sind; habt; bist; sind; haben; ist

3 a gemocht: I('ve) always liked mathematics. b können: We weren't able to go. c können: We won't be able to go.

4 ist

5 a Er wird um neun Uhr ankommen. b Sie wird das getan haben. c Du bist schnell gelaufen. d Die Eier sind gekocht worden. e Ich hatte ihm das Buch gegeben. f Wir sind zu Hause geblieben. g Wir werden uns am Strand entspannen. h Sie war

nach Krakau geflogen. i Er hat mich angerufen. j Du wirst diese Tabletten nehmen müssen.

Checkpoint 17 **Page 170**

1 nimm! nehmt! nehmen Sie!; warte! wartet! warten Sie!; schreib(e)! schreibt! schreiben Sie!; beeil(e) dich! beeilt euch! beeilen Sie sich!; wasch(e)! wascht! waschen Sie!; veränd(e)re! verändert! verändern Sie!; fang(e) an! fangt an! fangen Sie an!; studiere! studiert! studieren Sie!; zieh(e) dich an! zieht euch an! ziehen Sie sich an!

2 Gehen wir zurück!

3 a Der weinende Junge lief über die Brücke. b Ein Baum ist auf ein vorbeifahrendes Auto gefallen.

4 subjunctive only: er sei, sie ginge, wir hätten, ich müsse, es wäre, wir wüssten; indicative or subjunctive: ich habe, er wollte, wir kommen, sie werden

5 a Ich möchte/Ich hätte gern ein Glas Wein. b Ich wünschte, ich hätte mehr Geld. c Er tat, als ob er arbeitete. d Könnten Sie mir sagen, wie ich zum Bahnhof komme?

6 a 4; b 1; c 2; d 5; e 3

Checkpoint 18 **Page 184**

1 a 5; b 4; c 2; d 3; e 1

2 a lasse; b ist; c werden; d hast; e würde; f geht; g habt; h gibt; i freut

3 a möchte; b solltet; c willst; d konnten; e muss; f darf; g wollten; h kannst; i könnten; j mussten

4 a customer; b shop assistant

Checkpoint 19 Page 190

1   *a* über; *b* an; *c* für; *d* an; *e* um;
    f nach; *g* auf; *h* mit; *i* von; *j* auf

2   *a* Wartest du auf mich? *b* Ich
    interessiere mich für Sport.
    c Es kommt darauf an/Es hängt
    davon ab. *d* Erinnert sie sich an
    mich? *e* Er verlässt sich auf seine
    Eltern. *f* Ich habe Angst davor.
    g Woran denkst du/denkt ihr/
    denken Sie? *h* Sie bereiten sich
    auf ihre Prüfung vor. *i* Ihr müsst
    auf den Lehrer achten. *j* Sie hat
    alles bezahlt./Sie bezahlte alles.

3   We're looking forward to the
    course.

Index